Advance Praise for

25 Great Sentences and How They Got That Way

"Geraldine Woods gives new meaning to the term 'topic sentence' by turning the sentence itself into the topic. Using hundreds of examples from writers as diverse as Bruce Springsteen and Virginia Woolf, she articulates the precise ways in which a writer can send a sentence spinning. This book will give anyone who opens it a new appreciation for the glories of syntax, which can only increase one's capacity for creating them."

—**Mary Norris**, author of *Between You & Me: Confessions of a Comma Queen*

"On *Veep*, we would obsess over every sentence in the script. Word by word, we fine-tuned every straight line and joke right up to the moment we shot the show. It's comforting to know now that someone else is paying attention to sentences the same way we did. From James Joyce to Judy Blume, from Yoda to Toni Morrison, Geraldine Woods breaks down twenty-five of the greatest sentences in the history of the written word and obsesses over them in a way that writers and nonwriters can appreciate."

—**David Mandel**, Emmy–winning executive producer of *Veep*

"Finally, someone who appreciates the engine of a fine sentence and isn't afraid to tinker with all the parts! As Geraldine Woods writes in her introduction: 'A sentence is . . . the smallest element differentiating one writer's style from another's.' Her guidance will be so useful for anyone who enjoys writing and wants to take it all to the next level."

—**Brenda Miller**, author of *An Earlier Life* and coauthor of *Tell It Slant: Creating, Refining, and Publishing Creative Nonfiction*

"Geraldine Woods was the English teacher who made me fall desperately in love with grammar. Who knew such a thing was possible—especially at the age of fifteen? Ms. Woods's approach to the art of the sentence—and her methodology in imparting this approach—is on glittering display in this engrossing text. Her inspired dissection of beloved sentences makes you fall deeper in love with writers you've long cherished; you come to understand why exactly you cherished them in the first place, while becoming a better writer and more attuned reader yourself."

—**Halley Feiffer**, actor and playwright, author of *Moscow Moscow Moscow Moscow Moscow Moscow* and *The Pain of My Belligerence*

"Geraldine Woods is the awesome teacher you had in high school and wanted to keep for life. It's no surprise that she crafted an engaging, instructive manual for self-proclaimed 'word nerds' and those who aspire to write like them. If you want to enhance your confidence and craft as a writer, this is your book."

—**Lara Setrakian**, CEO and executive editor of News Deeply

"As a high school English teacher, this volume gives me exactly what I want my students to have in mind as they read and write. Woods considers structure, sound, grammar, diction . . . she deconstructs and explains, and then sends readers out to construct and create on their own. Thought-provoking. . . . Woods had me revisiting texts that I've taught before as well as thinking about my own writing process. This is a book I will be using in class, for sure!"

—**Alex Myers**, author of *Revolutionary*, *Continental Divide*, and *The Story of Silence*

"There's not a dull moment in this collection. Woods's selection of sentences is both varied and surprising, her analyses refreshing and illuminating, with sources like Virginia Woolf or John F. Kennedy. Have you ever needed a book without knowing it, until it's in your hands? *25 Great Sentences* is that book. You'll savor it. You'll pick it up again and again."

—**John Allman**, winner of the Pushcart Prize and Helen Bulls Prize for poetry, author of *Loew's Triboro* and *Clio's Children*

25 Great Sentences and How They Got That Way

25 GREAT SENTENCES

AND HOW THEY GOT THAT WAY

Geraldine Woods

W. W. NORTON & COMPANY

Independent Publishers Since 1923

Since this page cannot legibly accommodate all the copyright notices,
pages 299–301 constitute an extension of the copyright page.

For information about permission to reproduce selections from this book,
write to Permissions, W. W. Norton & Company, Inc.,
500 Fifth Avenue, New York, NY 10110

For information about special discounts for bulk purchases, please contact
W. W. Norton Special Sales at specialsales@wwnorton.com or 800-233-4830

Manufacturing by LSC Communications, Harrisonburg
Book design by Fearn Cutler de Vicq
Production manager: Lauren Abbate

Library of Congress Cataloging-in-Publication Data

Names: Woods, Geraldine, author.
Title: 25 great sentences and how they got that way / Geraldine Woods.
Other titles: Twenty-five great sentences and how they got that way
Description: First edition. | New York : W. W. Norton & Company, [2020] |
Includes bibliographical references and index.
Identifiers: LCCN 2019047655 | ISBN 9781324004851 (hardcover) |
ISBN 9781324004868 (epub)
Subjects: LCSH: English language— Sentences. | English language—
United States— Rhetoric.
Classification: LCC PE1441 W67 2020 | DDC 808/.042—dc23
LC record available at https://lccn .loc .gov/2019047655

W. W. Norton & Company, Inc., 500 Fifth Avenue, New York, N.Y. 10110
www.wwnorton.com

W. W. Norton & Company Ltd., 15 Carlisle Street, London W1D 3BS

1 2 3 4 5 6 7 8 9 0

For Harry,
who lives in my heart.

CONTENTS

PART IV: CONNECTION/COMPARISON

PART V: EXTREMES

ACKNOWLEDGMENTS

This book is a child of my mind, and it did indeed "take a village" to raise it. I'm grateful to the thoughtful readers and supportive friends who offered insight, encouragement, and invaluable suggestions. Here is a partial list, all of whom can claim credit and, if they wish, a celebratory dinner: Harriet Benzinger, Catherine Conley, Pilar Enright, Jacqueline Friedman, Matt Hedges, Karen Johnson, Deborah Kassel, Sharon Kunde, David Schiller, Wendy Steiner, Amanda Summers, and Don Yates. I also appreciate the efforts of Sophia Seidner, Carol Collins, Sara McBride Tuohy, and Nancy Palmquist—publishing professionals whose expertise is matched only by their kindness and diligence. Finally, I offer thanks to the writers whose work appears in this book. The beauty they've created is a gift to us all.

INTRODUCTION

S entences. When I was a kid, I had to label, diagram, and write them to fit my teachers' chalk-dusted definition: a subject/verb pair expressing a complete thought and ending with proper punctuation. I don't discount the value of those lessons; in fact, I'm grateful for them. But that definition—or, more accurately, prescription—is far too limited. Stay within its confines and you understand why the word *sentence* also applies to a jail term.

No one told me, in my school days, that sentences could be artful. No one had to. The writers I loved showed me what a sentence could achieve, how careful crafting could make a sentence great. This book is a celebration of those authors and many others who create with language—journalists, poets, lyricists, and orators.

Before I get to *great*, a subjective category if ever there was one, a redefinition of *sentence* is in order, one that pries the word away from grammar. Wendell Berry establishes a good starting point. To him, the sentence is "both the opportunity and limit of thought—what we have to think with, and what we have to think in." I agree with Berry in part: there is opportunity and limit in a sentence. But few people, if any, think in sentences. Words are more basic, and underlying words is a still more basic, nonverbal stew of ideas. Only with purposeful effort does a sentence emerge, which, in my view, is best defined as "a unit of discourse." A sentence is also the smallest element differentiating one writer's style from another's, a literary universe in a grain of sand.

And writers do hold sentences close to their hearts! Sylvia Plath hoped to "live, love, and say it well in good sentences." E. L. Doctorow faced the wall when he wrote, so that "the only way out is through the sentence." Barbara Kingsolver wakes up with sentences "pouring into" her head, as did Ernest Hemingway. Alice McDermott has to "hear the rhythm of the sentence . . . the music of the prose." Michael Cunningham, too, wants a sentence to "engage and delight the inner ear." Denis Diderot likened concise sentences to "sharp nails which force truth upon our memory."

A sentence-level approach to the craft of writing has limitations, I know. You can't grasp the rhythm of a paragraph or the rhyme scheme of a stanza in one sentence, any more than you can appreciate the full melodic structure of a song from a few bars. Nor can you trace the arc of a story or the logic of an argument. Nevertheless, there's value in a narrow focus. In one sentence you can appreciate the words an author selected, the order in which they appear, the connections they make, and the sound and visual effects they generate. In well-written sentences, form and meaning work together, in synergy. If you're eager for more when you read the sentences selected for this book, I hope you'll seek out the full works they come from.

WHY THESE SENTENCES?

While writing this book, I got into quite a few arguments over which sentences to include and which to cut. I won all those arguments, and I lost them all as well. This is what happens when you fight with yourself! At least I wasn't attempting to compile the *25 Greatest Sentences*—a truly impossible task. There's no accounting for taste, as the saying goes, so I imagine you'll relish some of my selections and tsk-tsk over others. Good thing, too. Life would be terribly boring without variety.

My standards for judging a sentence start with this foundation: a good sentence communicates clearly and fulfills the author's purpose, whatever that might be. The sentence should flow naturally and rest on a sturdy structure. Not much argument about these criteria, I imagine. Moving onward into more controversial territory: to rise from good to great, a sentence must be beautiful, creative, or resonant.

A beautiful sentence stops you cold. You savor it not just for what it says but also for how it's written. It's not always pretty, mind you. Keats was right: "Beauty is truth, truth beauty." A beautiful sentence gives you the sense that you've encountered something real and therefore important, however ugly that reality may be. The marathon-length sentence Dr. Martin Luther King Jr. wrote in "Letter from a Birmingham Jail," for example, lists the dangers and humiliations facing African Americans in a racist society. King's call for justice delivers a painful, necessary, and yes, beautiful punch. Less weighty but also beautiful are sentences that engage your senses. When Li-Young Lee refers to "the round jubilance of peach" in his poem "From Blossoms," you're right there in the orchard, experiencing a bite of summer fruit.

Great sentences tap the fountain of creativity. They don't aspire to novelty, if novelty is even possible after millennia of human expression. Instead, a creative sentence forces you to see the familiar in a different way. In Gish Jen's *Mona in the Promised Land*, for instance, the teenage title character experiences her first kiss. I laughed as I recognized the accuracy of her remark: the nose is indeed "inconveniently placed." A creative sentence may also spring from mystery, perhaps from the unconscious. When Jack Kerouac, in his novel *On the Road*, describes "the mad ones . . . who never yawn or say a commonplace thing," you know that he's reaching beyond reality, but it's a reach that says everything about human desire.

Another quality lifting a sentence to greatness is resonance. When you read a resonant sentence, you grasp the surface meaning immediately. Progressing through the work, you realize that the sentence carries more meaning—perhaps so much more that you have to double back to see what the author hid in plain sight. An example: in the first scene of Virginia Woolf's *Mrs. Dalloway*, a society woman muses about the end of the Great War. Only after finishing the book do you understand that Woolf's sentence encapsulates the psychology of her characters and the tragedy of her plot.

25 PLUS

Anyone opening a book entitled *25 Great Sentences* would reasonably expect to read an analysis of, well, 25 sentences. And each of the 25 chapters does indeed highlight one great sentence, which I selected because it exemplifies a distinct element of style. Being a literary glutton, however, I couldn't limit myself to just one example. Thus every chapter includes a dozen or so additional sentences that illustrate the same technique or variations of it.

A great sentence is great for more than one reason, of course, and my classifications are somewhat arbitrary. So, too, are the chapter groupings: structure, diction, sound, connection and comparison, and extreme creativity. The last category includes sentences that stretch the limits of conventional expression: visual art, for example, and extraordinarily long or tightly compressed sentences. I hope you'll take a moment to appreciate every sentence as a whole, regardless of the chapter or section I've placed it in and whether or not it's the featured sentence of the chapter.

A word about sources: I found great sentences in fiction, nonfiction, drama, poetry, song lyrics, speeches . . . in short, everywhere. At times they seemed unavoidable. One evening I sat down to watch a mindless television show as a break from a long stretch of research and writing. And there it was: a silly character in an absurd scene saying a great sentence. So much for my break! But that moment exemplifies the underlying premise of this book: language, regardless of where it appears, is open to the same possibilities, subject to the same limits, and shaped by the same techniques.

I cast a wide net while collecting sentences for this book, revisiting old favorites and sampling works I'd heard about but never read. I paced the halls of my local library and spent far too many hours bouncing around the internet. Much that I found was forgettable and occasionally regrettable, but I did discover gems from established writers and from some sources not usually associated with literary excellence (Phil Rizzuto, Mae West, and Abigail Adams, to name a few).

DIGGING DEEP, CAREFULLY

One question inevitably arises in any discussion of literature: "Did the author really intend to do that?" (Alternate version, with eye roll: "Aren't you stretching the point?") To which I reply, "Yes, the author really did intend to do that, but not necessarily consciously." Art has layers of meaning. To adapt a phrase from Walt Whitman: it contains multitudes.

I don't, however, discount the danger of overanalysis. I once spent an hour picking apart a poem with a group of students, trying to figure out why the personal pronoun *I* was capitalized in every line but one. A few days later, when the poet visited, we jumped at the chance to question him. "Typo," he said curtly, deflating our overblown theories and egos with a single word.

Despite that humbling experience, I'm convinced that analyzing language—digging deep, carefully—is a worthwhile task. Seeing how authors achieve the effects they desire not only enhances the reading or listening experience but also impairs the author's power to manipulate. Once you recognize techniques, you can peer through them and evaluate the content according to your own standards.

While I'm on the subject of technique: grammatical and rhetorical terms apply to every sentence I analyze in this book, but I mostly avoid them. I don't want to build a house that shelters insiders who are fluent in that vocabulary and leaves those who aren't out in the cold. I prefer that everyone confront the sentence directly, free from obstacles. A few labels are necessary, and some are intriguing. Those I use.

WHO I AM AND WHO I THINK YOU ARE

Speaking of labels, I claim this one with pride: "language enthusiast" (or, more colloquially, "word nerd"). During a recent visit to a museum in Ireland, for example, I noticed a sign cautioning visitors to "mind the plinth." *They think visitors know what a plinth is! Do I know what a plinth is? I wonder why it's* mind *instead of* beware? Lost in speculation, I nearly tripped over the plinth, which, by the way, is "a heavy base supporting a column, vase, or statue." I looked it up.

My point is that no matter what I'm doing, I think about language. That's why I've taught literature and writing classes throughout my adult life and why I became a writer myself. I imagine that you are also interested in language. Perhaps you started early, as I did, reading the text on the cereal box at breakfast instead of digging for the toy inside. Maybe you, too, fell down more than one staircase because you didn't want to stop reading long enough to look at the steps. And most likely you'll never declutter your bookshelves because they hold the mind-children of authors you care about. "Words matter," I hear you say, and I couldn't agree more.

I must admit that writing about reading, for an audience of readers, is daunting. I take courage from the fact that no matter how many times I've read a text and its attendant criticism, I find something new to think about when I discuss the work with students and colleagues. Someone may point out a detail I've overlooked or present an interpretation that differs from my own. It doesn't matter whether or not I agree with others' comments, because those conversations inevitably deepen my understanding, reconfirming or altering my view. If you run across sentences that are old friends, I hope you'll enjoy the encounter. Plus, I hope you'll find some authors or works you haven't read before, enriching your reading palette.

YOU, THE WRITER

When I tell people I'm a writer, I occasionally hear something like "You're so lucky! I can't write." But I don't believe that luck has anything to do with the writing process. Some would-be writers expect their own *Pride and Prejudice* or *Carrie* to flow smoothly onto the paper. It doesn't work that way! First, no one but Jane Austen can be Jane Austen, nor can anyone but the man himself be Stephen King. And why would you want to be? Oscar Wilde said it best: "Be yourself; everyone else is already taken." Further, not even great writers achieve a flawless first draft. They start, stop, erase, rewrite, polish, and eventually create great sentences.

So can you. I believe that in the right circumstances—when purpose, passion, and situation align—anyone can craft a great sentence. I'm not denying that some writers are geniuses. How else to account for Shakespeare or Toni Morrison? But with practice, you can improve your ability to write. With more practice, you can fashion and perfect your own unique style.

This is not to say that great writers have nothing to offer you. All of the sentences in this book may serve as models. Take some you like and some you hate. Rework them, or make them into trampolines that bounce you off into new territory. The results may be pleasing or the verbal equivalent of month-old sushi. No matter; you'll have flexed your writing muscles. To help you hone your writing skills, I've placed a "For the Writer" section in every chapter. There you'll find suggestions and exercises that prompt you to try various techniques.

ONE LAST THOUGHT

I hope this book inspires you to become a sentence collector, jotting down sentences you like on index cards, in a notebook, or in a computer file. When you need inspiration, distraction, or a dose of art, reread some. Share great sentences with others who love words, or keep your stash as a private treasure. Regardless, I hope this book will increase your appreciation of the myriad ways authors mesh content and technique.

More than anything else, I hope you enjoy reading *25 Great Sentences and How They Got That Way*. I certainly enjoyed writing it.

PART I STRUCTURE

POCKET

The War was over, except for some one like Mrs. Foxcroft at the Embassy last night, eating her heart out because that nice boy was killed and now the old Manor House must go to a cousin; or Lady Bexborough who opened a bazaar, they said, with the telegram in her hand, John, her favorite, killed; but it was over; thank Heaven—over.
                                                —Virginia Woolf, *Mrs. Dalloway*

Ask a few people what they carry in their pockets. Chances are you'll find mostly necessary items (keys) and an occasional object of little use but much meaning (a lucky pebble). Even a secret (a love note) may turn up. The contents tell you something about the owner's character.

Virginia Woolf's sentence is a pocket. It appears near the beginning of her novel *Mrs. Dalloway* and holds the thoughts of the title character, who sets out for a walk across London on a morning in June. Mrs. Dalloway, a society hostess, is giving a party that evening. Throughout the course of one day, she evaluates the choices she's made in her life. Entwined with her story is that of a veteran suffering from posttraumatic stress.

Published in 1925, the novel is set shortly after the end of World War I, a time of upheaval in Britain and throughout the world. The huge number of dead and wounded, casualties of the war and an epidemic of what was known as "Spanish flu," forced changes in class structure and traditions. Gender roles were also in flux: activists who had been campaigning for women's right to vote since the late nineteenth century intensified their efforts when the war ended. In so many ways, society was reconfiguring and reconstructing itself during the 1920s.

So was art. A group of writers and visual artists, the Modernists, experimented with form and method. Many—including Virginia Woolf—were influenced by Freud's theory of the unconscious mind, which was gaining popularity during this period. *Mrs. Dalloway* is the result of Woolf's deliberate effort to present her characters' thoughts, a stream of consciousness. Before turning to this technique, Woolf was tempted to abandon the project. Clarissa Dalloway embodied nearly every trait Woolf disliked. She was superficial and "glittering," Woolf wrote in her diary. But the author's creativity flowered when she presented the hidden memories, desires, and dreams of Mrs. Dalloway and other characters. The pocket structure of her sentence is perfectly suited to that content.

The sentence begins and ends with strong declarations:

The War was over
it was over; thank Heaven—over.

This pair forms the pocket. Inside are two small objects: Mrs. Dalloway's memories of *Mrs. Foxcroft at the Embassy last night* and *Lady Bexborough who opened a bazaar*. These thoughts are tucked away, out of sight, as the sentence is tucked inside Mrs. Dalloway's mind. But look at the contents of the pocket. Mrs. Foxcroft's War isn't over; she's *eating her heart out because that nice boy was killed*. Tucked inside that pocket is still another object, which for Mrs. Foxcroft is perhaps a greater tragedy. The link between a family and its ancestral land is broken (*and now the old Manor House must go to a cousin*). Lady Bexborough, too, is hiding. Despite her grief, she dutifully conducts a meaningless ceremony with *the telegram in her hand*, the piece of paper informing her of the death of *John, her favorite*. Mrs. Dalloway doesn't rummage around in these dark spaces. She buttons up the pocket with a determined return to her initial declaration.

Woolf has fashioned the pocket from independent clauses, subject-verb statements that can stand alone as complete sentences. This sort of grammatical element generally carries the most important ideas, so you'd expect this structure to emphasize that Mrs. Dalloway has moved on and that her resolute drive to put the War behind her has succeeded. But has it? Repetition reveals Mrs. Dalloway's doubts. Three *overs* in one sentence! She's working hard to convince herself.

Look again. Right before the last clause is *but*, a word that signals a change in direction, the beginning of an exception or an argument. Mrs. Dalloway has been thinking of Mrs. Foxcroft and Lady Bexborough. She shoves them aside with *but* and reassures herself: the War was *over*.

What about that dash? A dash may indicate an interruption, an extra detail:

Luke bought eggs—he'd been to the farmers' market—and made an omelet.

or a trailing thought:

If you really have to go—

In Woolf's sentence, the dash dares the reader to decide. Is the War *over* for Mrs. Dalloway? Are her memories of Mrs. Foxcroft and the rumor about Lady Bexborough interruptions in her life? Or does she break off her train of thought because it's too difficult? A comma wouldn't take you into this dilemma. A dash leaves you there, wondering.

Take another look inside the pocket. Notice this long string of phrases:

except for some one like Mrs. Foxcroft at the Embassy last night

Phrases add information to a base, and most people see them as less important than a clause. "The vase shattered" (clause) arguably carries more meaning than "on the shelf" (phrase), which simply tells you which vase broke or where the accident happened. In Woolf's sentence, though, the phrases go on and on, adding Mrs. Foxcroft and Lady Bexborough as examples of people whose suffering hasn't stopped. By placing this information in a lesser grammatical structure, Woolf, in a sense, is stuffing it into a smaller place—a pocket in the sentence.

Woolf also attaches a description to Lady Bexborough: *who opened a bazaar . . . with the telegram in her hand, John, her favorite, killed.* That several words in the description are implied but not stated suits the meaning: Lady Bexborough doesn't speak of her pain, but the words appear on the telegram. They exist, as does the reality they reveal, even though they're not acknowledged.

There's one more statement in this pocket: *they said.* Its presence emphasizes that Mrs. Dalloway herself hasn't experienced pain from the War. Her understanding of it comes from others.

Woolf could have presented the same information in a more conventional way, writing something like this:

> "The war was over," Mrs. Dalloway thought. The previous night she had attended a party at the embassy, where Mrs. Foxcroft had talked with obvious pain about the death of a young man. His cousin would now inherit the Manor House. Someone had also told Mrs. Dalloway about Lady Bexborough, who had opened a bazaar while holding the telegram notifying her of the death of her favorite son, John.

All the facts are here, but not much else. The reader grasps the information about three characters (*Dalloway, Foxcroft,* and *Bexborough*) and moves on. Because Woolf turns the sentence back on itself, the reader can easily imagine that Mrs. Dalloway will thrust her hand into that pocket again, fiddling with the contents. And, indeed, in the course of the novel, Mrs. Dalloway returns over and over to the theme of mortality. She's getting old, and she's been ill. During the party she learns of a suicide, and just for a moment she admires the dead man, who has "thrown it all away." Mrs. Dalloway's pocket, and the sentence that creates it, mirror her mind and go even further. They reflect the way all minds work.

A few more words about punctuation: The description (*who opened a bazaar . . . killed*) would normally be set off by commas, because *Lady Bexborough* has already been identified. Generally, identifying information appears without commas; nonessential information is surrounded by commas. By omitting the first comma, Woolf turns *Lady Bexborough* into an interchangeable noble. Her name isn't important. She could be anyone of rank, performing any duty. But the death is essential; it's the whole point of mentioning this woman.

One final thought about *Lady Bexborough*: Woolf refers to her and to *Mrs. Foxcroft* as *some one*, creating a small but significant difference from the more common term, *someone*. As one word, *someone* applies to any individual in a group. *Some one*, on the other hand, singles out a specific member of the group. This pronoun choice appears to contradict the idea that *Lady Bexborough* as an individual is not important. In fact, *some one* reinforces the meaning created by the missing comma. War affects the lives of particular individuals, but it strikes randomly.

MORE POCKETS

Pocket sentences are surprisingly common, once you look for them. With this structure, writers insert extra information, create comparisons, reveal a character's hidden thoughts or emotions, and achieve many other effects.

Justification

This one comes from Phil Rizzuto, a legendary baseball player and broadcaster. Instead of reflecting his hidden thoughts, the pocket contents justify an assertion:

When I was in New York at the time I played for the Yankees, I mean when I finally came up, it was the baseball universe—I mean, the Dodgers were there, the Giants were there, the Yankees were there—you could walk down any street in Brooklyn or New York and never miss an inning or a pitch—somebody had the radio on all the way down the block, and it was just, you know, it was so great, the baseball was so great.

Rizzuto's sentence, from his speech at his 1994 Hall of Fame induction, brings listeners into the New York City of the 1930s and 1940s. (To clarify one point: While Brooklyn has been a part of New York City since 1898, Rizzuto separates it. Perhaps to him Brooklyn felt like the independent city it once was.)

The pocket sets forth an opinion:

it was the baseball universe
the baseball was so great

Within the pocket are supporting statements:

the Dodgers were there, the Giants were there, the Yankees were there
you could walk down any street in Brooklyn or New York and never miss an inning or a pitch [because] somebody had the radio on all the way down the block

The presence of three teams and the fans' enthusiasm fill the pocket and, for Rizzuto, justify why he viewed New York as *the baseball universe* that was *so great*.

Argument

These lyrics from "Farmer Refuted," a song in the play *Hamilton* by Lin-Manuel Miranda, present an argument:

Yo, he'd have you all unravel at the
Sound of screams but the
Revolution is comin'
The have-nots are gonna
Win this it's hard to listen to you with a straight face.

The words come from the title character, who answers Samuel Seabury, a farmer urging the crowd to abandon the budding American Revolution and remain a British territory. The pocket attacks Seabury:

> he'd have you all unravel
> it's hard to listen to you with a straight face

The contents of the pocket express an opposing idea:

> Revolution is comin'
> The have-nots are gonna
> Win this

The *you* in the first and last lines unify the pocket, but they're not the same. In the first line, *you* refers to the crowd, the audience for these arguments. The second *you* is Seabury. By giving the same pronoun different meanings, Hamilton creates a separation. Seabury appears to be one of the group, but he's really an outsider. Hamilton's statements are stark and forceful. He's asking the first *you* to believe that war and its outcome are inevitable and to reject the ideas of the second *you*, the loyalist.

Here's another example of argument from a speech Abraham Lincoln delivered in 1860, arguing that no compromise would satisfy those who supported the extension of slavery:

> Most of them [proslavery politicians] would probably say to us, "Let us alone, *do* nothing to us, and *say* what you please about slavery"; but we do let them alone—have never disturbed them— so that, after all, it is what we say which dissatisfies them.

The beginning and the end of these two closely linked sentences contain the word *say* and thus define the pocket. In between is Lincoln's argument, which he sums up later in his speech: "Their thinking it [slavery] right, and our thinking it wrong, is the precise fact upon which depends the whole controversy." Lincoln's view—that slavery is morally wrong—is what offends the opposition, and nothing short of saying that slavery is morally right will appease them.

Comparison

Calvin Trillin stashes a dose of humor in this pocket from an essay about his wife, Alice. Earlier he explains that his father told him to marry someone with good teeth in order to avoid large dental bills. Then this sentence appears:

> About the time the dentist who had been treating Alice seemed to start counting on one of her wisdom teeth as a sort of small second income—the way that someone who works in a corporate auditing office might figure on picking up some extra money doing income-tax returns on the side, or the way a mildly corrupt policeman might begin to include some free lunches in his budget—it occurred to me that I had neglected my own father's advice.

The pocket begins with a statement about extensive dental work and ends with the same issue, by referring to the father's advice. Though the essay is nonfiction, the pocket contents are a comically exaggerated comparison.

Description

John Updike fills this pocket sentence from "The Dogwood Tree" with physical detail:

> A little gravel alley, too small to be marked with a street sign but known in the neighborhood as Shilling Alley, wound haphazardly around our property and on down, past an untidy sequence of back buildings (chicken houses, barns out of plumb, a gun shop, a small lumber mill, a shack where a blind man lived, and an enchanted grotto of a garage whose cement floors had been

waxed to the luster of ebony by oil drippings and silver water so cold it made your front teeth throb) on down to Lancaster Avenue, the main street, where the trolley cars ran.

The pocket locates the beginning and end of Shilling Alley; the contents tell you what appears along the way.

Correction

You can't store much in a small space, so pocket sentences tend to be long. But Frederick Douglass, in this sentence describing the hardship and danger that enslaved people undergo, tucks a short but crucial correction into this one:

> I felt glad that they were released from prison, and from the dread prospect of a life (or death I should rather say) in the rice swamps.

Douglass changes the focus from "life" to "death" with the words that appear in parentheses, altering his initial statement and emphasizing what's really at stake for the prisoners he discusses.

George Bernard Shaw, in his play *Man and Superman*, also uses a pocket sentence to make a correction. The state of the character's marriage forms the pocket, with the correction inside:

> When I married Ana's mother—or perhaps, to be strictly correct, I should rather say when I at last gave in and allowed Ana's mother to marry me—I knew that I was planting thorns in my pillow, and that marriage for me, a swaggering young officer thitherto unvanquished, meant defeat and capture.

Contradiction

Elizabeth Bishop, in her poem "One Art," needs only two words to undermine her statement that "the art of losing is not too hard to master":

... the art of losing is not too hard to master
though it may look like (write it!) like disaster.

The command—*write it!*—is pocketed between two *likes*. Bishop's structure creates a stutter and a determined mood, the way you feel when you're convincing yourself of something you know isn't really true.

Drama

This sentence from science writer Bianca Bosker appears in an article entitled "What Really Killed the Dinosaurs":

NASA initiated Project Spacewatch to track—and possibly bomb—any asteroid that might dare to approach.

The pocket portion is almost ho-hum: NASA, the space agency, has a program to track asteroids approaching the Earth. The contents (pardon the pun) drop a bombshell into the statement: NASA foresees a potential threat to the planet and is prepared to blow up an asteroid.

Imitation of Reality

In this sentence from a review by Jennifer E. Smith of a museum exhibit on J. K. Rowling's *Harry Potter* series, the pocket structure imitates reality. Rowling worked on the *Harry Potter* story for years, jotting ideas and sketching scenes from the book on scrap paper, which, judging from the creases and crinkles of the museum exhibits, she most likely tucked into her pockets. Smith's sentence refers to Rowling's drawing of the main characters:

But to imagine her painstakingly adding the stripes on Harry's shirt or the freckles on Ron's face long before she could've guessed that anyone would care—there's something profoundly moving about that.

Two references to Rowling's commitment to *Harry Potter* create the pocket: *painstakingly adding* (a reference to her carefully detailed sketching) and the pronoun *that*, which refers to the act of *painstakingly adding*. Within the pocket are the details that Rowling drew (*the stripes on Harry's shirt, the freckles on Ron's face*).

Context

In this sentence from Tara Siegel Bernard's *New York Times* article entitled "How to Land Your First Job, on Your Terms," the pocket contents provide context for advice about salary negotiations:

> Instead of accepting the offer—as many first-time applicants, especially women, do—she researched what the job paid in Los Angeles, on average, and countered with a number just above the higher end of the firm's posted range.

The pocket is shaped by two references to salary (*offer* and *number . . . range*). Within the pocket is just one idea, but it's important. The statement about a tendency of *first-time applicants, especially women* to accept the company's initial salary offer shows the reader a common shortcoming that one job seeker (*she*) avoided and sets the stage for the author's recommendation that applicants research the competition and request more money.

Character Development

In this sentence from Neil Gaiman's novel *Anansi Boys*, a character's perception slips into a pocket made from references to *Macbeth*:

> It was sort of like *Macbeth*, thought Fat Charlie, an hour later; in fact, if the witches in *Macbeth* had been four little old ladies, and if instead of stirring cauldrons and intoning dread incantations they had just welcomed Macbeth in and fed him on turkey, and rice and peas, spread out on white china plates on a red-and-

white patterned plastic tablecloth, not to mention sweet potato pudding and spicy cabbage, and encouraged him to take second helpings, and thirds, and then, when Macbeth had declaimed that nay, he was stuffed nigh unto bursting and on his oath could truly eat no more, the witches had pressed upon him their own special island rice pudding and a large slice of Mrs. Bustamonte's famous pineapple upside-down cake, it would have been exactly like *Macbeth*.

Clearly, nothing in the pocket pertains to the Shakespearean play. Yet the detailed description of an immense meal and overwhelming generosity is vivid and tells the reader a lot about Fat Charlie's imagination.

Hierarchy

John Adams, the second president of the United States, uses one word (*facts*) to create his pocket:

Facts are stubborn things; and whatever may be our wishes, our inclinations, or the dictates of our passions, they cannot alter the state of facts.

In Adams's sentence, *wishes, inclinations,* and *passions* are inside the pocket, but they cannot alter the nature of the pocket (*facts*). Adams asserts the primacy of objective reality, which exists whether we want it to or not.

Emphasis

Edward Gorey, artist of the surreal and macabre, expressed his dismay to an interviewer about a Broadway production of *Dracula* featuring his sets. He describes seeing them for the first time:

I practically had cardiac arrest, is what I practically had.

The pocket catches your attention and emphasizes Gorey's extreme reaction, *cardiac arrest*.

FOR THE WRITER

Pocket sentences aren't hard to write; they're just hard to write well. With practice, though, any writer can master the pocket structure. The guiding principle is that form should support and reinforce content.

POCKET CHANGE

Keep the pocket but change the contents of Virginia Woolf's sentence. Don't worry about being consistent with the character and book that Woolf wrote. You're simply practicing, not rewriting the novel.

The War was over _____ over.

What would you add if you wanted to emphasize the character's certainty that the War really had ended? What would you add if you wanted to reveal survivor's guilt? pride? regret? Select any emotion, or more than one, and create contents to tuck into Woolf's pocket.

FILLING UP

Below are some empty pockets. Think about what you might put in them. Consider adding information, description, clarification, thoughts, and anything else that strikes you as interesting and appropriate. Try a few variations for the same pocket.

Doreen stared at the closet _____ she saw it clearly.

The cave painting was simple but realistic _____ the animals looked natural and alive.

THE HOGARTH PRESS

In 1917, Virginia Woolf and her husband, Leonard, purchased a printing press and a sixteen-page pamphlet that promised to teach them how to use it. Virginia was struggling with bipolar disorder while producing an extraordinary number of novels, stories, essays, and letters. Leonard's goal was to calm his wife during her manic periods with the simple, mechanical work of placing metal letters in a frame. Both hoped that owning a printing press would free them from the constraints imposed by established publishing firms.

Typesetting was tedious—Leonard gave up almost immediately—and the task did not prevent Virginia from thinking obsessively about her writing, as Leonard had hoped. Instead, she pondered each word and punctuation mark. In an essay entitled "How Should One Read a Book?" Virginia declares, "Books are made of tiny little words, which a writer shapes, often with great difficulty, into sentences of different lengths, placing one on top of another, never taking his eye off them, sometimes building them quite quickly, at other times knocking them down in despair, and beginning all over again." Can anyone doubt that this conception of writing was influenced by her experience setting type? Or that the statement itself illustrates the technique she describes?

The printing press did, however, allow the couple to achieve the second, more important goal. Because she self-published, Virginia Woolf was free to experiment and ultimately to fashion the startling sentences of *Mrs. Dalloway*. As she wrote in her diary, she considered herself "the only woman in England free to write what I like."

"Time to go," said Arthur _____ ; "we have to leave now."

The jury found him guilty _____ definitely guilty.

STREAMING

Because Woolf's technique for presenting thoughts is effective, you may want to try it yourself. Set a timer for five minutes and type or write everything you're thinking. Don't worry about complete sentences, punctuation, or anything else. The only requirement is to write without stopping for five minutes.

When the time is up, read what you've written. Did you refer to something in the present, to a memory, or to the future? Did you make an oblique reference that a reader wouldn't catch? Are there any secrets on the paper? Any lies or wishes? Most likely you'll discover that regardless of detail, you've roamed around quite a bit. Woolf did so, too. Now take stock of the emotions you experienced while writing. Perhaps you were frustrated that writing is so much slower than thinking. Did you self-censor, despite knowing that no one else would see your words?

Now look back at Woolf's sentence. Does it resemble anything you wrote? Probably not, because Woolf took the raw material of her character's inner life and deliberately shaped her sentence to reflect Mrs. Dalloway's personality, emotions, and ideas. She didn't represent reality in all its messiness. She created art. Using her pocket as a model, comb through what you wrote for phrases that reveal your true self. Fashion a pocket and tuck them in.

POCKETING A BRAINSTORM

Choose one or more of these ideas or choose another starting point: friendship, uncertainty, patriotism, grit, happiness. Write everything that comes into your mind when you think about your chosen topic. Circle the best of what you wrote; that's the contents. Now design a pocket. You can opt for fiction, adding a character who's thinking about or acting on your topic, or you can write a nonfiction statement, which the contents illustrate or modify.

CROSSED SENTENCE

Ask not what your country can do for you; ask what you can do for
your country.

—John F. Kennedy, Inaugural Address

Opposing views. Free will. Wordplay.

All three are in the mix when you cross a sentence, as President John F. Kennedy did in this famous declaration from his 1961 inaugural address.

Kennedy's speech took place when the nation, too, was at a crossroads. At forty-three, Kennedy was the youngest man ever elected president and the first born in the twentieth century. His relative youth and energy were a marked contrast to the elderly men who preceded him as president: Dwight D. Eisenhower, Harry Truman, and Franklin Roosevelt. Behind Kennedy were the Great Depression, World War II, and the postwar reordering of power that triggered the Cold War between the two reigning superpowers: the United States and the Soviet Union. Richard Nixon, Eisenhower's vice president, had lost to Kennedy by a narrow margin in the 1960 presidential race. Nixon's campaign promoted continuity and stability, but Kennedy proposed a shift to activism, a change that was already taking place. The modern civil rights movement was gaining strength, the power of television to influence politics was growing, and a huge group of young people—the "baby boomers"—would soon be old enough to vote. The structure of Kennedy's statement, and of the entire speech, reflects the historical moment.

Two views of citizenship appear in this sentence, tucked into statements beginning with *what*:

what your country can do for you
what you can do for your country

The words in each arm of Kennedy's sentence are exactly the same, but the change in word order creates a crossroads, each arm marking the path to a different philosophy. The first statement centers on the individual and stresses that elected officials should focus on *you* and what *you* need or want. It's the platform of self-interest, of a belief that government should fulfill one's personal needs. The second statement is a declaration of an individual's responsibility to the greater good, an appeal to take personal responsibility for the well-being of the nation.

In each statement, *can do* is the verb, the action in the sentence. In the first statement, *country* is the subject. In the second, the subject is *you*. Subjects perform the action, those who *can do*. The change from *country* to *you* marks the difference in the paths presented. Another switch occurs in the phrases:

for you
for your country

In the first phrase, *you* receive; in the second, *your country* receives. Aligning grammar with content strengthens Kennedy's message.

Kennedy's "ask not" sentence is the most famous cross, but his speech is filled with paired and opposing ideas, echoing and reinforcing the theme of critical choices:

- "not a victory of party but a celebration of freedom"
- "an end as well as a beginning"

- "the power to abolish all forms of poverty and all forms of human life"
- "united there is little we cannot do . . . divided there is little we can do"
- "if a free society cannot save the many who are poor, it cannot save the few who are rich"
- "only when our arms are sufficient beyond doubt can we be certain beyond doubt that they will never be employed"
- "Let us never negotiate out of fear. But let us never fear to negotiate"
- "explore what problems unite us instead of belaboring those problems which divide us"

Video and a transcript of the entire inaugural address are available at the John F. Kennedy Library website (www.jfklibrary.org). In the video clip, the "ask not" sentence appears at minute 14.

The power of Kennedy's sentence arises from its structure. Consider these statements, each with the same content as Kennedy's sentence:

People expect their country to take care of them when it should be the other way around.

What can America do for me? Don't ask that. Instead, ask how you can serve the nation.

Assess your talents and use them for the benefit of the country. Do not let self-interest dominate your actions.

Not exactly inspiring, right? The rewritten sentences lack the drama created by the cross pattern, as well as an important effect the cross creates, which is to place the reader at a fork in the road, showing competing values and contrasting worldviews. Yet the repetition—either the same words, as in Kennedy's statement, or words that vary slightly—keeps the crossroads in a shared reality. For the shortest moment, both paths seem possible. Then the cross nudges the reader in one direction. No one can read Kennedy's statement as neutral. He's clearly in favor of the second choice, and not simply because the sentence takes the form of a negative command (*Ask not*). His words frame the debate as a choice between selfishness and patriotism. And the person who frames the debate influences its result. If, for example, you ask:

Is it proper to smoke while praying?

most people say no. If the question is worded this way:

Is it proper to pray while smoking?

most people say yes.

Seven words. No more, no less, and only slightly different (*to smoke/smoking, to pray/praying*). But their order sets up two scenarios, switching the primary activity with the word *while*. In the first question, you imagine someone taking out a pack of cigarettes and disrespectfully lighting up, despite the presence of other worshippers in a sacred setting. You can almost hear a tsk-tsk. In the second, you envision someone puffing away, either alone or in a crowd. Suddenly, you see a thoughtful expression on the smoker's face, revealing the urge to pray. There's no disrespect in this picture—just human need and faith.

It's important to note that a crossed sentence only adds to the appeal of one choice. Free will still exists. Ultimately, the reader or listener decides.

———

Not every cross is a sentence. Here's a line from Oliver Goldsmith's poem "The Traveller":

to stop too fearful, and too faint to go

In the poem, a traveler surveys various countries and concludes that "laws or kings" play only a small part in "all that human hearts endure." Brief but powerful, these words cross two infinitives (*to stop*, *to go*) and two descriptions (*too fearful*, *too faint*), reversing the order:

infinitive description / description infinitive

Adding to the effect, the infinitives themselves are opposites (*stop* and *go*). Plus, Goldsmith's line links the ideas by sound (*too*, *to*). The balance in this cross is like a seesaw frozen in a horizontal position. It emphasizes Goldsmith's belief that traveling in search of a perfect system of government is futile.

Now to Shakespeare, whose wide-ranging genius provides examples of nearly every element of style a writer may need, including this cross from *Macbeth*. The king of Scotland has just been murdered and his sons decide to flee:

MALCOLM: I'll to England.
DONALBAIN: To Ireland I.

The subject, *I*, is followed by the destination in Malcolm's line. In Donalbain's line, the destination precedes the subject, also *I*. The cross emphasizes the linked fates of the king's sons. The first son, Malcolm, returns in the last act to avenge his father and retake the throne. The small change from *England* to *Ireland*, as well as the placement of Malcolm's statement before his brother's, emphasizes the primacy of England and English rule, an often-disputed topic in Elizabethan times.

CROSSES EVERYWHERE

This sentence pattern is so popular that it appears in music, politics, philosophy, comedy, and many other genres. You can find crosses in ancient texts and contemporary rap lyrics, and from nearly every area of the world.

They define and compare:

Painting is poetry that is seen rather than felt, and poetry is painting that is felt rather than seen.

—Leonardo da Vinci (Renaissance artist)

The art of progress is to preserve order amid change and to pre-serve change amid order.

—Alfred North Whitehead
(British philosopher, twentieth century)

In peace, sons bury their fathers; in war, fathers bury their sons.

—Croesus (king of Lydia, sixth century BCE)

or present a philosophy of life:

Money will not make you happy, and happy will not make you money.

—Groucho Marx
(comedian and filmmaker, twentieth century)

Failure is the foundation of success; success is the lurking-place of failure.

—Lao Tzu (Chinese philosopher, sixth century BCE)

It is not the oath that makes us believe the man, but the man the oath.

—Aeschylus (Greek playwright, fifth century BCE)

One should eat to live, not live to eat.

—Cicero (Roman philosopher, first century BCE)

We should behave to our friends as we would wish our friends to behave to us.

—Aristotle (Greek philosopher, fourth century BCE)

The earth does not belong to the man; man belongs to the earth.

—attributed to Chief Seattle

(Native American leader, nineteenth century)

Many comment on politics and government:

Advance the honest over the crooked and the people will be loyal; advance the crooked over the honest and the people will be disloyal.

—Confucius (Chinese philosopher, sixth century BCE)

America did not invent human rights. In a very real sense . . . human rights invented America.

—Jimmy Carter (president of the United States, 1977–81)

A statesman is a politician who places himself at the service of the nation. A politician is a statesman who places the nation at his service.

—Georges Pompidou

(prime minister and president of France, twentieth century)

Nations do not mistrust each other because they are armed; they are armed because they mistrust each other.

—Ronald Reagan (president of the United States, 1981–89)

Better have as king a vulture advised by swans than a swan advised by vultures.

—the *Panchatantra*

(collection of fables from India, fourth century BCE)

Happy is the time where the great listen to the small, for in such a generation the small will listen to the great.

—the Talmud (collection of Jewish writing dating from the fifth century CE onward)

Crossed sentences also describe:

> No woman has ever so comforted the distressed—or so distressed the comfortable.
> —Clare Boothe Luce (author and diplomat),
> speaking of Eleanor Roosevelt (former first lady and diplomat)

and entertain:

> I'd rather be looked over than overlooked.
> —Mae West (American actor, twentieth century)

or challenge:

> Are we a nation of states? What's the state of our nation?
> —Lin-Manuel Miranda (American playwright and actor)

and often play with sounds:

> I'd rather have a bottle in front of me than a frontal lobotomy.
> —Winston Churchill
> (prime minister of Britain, twentieth century)

FOR THE WRITER

Crossed sentences are the neon signs of the sentence world. They attract attention—unless everything around is also in neon. Save a crossed sentence for the most important point or use it sparingly for statements that reinforce the main idea. Before you can limit your use of this sort of sentence, though, you have to become comfortable with the pattern. Here are a few suggestions to get you started.

SANDBOX

To a writer, a blank page can be a sandbox where words are toys that sift and shift until a pleasing construction emerges. Time to play in the sandbox! Below are three bundles of words. Some appear twice because they're present in both arms of the crossed sentence. Move them around until you come up with a crossed statement or question. These are all words that have appeared in other writers' work. Answers appear at the end of this chapter.

Bundle #1
    or kiss kiss never you you fool fool a a let

Bundle #2
    never winners never and quitters quit win

Bundle #3
    afterwards us we shape shape our our and buildings buildings

DEFINITION

Not just neutral explanations that pop up on the screen when you type in the search term, definitions may also reflect a worldview, an opinion of the nature of something. When you cross a definition, you state what that thing *is* and also what it *isn't*. In doing so, you reveal your values and beliefs.

Try your hand at crossing definitions of one or more of these words, or a word that you yourself supply:

happiness, leader, honor, evil, home, art

Once you've made your choice, follow these steps:

- Brainstorm qualities associated with the word you've selected. Don't limit yourself to the literal. Metaphors and similes are helpful, too.

A GREEK CROSS

The cross pattern has a name—two names, actually: *chiasmus* and *antimetabole*. *Chiasmus* comes from the Greek letter *chi*, which resembles the letter *X* and reflects the crossed paths the sentences present. With chiasmus, the order flips but some of the words may differ, as they do in this statement from Mary Leapor, an eighteenth-century writer and feminist, about a woman's fate:

Despised, if she's ugly; if she's fair, betrayed.

Kennedy's sentence follows a tighter pattern, *antimetabole*, in which the same words appear in each arm of the cross, but in a different order.

- Make several separate statements that are true about your chosen word.
- Pick a couple of promising statements and state the opposite. For the moment, don't worry about using words that are the same or similar to the words in your "true" batch.
- Fiddle with the words until you play the "true" statement off the "false" statement. Think of the template this way:
  _____ is/does _____ not _____
- Formulate your definition so it resembles a cross.

I HAVE ISSUES

What do you care about? What possible futures do you envision for yourself, your community, or the world? To convince others that your path leads to a successful outcome—and that an alternative path leads to problems—create a crossed thesis statement, the assertion you intend to prove.

- Think of an idea or an issue you're passionate about—the environment, human rights, the best superhero film . . . whatever.
- Imagine a speech that would convince others to share your views. Your intended audience includes those who haven't thought about the issue at all, those who are on the fence, and those who actively oppose your position. You have to reach them all.
- Brainstorm for a few moments. What words come to mind when you think about this topic? Write the words without judging whether they'll be useful or not.
- Consider opposite approaches to the issue. What would someone who does not agree with you say?
- When you think about this issue, what does the future hold? Imagine a few possible scenarios. Then select two, one you hope for and one you dislike.
- Circle a few words that might express your meaning. Be open to changes; new words may pop up as you look at what is already there.
- Now treat the words as if they were magnets on a refrigerator. Rearrange them. Keep adding and subtracting until they start to make sense.
- Play with the words until you create a "cross" of opposites.
- Move the arms of the cross around, so that listeners are subtly urged toward your position.
- Evaluate your sentence. Could it serve as a springboard for a persuasive speech or essay?

PERSONAL NARRATIVE

Have you ever come to a crossroads in your life? Think about the choices you faced. Create a crossed sentence to anchor the moment and state the theme. Now describe what happened, using dialogue and description to set the scene. Give your reader some context for the choice—what was going on in your life that led you to this point. Explain which path you chose, and why. Evaluate the consequences of your decision.

Sandbox answers: (1) "Never let a fool kiss you or a kiss fool you."—comedian Joey Adams (2) "Quitters never win and winners never quit."—football coach Vince Lombardi (3) "We shape our buildings, and afterwards our buildings shape us."—British prime minister Winston Churchill

PARALLELISM

O, to take what we love inside,
to carry within us an orchard, to eat
not only the skin, but the shade,
not only the sugar, but the days, to hold
the fruit in our hands, adore it, then bite into
the round jubilance of peach.

—Li-Young Lee, "From Blossoms"

M any of us yawned through grammar lessons on parallelism—how
to avoid sending a sentence off track with something like "Gina
enjoyed skiing, to play hockey, and raising tulips." (In case your school
avoided this topic, "to play hockey" ought to be "playing hockey.") But
parallelism isn't just a meaningless rule that English teachers foist on
their pupils. It's a stylistic device that unifies ideas and gives them equal
importance, builds tension within a train of thought, or creates a path
for the reader. Parallel elements balance a sentence and satisfy the taste
for symmetry. Also useful are deliberately *non*parallel elements, which
jar the reader and call attention to a misfit phrase.

In the featured sentence, excerpted lines from Li-Young Lee's poem
"From Blossoms," a list of infinitives lay parallel tracks to carry the
reader into *the round jubilance of peach*, from tree to taste buds. The
infinitives are *to take, to carry, to eat, to hold, adore*, and *bite*. The first
four fit the "to + verb" pattern, and the last two break it. This isn't a random variation.

The sentence begins with *O*, an expression of yearning. Then come
the actions the implied speakers (*we*) ache for. (I say "implied" because
there's no way to know if one speaker represents a group or if the group

itself forms a collective speaker.) The first action, *to take what we love inside*, isn't peach-specific. It hints at the sexual, the desire to engulf and absorb *what we love*. The second, *to carry within us an orchard*, also expands outward from the *peach*. Here's the desire for more, not just for a piece of fruit but for all fruit, for nature itself. This parallel infinitive has parallel modifiers: *not only the skin, but the shade, / not only the sugar, but the days*. Sensual details apply to a peach (*skin, sugar*) but also bring bodily pleasure to mind. Yes, that's sex again, but not only sex. Lee's sentence calls to mind the relief of *shade* in the warm season when peaches ripen. *Days* may suggest hours spent outside in the orchard, a time of *jubilance*. The next link in the parallel chain is *to hold*. No one can *hold* without a conscious act of will; *to be held* is the form showing lack of power. In this portion of the sentence, too, a peach is more than a literal peach. It's the equivalent of *what we love* and desire *to hold*.

Now the parallel pattern breaks, because the last two infinitives (*adore, bite*) lack *to*. Why the change? Perhaps free will has given way to compulsion. Emotions come unbidden. Once *the fruit* is *in our hands*, we can't help how we feel. We *adore it. Bite* is problematic. If that action, too, is compulsive, the reader may be complicit in a forced act: we *adore*, therefore we *bite*—consume *what we love*. Maybe that last word is the logical conclusion of a process, something that happens almost without thought. Almost.

The poem's other stanzas allude to life and death. In both Chinese and Japanese culture, the peach is a symbol of long life or immortality. Just before the featured sentence are these words: *dust we eat*. Literally, the dust is on a peach freshly picked and consumed at a roadside stand. No chance to clean it! Figuratively, *dust* is what we return to after death, according to the Bible. In the featured sentence, *shade* and *days* evoke the passage of time. Also, Lee reinforces the cycle-of-life theme in the last stanza of the poem, citing "days we live as if death were nowhere." But death isn't nowhere. Instead, life comes "From Blossoms" (the title of the poem) and moves forward toward death. Everything that matters lies in the middle and, in the featured sentence, is represented by parallel infinitives.

One more thought: T. S. Eliot, in "The Love Song of J. Alfred Prufrock," poses the question "Do I dare to eat a peach?" I imagine that Li-Young Lee would answer, "Why not?" His poem advocates going from "joy / to joy to joy" while we can.

PARALLEL PRINCIPLES

Sweeping statements of principle are perfectly suited to parallel structure. Here's a sentence from the *King James Bible*, Ecclesiastes 3:1–8:

> To every thing there is a season, and a time to every purpose under the heaven:
> A time to be born, and a time to die; a time to plant, and a time to pluck up that which is planted;
> A time to kill, and a time to heal; a time to break down, and a time to build up;
> A time to weep, and a time to laugh; a time to mourn, and a time to dance;
> A time to cast away stones, and a time to gather stones together; a time to embrace, and a time to refrain from embracing;
> A time to get, and a time to lose; a time to keep, and a time to cast away;
> A time to rend, and a time to sew; a time to keep silence, and a time to speak;
> A time to love, and a time to hate; a time of war, and a time of peace.

The sentence, grammatically, is one independent clause—a subject/verb statement that expresses a complete thought. The opening statement, all by itself, qualifies as an independent clause:

> To every thing there is a season, and a time to every purpose under the heaven:

As a separate sentence, these words would end with a period. But here you see a colon, the traditional way to begin a list, in this case, a parallel list of *times*. Each of the *time* statements elaborates on the meaning of the first *time* (*a time to every purpose under the heaven*). Furthermore, within each *time* statement are more parallels: *a time to cast away stones* is parallel to *a time to gather stones together*. Though the listed *times* appear to focus on details, they represent something larger and more general. *A time to rend, and a time to sew*, for example, implies all destruction (*rend*) and creation (*sew*). The main idea, that everything *under the heaven* is part of the Creator's plan, is reinforced by the parallel structure of the sentence, which gives both tragedy and joy equal importance.

––––––––

The American Declaration of Independence begins with a parallel statement of principle:

> We hold these truths to be self-evident, that all men are created equal, that they are endowed by their Creator with certain unalienable Rights, that among these are Life, Liberty and the pursuit of Happiness.

Three statements beginning with *that* parallel one another and create a staircase of logic. The first step is *that all men are created equal*. What does that idea mean, in a practical sense? The second step answers: *that they are endowed by their Creator with certain unalienable Rights*. Now the next step: which *Rights*? And the answer: *Life, Liberty and the pursuit of Happiness*, among others. Just as a good staircase is constructed from even, equal steps, so is this sentence.

––––––––

Not quite a century later, President Abraham Lincoln spoke at Gettysburg, the site of a bloody battle of the Civil War, where land had been set aside for "a final resting place for those who here gave their lives." His address contains this sentence, the heart of his tribute:

But, in a larger sense, we can not dedicate—we can not consecrate—we can not hallow—this ground.

The "brave men, living and dead" had already consecrated the land, Lincoln explained, "far above our poor power" to do so. The parallel verbs
are very close in meaning:

> dedicate—to set apart for a purpose, to devote to God or a
>   sacred being
> consecrate—to set apart as sacred to God, to make holy
> hallow—to make holy, to purify

Though these three are often considered synonyms, shades of meaning
create a chain, with each link intensifying Lincoln's point. *Dedicate* is
appropriate for a nonreligious action, but *consecrate* and *hallow* are not.
Consecrate and *hallow* "make holy," but only *hallow* purifies. Lincoln
uses all three negatively to emphasize that politicians can't do what soldiers did on that battlefield.

———

Much more concise, but still a statement of principle, is this remark from
Ronald Reagan:

> How can we love our country, and not also love our countrymen?

———

Similarly, Francis Bacon gets right to the point in his essay "Of Studies":

> Reading maketh a full man, conference a ready man, and writing
> an exact man.

Conference, as Bacon uses it here, means "speaking with others, seeking
counsel." *Ready* is "knowledgeable, prepared," and *exact* is "accurate."

———

Bacon omits *maketh* in the last two portions of his sentence, relying on the reader to supply the missing verbs. But Wole Soyinka prefers an almost chantlike repetition. This sentence from a character in his play *Death and the King's Horseman* explains how life remains in balance. Fittingly, Soyinka makes his point with parallel statements:

> There is only one home to the life of a river-mussel; there is only one home to the life of a tortoise; there is only one shell to the soul of man; there is only one world to the spirit of our race.

———

American philosopher Ralph Waldo Emerson comments on priorities:

> What lies behind us and what lies before us are tiny compared to what lies within us.

Three iterations of *what lies* illustrate where an individual might invest emotional energy. In Emerson's view, events in the past and future are much less important than an individual's strength of character.

PARALLEL DESCRIPTIONS

Biographers and other writers often weigh character traits and accomplishments. Is their subject mostly cruel but occasionally kind? Are actions balanced between justice and mercy, or tending toward one or the other? Parallel structure supports the writer's assessment.

Consider this sentence from a eulogy President Barack Obama gave for Nelson Mandela of South Africa, who led his country as institutionalized segregation (apartheid) ended:

> It took a man like Madiba [Nelson Mandela] to free not just the prisoner, but the jailer as well; to show that you must trust oth-

ers so that they may trust you; to teach that reconciliation is not a matter of ignoring a cruel past, but a means of confronting it with inclusion and generosity and truth.

Each parallel element of Obama's list begins with an infinitive (*to free, to show, to teach*). Thus Mandela's three major accomplishments have equal importance. Within those elements are other parallels (*not just the prisoner but the jailer, that you must trust others . . . that they may trust you, ignoring . . . confronting*). By placing these paired ideas in parallel, Obama shows that Mandela deemed both elements of each pair to be essential.

———

This assessment of women comes from a character in Edith Wharton's short story "The Fullness of Life":

> But I have sometimes thought that a woman's nature is like a great house full of rooms: there is the hall, through which everyone passes in going in and out; the drawing-room, where one receives formal visits; the sitting-room, where the members of the family come and go as they list; but beyond that, far beyond, are other rooms, the handles of whose doors perhaps are never turned; no one knows the way to them, no one knows whither they lead; and in the innermost room, the holy of holies, the soul sits alone and waits for a footstep that never comes.

A house as a metaphor for women is not uncommon, but Wharton's twist is unusual. She takes her readers on a tour through what the character sees as women's nature—what modern readers may view as society's rigid gender roles. Two of the three named rooms, the *drawing-room* and *sitting-room*, are cited in conjunction with the duties of an upper-class woman of Wharton's era: nurturing family and welcoming visitors. The other, *the hall*, is open to everyone because nothing happens there except movement in and out.

The "room" elements are parallel, with the function following each name. Fittingly, the two associated with female duties have the strictest parallels; both are descriptions beginning with *where*. After these named rooms—*beyond that, far beyond*—the rooms have no names, and their descriptions aren't strictly parallel. Through this structure, Wharton shows outward conformity and inner variety.

————

Another description, this time of a country:

> This royal throne of kings, this sceptred isle,
> This earth of majesty, this seat of Mars,
> This other Eden, demi-paradise,
> This fortress built by Nature for herself
> Against infection and the hand of war,
> This happy breed of men, this little world . . .
> This blessed plot, this earth, this realm, this England.

These often-quoted lines from Shakespeare's *Richard II*, spoken by John of Gaunt, describe an ideal: England as it should be. The parallel descriptions (*this royal throne, this sceptred isle*) link kingship to the land (*earth, plot*) and people (*happy breed of men*).

————

Smaller, both in subject and in length, is Jan Morris's description of Washington, DC:

> Down the great thoroughfares we drove, and all the memorials
> of the American splendour passed us one by one, granite and
> concrete, obelisk and colonnade.

The *memorials of the American splendour* are defined by four nouns: *granite, concrete, obelisk,* and *colonnade.* Those four are broken into pairs, the first of building materials and the second of forms. It's interesting that *one by one* precedes this list. That's how Morris perceives the memorials, but the list is two by two. The sentence is more parallelogram than parallel, with two sets of parallel lines meeting, but slightly askew. How much of politics, the primary business of Washington, resembles this sentence?

Now to a parallel, house-level description, also from Jan Morris:

> He took me to the small, square house where he and his wife lived and, merciful heavens, the moment he opened the front door for me I found myself hemmed in, towered over, squashed in, squeezed down by an almighty multitude of books.

The *he* of Morris's sentence is, not surprisingly, a writer.

MORE PARALLELS

A few more parallels, the first from Dylan Thomas's *A Child's Christmas in Wales*:

> I can never remember whether it snowed for six days and six nights when I was twelve or whether it snowed for twelve days and twelve nights when I was six.

I could make a serious point about memory here, but serious is beside the point. Thomas is having fun in this sentence, as is the reader.

More parallel verbs, from Ransom Riggs's novel *Miss Peregrine's Home for Peculiar Children*:

> We picked our way down to the beach, where what seemed to be an entire civilization of birds were flapping and screeching and fishing in tide pools.

Though I selected this sentence for its parallel verbs (*flapping, screeching, fishing*), what makes me smile, I must admit, is *civilization*. What a brilliant word choice!

———

Totally serious is this sentence from President George W. Bush's speech after the attacks of September 11, 2001:

> We've seen the unfurling of flags, the lighting of candles, the giving of blood, the saying of prayers—in English, Hebrew, and Arabic.

Four parallel verb forms (*unfurling, lighting, giving, saying*) at first appear equal. But the last one comes with a parallel set of qualifiers, an arrangement that gives the saying of prayers more importance. Further, the parallel list of languages emphasizes the unity of purpose in three major faiths.

FOR THE WRITER

You write parallels all the time, if your sentences conform to the traditions of standard English. But do you get top value from each parallel you write? To do so, you must consider the equality or hierarchy of the parallel elements. These exercises may help.

FILL IN THE BLANKS
Take these general sentences and fill in the blanks with parallel elements:

Elena sang _____ but _____.

What _____ and what _____ didn't matter to his father.

In the town where _____, where _____, and where

_____, the citizens were prosperous.

Some _____, but some _____.

Recycle this exercise by doing it several times, changing your answers again and again.

GROCERY LIST

Write a list, with reasons, of all the things you should buy. Make your reasons parallel for items of equal importance and *not* parallel for trivial purchases. Here's an example:

> **new key**, because I lost my old one and I can't get in when
>   Fred's not home
> **pepper spray**, because three people on the block were
>   mugged last week
> **cell phone charger**, because my phone went dead and I
>   need it
> **almonds**, which I like to snack on
> **orange juice**, if I have a coupon

As you see, the first three items are significant and parallel to each other. The last two pale in importance in comparison to the first three. I've broken the parallel pattern in writing them.

CLOSET

What would I see if I looked in your closet (attic, garage, cabinet, whatever)? Describe the mess using some parallel descriptions. To start you off:

> In the hall closet are two pairs of sheets, one embroidered in
> fanciful patterns by my grandmother and the other machine-
> printed in garish colors by some mega-corporation.

Claim the fiction writer's privilege and lie as much as you want for this exercise.

PHILOSOPHY

What principles guide your life? Taking your cue from the philosophers in this chapter, fashion a few parallel statements that reflect what matters to you. Start each statement with "I believe that."

REVERSED SENTENCES

Much to learn, you still have.
—Yoda, *Star Wars* character created by George Lucas

To paraphrase the most common dictionary definition: a "work-horse" is someone or something relied on to do a lot of work, especially of a type that is necessary but not interesting. The workhorse of English expression is

subject—verb—object

with the *subject* being who or what performs the action expressed by the *verb*, and the *object* receiving the action. (Some sentences express a state of being instead of an action, but that's not the situation in the featured sentence.)

If Yoda were riding the workhorse, he would have said:

You still have much to learn.

You don't need grammatical terminology to understand that Yoda has reversed the usual order. But if you care, here it is: Yoda's statement places the object (*much*) before the subject-verb pair (*you have*). The reversal makes Yoda sound odd, but also funny and appealing. How can you not like a character who says, "When nine hundred years old you reach, look as good, you will not"? Yoda's physical traits—tiny, with bulging eyes, bat-wing ears, and the number of wrinkles you'd expect to see on a nine-hundred-year-old—join his sentence structure in signaling that Yoda is an alien. That's why the featured sentence works so well. Sentences with scrambled word order aren't absent in English, but they're not common either. They call attention because they're different, just as Yoda is.

The reversed order of Yoda's statement also shines a spotlight on his role. He trains prospective Jedi knights, teaching them to access "the Force," a mystical web uniting all life forms, and use it for the greater good. But Yoda isn't always successful; he makes his statement in a confrontation with Count Dooku, a former student who has gone over to "the Dark Side." Though Dooku brags to Yoda that he is "more powerful than any Jedi knight, even you," Yoda easily counteracts and contains Dooku's attack. By starting with *much to learn*, Yoda highlights the underlying principle of the Jedi code: personal identity (*you*) is less important than the collective knowledge and power of the Force.

BEGINNINGS, WITH EMPHASIS

Writers not in a *Star Wars* "galaxy far, far away" also reap benefits from reversed sentences. Authors can direct the reader's focus to the key idea by moving it to the beginning of the sentence. Here's the first line of Robert Frost's poem "Stopping by Woods on a Snowy Evening":

Whose woods these are I think I know.

The speaker makes this statement while pausing on the "darkest evening of the year" to look at the *woods*, which are "lovely, dark, and deep." After a few minutes and a reproachful harness shake from "my little horse," the speaker moves on because of "promises to keep, and miles to go before I sleep."

You can read this poem as nothing more than a traveler's moment of rest, but the structure of the first line hints at something else. In ordinary speech, you'd expect to hear "I think I know whose woods these are" or "I think I know who owns these woods." Either way, *I* comes first. But Frost moves the *I* statement to the end of the sentence. One reason for doing so is to adhere to the poem's pattern of rhyme and rhythm. But meaning also plays a role. The first words concern ownership, literally of one patch of woods, but perhaps also of nature itself. Who owns the beauty of a snowfall, the peace of the silent scene? The one who stops to enjoy it? Or the one with legal title, whose house is "in the village"?

Of course, other interpretations are plausible, too. Some readers connect this poem, with its "dark and deep" *woods*, to depression or even suicide. Others see a conflict within the speaker, who wants a quiet life but cannot neglect work and other obligations. Perhaps Frost's *I think I know* is the most any reader can say about the meaning of "Stopping by Woods on a Snowy Evening."

Moving indoors, but still reversing for emphasis, is Winston Churchill, who said these words during an address in London shortly after World War I began:

Sure I am of this, that you have only to endure to conquer.

For an audience perhaps fearful of war, *sure* is a good way to begin a sentence about victory (*to conquer*).

Now to Shakespeare. In this line from *The Tempest*, the Bard aligns form with content. A key moment in the play is, as the title suggests, a dangerous storm. The boatswain, frantically trying to keep the ship afloat, has little patience for his noble passengers. He shouts at them:

What cares these roarers
for the name of king?

These roarers are the waves threatening the boat. Shakespeare matches *roarers*, the subject, with the verb *cares*. Today's writers would put the boatswain's question this way: "What do these roarers care for the name of king?" The subject, *roarers*, precedes the main verb, *care*, in the modern version, but not in Shakespeare's line. By placing his verb first, Shakespeare upends the common order of words. The traditional order of authority is also upended in this scene. The boatswain ranks below the people around him, but in an emergency, he assumes authority. The reversed sentence mirrors the reversed hierarchy.

———

A modern bard, Bruce Springsteen, writes in his autobiography, *Born to Run*:

> From Phil Spector came the ambition to make a world-shaking mighty noise.

This sentence is one of several with the same pattern, all beginning with *from* and all listing important influences on Springsteen's career. In addition to Spector, a record producer, Springsteen cites musicians Duane Eddy, Roy Orbison, Elvis Presley, and others. The placement of *From Phil Spector* emphasizes the fact that Spector and the musicians came first chronologically and that Springsteen drew from their work to develop his own musical style.

———

Edgar Allan Poe's reversals in the first paragraph of his short story "The Tell-Tale Heart" reveal the narrator's disordered mind:

> True!—nervous—very, very dreadfully nervous I had been and am. . . . Above all was the sense of hearing acute.

The narrator, who murdered and dismembered an old man and hid body parts under the floor planks, has every reason to be *nervous*. It's fitting that this word precedes *I had been and am*, because this feeling has taken over the narrator's mind. As the police question him, the narrator hears the beating of the dead man's heart, louder and louder. Others in the room perceive nothing; what the narrator "hears" is his own guilt. Eventually, he confesses. By placing *Above all* first, Poe directs the reader's attention to the narrator's *sense of hearing*, which is not *acute* but delusional.

MOVING PAST FIRST

Authors sometimes reconfigure the middle of a sentence to spotlight or bury an idea. Here is a sentence from Mary Shelley's novel *The Last Man*:

Fools that we were not long ago to have foreseen this.

The Last Man describes an apocalyptic plague that eventually kills every human being except for one, the title character. Shelley places an important word, *Fools*, at the beginning of the sentence. Equally important is that she inserts a phrase about time (*not long ago*) in the middle of her sentence. This placement creates ambiguity. The phrase may be attached to *were*, meaning *not long ago we were fools*. Or it may belong with *to have foreseen this*, meaning *we were fools not to have foreseen this long ago*. Both interpretations have merit. The characters in Shelley's novel closely resemble real people, including her husband, Percy Bysshe Shelley, and their friend Lord Byron. These men died young as a result of arguably foolish activities: Shelley's sail during a storm and Byron's ill-prepared trip to a war zone. Thus, *not long ago we were fools* makes sense. But so does the second interpretation. Despite warning signs, the characters in the novel do not recognize the danger of the plague until it's too late. They *were fools not to have foreseen this long ago*.

———

Also tinkering with the middle is Truman Capote. His true-crime book, *In Cold Blood*, relates the murder of the Clutter family of Holcomb, Kansas, and the subsequent investigation. Capote writes:

Like the waters of the river, like the motorists on the highway, and like the yellow trains streaking down the Santa Fe tracks, drama, in the shape of exceptional happenings, had never stopped there.

Three long phrases beginning with *like*, as well as another phrase (*in the shape of exceptional happenings*) nearly eclipse the subject, *drama*. That structure supports Capote's point. Everything—*waters, motorists, trains*—sped through the rural area where the Clutters lived. Nothing out of the ordinary happened until two men on parole *stopped there* to rob and murder four people. *Drama* is in an unexpected place, just as the murders were.

———

E. F. Benson, in *Lucia in London*, employs the same device by situating the subject of the sentence, always an important word, in the middle:

By the fireplace was standing the Royal lady, and that for the moment was the only chagrin, for Lucia had not the vaguest idea who she was.

Lucia is a small-town girl desperate to climb the social ladder. She's crashed a party and worked her way through the crowd, searching for dignitaries. Unfortunately, it's hard to brag about meeting *the Royal lady* without knowing the woman's name.

———

Walt Whitman's haunting poem about the death of Abraham Lincoln, "When Lilacs Last in the Dooryard Bloom'd," includes these lines:

Ever-returning spring, trinity sure to me you bring,
Lilac blooming perennial and drooping star in the west,
And thought of him I love.

Ever-returning spring is a direct address. (In this case, the speaker addresses *spring*, which is personified.) Next comes the reversal: *trinity sure to me you bring.* The nonpoetic version is "you surely [always] bring a trinity to me." The phrase *to me* is sandwiched between elements that never change: *trinity* and *you* (the *ever-returning spring*). Whitman defines the *trinity* as a flower, *lilac*, which blooms in the spring; a *drooping star in the west*, a reference to the spring sky; and the *thought of him I love*. Two elements are natural, and perhaps the third—the implied grief of *thought of him I love*—is as well. By burying *to me* between powerful images, Whitman shows that the speaker feels overwhelmed.

———

Now to the end of the sentence, which writers know is valuable real estate. Take a look at this sentence by J. R. R. Tolkien, author of *The Hobbit, The Lord of the Rings,* and *The Silmarillion*:

In a hole in the ground there lived a hobbit.

Tolkien claimed that this sentence sprang into his mind while he was reading student essays. If Tolkien's account is true—how many origin stories are myths?—his fantasy novels and the extremely profitable film series based on them arose from the tedium of paper grading. Perhaps Tolkien was hoping to find a spark of inspiration in the pile of student writing, akin to discovering a hobbit *in a hole in the ground.* True or not, Tolkien's reversed sentence is much more effective than "A hobbit lived in a hole in the ground." Tolkien draws you into the setting and then introduces you to the creature who lives there.

———

Another effective ending is this one from Gish Jen's novel *Mona in the Promised Land*:

And how inconveniently placed is the nose.

Readers, as well as the middle-schoolers experiencing their first, far-from-perfect kiss, bump right into that *nose*.

PAIRS

Two-line reversals double the impact of unusual word order. Nilo Cruz, in his play *Anna in the Tropics*, pairs a straightforward sentence with its reversal to reveal the nature of a relationship. A married couple, Santiago and Ofelia, fight about nearly everything. After an argument, the husband makes a statement and the wife reverses his words:

> SANTIAGO: He's good. He has a solid voice. . . .
> OFELIA: Yes, a solid voice he has. . . .
> SANTIAGO: You're right . . . I shouldn't drink.
> OFELIA: That's right, drink you shouldn't.

The words the husband and wife say indicate agreement, but the reversal emphasizes that they approach life in fundamentally different ways.

———

British writer William Makepeace Thackeray also pairs statements in this sentence from a letter he wrote to a friend during a trip to New York City:

> Nobody is quiet here, no more am I.

Nobody is quiet here follows the usual order. That last bit, *no more am I*, doesn't. The reversal comes as a surprise to the reader. Perhaps Thackeray himself was a little surprised at the city's effect on his behavior.

FOR THE WRITER

All competent writers vary sentence patterns, but reversed sentences take variety to a whole new level. Here are a few exercises that may inspire you to try reverse gear.

OVERUSE

Done too frequently, reversals quickly become annoying. (Yoda, of course, is an exception.) In your own work, take care not to inspire a comment like this one from Wolcott Gibbs, who parodied the writing style of a popular magazine: "Backward ran sentences until reeled the mind."

The easiest way to see the perils of reversal is to reverse *everything*. Select a paragraph from a fiction or nonfiction work or a few lines from a play. Tinker with word order: Place a subject after its verb, bury an important word in the middle, or hit the reader with a surprising end. Read what you wrote. It will be awful, and that's the point. Once you see excess, you appreciate moderation. Plus, you'll have practiced writing reversed sentences. As Yoda would put it: "Writing reversed sentences, you'll know how to do."

QUESTIONS

How, *when*, *where*, *why*, and *who* are common question words. They usually appear at the beginning of the sentence:

> *Where* are you going?
> *Why* should I go with you?
> *How* will we get there?

and so forth. If you move the key word to the end of the question, the tone changes:

> You are going *where*?
> I should go with you *why*?
> We will get there *how*?

Depending on the context, these reversed questions add snark, skepticism, defiance, or other emotions. Write a few reversed questions, perhaps in a scene or a character sketch. Keep the emotional context in mind as you write, so that the reversal illuminates the character trait or situation you envision.

MIDDLES

If you're a public figure who must admit something you hope will be ignored, Saturday night is the best time to issue a press release. The story may go viral anyway, but mid-weekend news tends to fade into the background. With this in mind, think of some information that you can bury in the middle of a sentence, with lots of distracting phrases before and after. These scenarios may inspire you:

A child has broken something and must tell the babysitter what happened.

The mayor did not, in fact, stay within budget in redecorating City Hall.

That text wasn't meant for you. Honestly, I can explain!

POEM CHANGES

Find a poem with unusual word order. (This shouldn't be too hard.) Rewrite the poem in standard, workhorse-style sentences. Compare the original and your version. How does each affect the reader? Don't judge. Concentrate on the differing impact of standard and reversed order. Additional challenge: Figure out why the poet changed the order. If the poem is good, you should be able to identify the reason.

SURPRISE

She had found some acquaintance, had been so lucky too as to find
in them the family of a most worthy old friend; and as the completion
of good fortune, had found these friends by no means so expensively
dressed as herself.

—Jane Austen, *Northanger Abbey*

The only image that without doubt depicts Jane Austen is a sketch
her sister Cassandra drew. It shows a sweet-faced woman wearing a
demure cap and a high-necked gown. There's no scalpel in the picture,
but I like to think Jane had it on her somewhere, the better to lacerate
her characters with. Such was her skill that her victims, had they been
alive and not fictional, would not have noticed the cut until they'd been
surgically, and literarily, dissected. I like to imagine their surprise on
discovering that an outwardly prim author could be so vicious.

Surprise is there for Austen's readers, too. Not in her plots, which
are simple enough to be written on an index card: a couple meets, faces
obstacles in their relationship, matures, and makes a solid match. The
surprise comes from Austen's writing style, which has more masterful
elements than I can discuss here. One especially elegant technique is to
start a sentence off in one direction and then spin it into a U-turn. The
humor is all the more effective because it's unexpected.

The featured sentence comes from *Northanger Abbey*, not as well
known as Austen's masterpiece, *Pride and Prejudice*, but nevertheless
a work that showcases her style and explores serious ideas. *Northanger
Abbey* is Austen's take on the Gothic novel, a genre that was popular

from the mid-eighteenth to the early nineteenth century—a little longer than the span of Austen's life. The conventions of the form include mystery (what's in this locked chest/cupboard/tower? what caused that "natural" death?) and horror (terrifying answers to those questions, and more). Austen sends Catherine Morland, a naive young woman who has read many such novels, into a truly horrifying setting: social gatherings of the British gentry. There Catherine applies the rules she's gleaned from novels to other mysteries, such as how to talk to an attractive man and how to distinguish genuine friendship from exploitation. The results are only mildly disastrous, *Northanger Abbey* being a comedy of manners and not an actual Gothic novel.

The *she* of the featured sentence is Mrs. Allen, a neighbor who chaperones Catherine in Bath, a popular English resort. The trip is not solely a vacation; Mrs. Allen's role is to help Catherine meet people beyond the rural community they both live in. Unspoken but understood is that Catherine may find a husband in Bath. Unfortunately—as Mrs. Allen says repeatedly during their first few days there—they know no one at the resort, and etiquette prohibits random interactions. Those frequenting the "Assembly Rooms" can talk with people they already know, but not with strangers. They must be introduced by a mutual friend or the Master of Ceremonies, whose role is to ease social interactions and keep the peace among the social-climbing, spouse-hunting crowd.

After a few contact-less days, Mrs. Allen meets someone she went to school with, Mrs. Thorpe. Austen notes that their happiness at seeing each other was great "since they had been contented to know nothing of each other for the past fifteen years." That last bit is an example of an Austenian U-turn, as is the final portion of the featured sentence: Mrs. Allen's *good fortune* in finding *these friends by no means so expensively dressed as herself*.

What's interesting about this sentence is the way in which it proffers and then subverts the values of society. Mrs. Thorpe is at first referred to as an *acquaintance*, a word that originally applied to a close connection but, by Austen's time, implied a slight, superficial relationship. And this is a society of surfaces, as *expensively dressed* underscores. Mrs. Allen is in charge of Catherine at a crucial moment in the young woman's life. Yet all Mrs. Allen talks about is clothing, even when Catherine turns to her for serious advice. (Lest the modern reader feel superior, Instagram and selfies show that only the medium, not the message, is different now.)

Digging deeper into the sentence: Austen attaches *some* to *acquaintance*, revealing that it doesn't matter to Mrs. Allen who the *acquaintance* is. She just wants someone to talk to. It's a plus that Mrs. Allen deems Mrs. Thorpe and her grown children *most worthy*, with no basis for that judgment except an *old* connection. Furthermore, whatever qualities Mrs. Allen saw in Mrs. Thorpe during their school years are now projected onto the entire Thorpe *family*—and family is a revered institution in this society. Many of Austen's characters speak about a "good" family as if that quality were a collective, inherited trait. But the author has a different view. Nearly every Austenian family has a lemon in it—some a groveful—and the Thorpes are no exception. By the end of the sentence the Thorpes are *friends*. Why? Austen explains that Mrs. Allen and Mrs. Thorpe talk constantly, each "far more ready to give than to receive information, and each hearing very little of what the other said"—still another Austenian surgical strike.

Austen's choice of *good fortune* instead of an expression like *good luck* is also relevant, as is her use of *by no means*. In Austen's world, yearly income and property went a long way toward determining one's status. Thus *good fortune* is a sly reference to the fact that Mrs. Allen has money and doesn't hesitate to spend it. Mrs. Thorpe, on the other hand, is associated with the expression *by no means*. Austen milks the double meaning: the Thorpes are not people of *means*. This fact makes the children's marriage prospects precarious, but it also makes Mrs. Thorpe the perfect pal for Mrs. Allen, who notes that Mrs. Thorpe isn't *so expensively dressed*. The U-turn takes readers exactly where Austen wants them to go, beyond the stated values of society into undeniable hypocrisy. After paying homage to decorum and family in the first part of the sentence, Austen reveals the real priority at the end: to have someone to look down on, someone with a lesser *fortune.*

SURPRISES ON THE FAMILY TREE

Robert Caro writes biographies, not novels, but like Austen he enjoys ambushing readers, as in this sentence from *The Passage of Power,* one of his books about President Lyndon Johnson:

> They felt those roots lay in the little house—a shanty, really, a typical Texas Hill Country "dog run": two box-like rooms, each about twelve feet square, on either side of a breezeway, two smaller "shed rooms" and a kitchen, all connected by a sagging roof—where Lyndon Johnson had lived from the age of eleven until just after his fourteenth birthday, for it was there that his father had failed.

The reader begins this sentence expecting something positive about *roots.* This is, after all, the story of a man who rose from *a shanty* to the White House. It's tempting to connect Johnson's boyhood home to Abe Lincoln's log cabin. But Johnson's *roots* come from the place where *his father had failed.* With those words, along with the evidence of poverty embedded in the house description, so much of Johnson's life comes into focus: his drive to succeed and to crush all opposition, his need for control and legitimacy, even his signature policy initiative, the War on Poverty. Caro surprises readers by presenting what is obvious to them in retrospect.

———

Another U-turn comes from N. Scott Momaday, who imagines his great-grandfather, waking up one morning and standing outside, musing:

> At times you can hear the wind, for it runs upon the walls and moans, but you cannot know it truly until you are old and have lived with it many years; so they say, who are old.

Up until the semicolon, the reader coasts on a bromide—we gain knowledge as we age. But the last portion of this sentence from Momaday's memoir, *The Names*, changes the path by citing an unreliable source. How can readers, or the great-grandfather, trust that *you cannot know it truly until you are old* when the only people who can attest to it are those who have a vested interest in sounding wise: *they . . . who are old*?

———

Larry McMurtry also explores his roots in "Take My Saddle from the Wall":

> That their names are not writ large in the annals of the Highway Patrol is only due to the fact that they lived amid the lightly habited wastes of West Texas and were thus allowed a wider margin of error than most mortals get.

With this statement McMurtry describes the older generation of his family, men with bowed legs and minimal driving skills whose only comfortable mode of transportation was a horse. They don't die on the road because there's not much to crash their cars into, but, McMurtry explains, he knew even as a boy that he was "witnessing the dying of a way of life." The surprising *wider margin of error than most mortals get* comes, literally, from *the lightly habited wastes of West Texas.* McMurtry hints that they have another *margin of error*: "the myth of the cowboy [that] grew purer every year because there were so few actual cowboys left to contradict it."

———

Maxine Hong Kingston, too, considers her forebearers in *China Men*, which interweaves biographies of her male ancestors with both American and Chinese myths. In a chapter entitled "American Father," young Maxine looks into what appears to her as a bottomless well in the basement of her home. She imagines "a long, long fall" that would take her "feet first" into China, where "the Chinese would laugh." She adds:

The way to arrive in China less obtrusively was to dive in head first.

Her premise—that she can fall through the world and come out on the other side—is plausible to a young child and amusing to adult readers. But the sentence delivers a shock. Expecting an "isn't-that-cute" comment, readers instead hear that it would be better *to dive in head first.* And that's what Kingston does in *China Men.* Her goal is to understand both the Chinese and the American portions of her identity. She does dive in, examining family stories, historical accounts, laws, and myth. Despite these efforts, Kingston can't put together a clear picture. No wonder she writes that the well is as murky as "black jello."

CHARACTER REVELATIONS

Writers are often advised to select just the right detail to bring a character to life. Joan Didion, in her 1977 novel, *A Book of Common Prayer,* does exactly that. The book recounts the life of Charlotte Douglas, whose daughter participates in the bombing of a skyscraper in San Francisco and then disappears, with the FBI in pursuit. Charlotte deals with uncomfortable truths by ignoring them. Another character calls her "immaculate of history, innocent of politics." The daughter, Marin, is a self-styled revolutionary, vaguely Marxist but so muddled that she plagiarizes her manifesto. This sentence reveals much about both characters:

> The agents had taken Charlotte to see the house on Grove Street in Berkeley where they had found the cache of .30-caliber Browning automatic rifles and the translucent pink orthodontal retainer Marin was supposed to wear to correct her bite.

Post-bombing, the rifles aren't a surprise. But the retainer? That's a remnant of the childhood Marin has rejected, along with a gold bracelet that she calls "dead metal" and attaches to the explosive device. Charlotte's state of mind is tucked into that retainer, too. Charlotte thinks that

Marin was supposed to wear it. Marin also was supposed to not bomb buildings. Traumatized, Charlotte is caught between the life she imagined for her daughter and the one her daughter chose for herself.

———

Ian Frazier recounts another act of violence, this time a real one, in "The Last Days of Stealhead Joe":

> Hanging from the inside rearview mirror was a large, red-and-white plastic fishing bobber on a loop of monofilament line, and on the dash and in the cup holders were coiled-up tungsten-core leaders, steelhead flies, needle-nose pliers—"numerous items consistent with camping and fishing," as the police report would later put it.

Frazier started out to write an article about fishing and did in fact fish with Stealhead Joe, a legendary guide who specialized in "steelheads." (Stealhead Joe changed the spelling on purpose, to reflect the fact that he often broke fish-and-game laws.) Six months after Frazier rode in Joe's truck, however, the colorful river guide committed suicide. Frazier builds his sentence by adding detail after detail (*the red-and-white fishing bobber*, the *monofilament line*, and so on). Then the sentence hits a wall: the *police report*. Frazier's profile of Stealhead Joe follows the same pattern. You're reading about an eccentric fellow who loves to fish—and then you're not. Instead, you're reading about a mentally ill man who takes his own life.

———

A few more character descriptions with a twist, the first a description of a woman hearing the latest gossip from her housekeeper:

> Mrs. Hopewell had no bad qualities of her own but she was able to use other people's in such a constructive way that she never felt the lack.
>
> —Flannery O'Connor, "Good Country People"

———

Here's a comment from Lena Dunham in her memoir, *Not That Kind of Girl*:

> One minute I was passionately engaged with my new friend Katie, and the next I was convinced she had the IQ of a lima bean.

I'm not sure whether this reveals more about Dunham or Katie—perhaps a bit of each?

———

This sentence tells you all you need to know about author Rachel Rieder-er's courage:

> It's easy to be calm because I cannot really have been run over by a bus.

But she has, and the rest of the essay, "Patient," describes her treatment and recovery.

———

Here's a sentence from Kevin Kwan's *Rich People Problems* describing the "Michelangelo of Botox" that some of his wealthy characters frequent:

> So deft were his hands at plunging needles into fine lines, fragile cheekbones, and delicate nasolabial folds, even his patients with the thinnest skins never bruised, and so subtle was his artistry that every patient visiting his clinic departed with the guarantee that they would be able to close both eyelids completely should they ever choose to blink.

The novel skewers these *rich people* as neatly as the plastic surgeon he describes.

———

I sincerely hope this last one isn't true:

The literary life, in this country, begins in jail.

This sentence comes from a letter written by E. B. White, most famous for *Charlotte's Web*. Writing to a friend, White explains that he feels "a little more like an author now" because the army and navy have banned one of his books.

SURPRISE AND DELIGHT

Surprise often sparks amusement; sometimes just a smile but occasionally a real belly laugh. To dissect humor is to kill it, so I'll present these sentences without comment and let your funny bone do the rest of the work:

Being Irish, he had an abiding sense of tragedy, which sustained him through temporary periods of joy.

—attributed to William Butler Yeats (Irish poet)

The secret to staying young is to live honestly, eat slowly, and lie about your age.

—Lucille Ball (actor)

I didn't like the play, but I saw it under adverse circumstances— the curtain was up.

—Groucho Marx (comedian)

Dress code: chic devastated.

—Mindy Kaling
(author and actor, from "Strict Instructions for My Funeral")

I learned three important things in college—to use a library, to memorize quickly and visually, to drop asleep at any time given a horizontal surface and fifteen minutes.

—Agnes de Mille (author and choreographer)

Blackstone declined to turn Sarah into an elephant—either he couldn't or he wouldn't, I've always said in my carefully balanced account of the incident—but he declined with great aplomb, pointing out to me that an elephant is one of the few beasts that require more upkeep than a teenager.

—Calvin Trillin (author)

Cleaning your house while your kids are still growing is like shoveling the walk before it stops snowing.

—Phyllis Diller (comedian)

FOR THE WRITER

Surprise your reader, and perhaps yourself, by constructing some sentences that change course at the last minute or deliver a punch. Here are a few ways to start.

DEFINITION

Open any handy dictionary and select a common word. Restate the definition in your own words, and then restate it again so that it matches your idea of what the word *really* means. For example:

Insurance is "protecting against potential harm"—wearing suspenders and a belt plus clean underwear, in case of wardrobe malfunction.

Education is "systematic instruction," the planting of seeds in the hope that some will eventually sprout.

Need some suggestions? Try *age, quarrel, party, snob, peanut butter, computer,* and *dance.*

SNEAK ATTACK

Thumb through your memory bank and locate a situation that turned out differently from what you expected—or one that you wish had turned out differently. Write a sentence with the unexpected element at the end. For example:

The real estate agent had told Mark that the apartment was "steps from Central Park," and it was, but somehow Mark had imagined fewer than 9,371 strides.

"No photos! No interviews!" the press agent shouted as his client moved through the hotel lobby, but no matter how loud he was, not a single guest noticed the actor.

MYSTERY

Sometimes it's fun to tease readers, leaking out a detail at a time before placing it in context. Who doesn't want to solve a mystery? So daydream a bit. Imagine a character and come up with as complete a background as possible. This sort of daydreaming is a great way to get through an annoying event (root canal, your third cousin's wedding, the Department of Motor Vehicles line, and so forth). Now write a sentence that represents one small piece of the puzzle that is your character. For example:

Marcia signed the lease, unpacked the moving boxes, and went to the grocery store, during which she would buy, for the first time in her life, her own container of salt.

I hope you're intrigued. Here's the backstory: Marcia is a young woman who lived first with her parents, then moved in with roommates, and eventually found Alex, who asked her to leave one Valentine's Day, when she was expecting a marriage proposal. Because she had always lived in someone else's house, she had never needed to purchase kitchen staples, like salt. *Her own container of salt* hints at a new stage in life for this character.

QUESTIONS

Are you there God? It's me, Margaret.

—Judy Blume

As all parents know, one of the more annoying stages of childhood occurs when kids ask "why?" every two minutes. Parents either spend an entire day explaining the world or pretend they haven't heard the question. The latter choice is understandable but unfortunate. Would you like your questions ignored? Don't answer that! It's a rhetorical question, not a real inquiry. Rhetorical questions introduce the point the writer wants to make, either explicitly or by implication. When H. L. Mencken asks, "Marriage is a wonderful institution, but who would want to live in an institution?" he lays the groundwork for a negative response.

All questions, rhetorical or not, engage the audience, because it's difficult to hear a question without supplying an answer. Good writers create questions not only to forge this connection but also to highlight a character trait or open a door to a chain of events and ideas.

Take the title of Judy Blume's novel *Are You There God? It's Me, Margaret.* Those two short sentences appear regularly within the book, whenever the narrator (Margaret) begins one of her highly personal conversations with God. Margaret has been raised without formal religion by a Jewish father and a Christian mother. Whatever their private beliefs, Margaret's parents practice neither faith and tell Margaret that she can choose a religion herself, when she is older.

As she approaches her twelfth birthday, Margaret struggles to define her identity in many ways, including religion. For a school project she studies several faiths, attending services, inquiring about the beliefs of participants, and waiting for a signal that she's found the religion that's right for her. Getting a head start on a contractual obligation of adolescence, Margaret sees her parents as clueless and irrelevant. Instead of talking with them, she turns to God every time she has a question or a request, such as when she'll begin to menstruate and would God please ensure that Margaret isn't the last of her friends to reach that milestone.

There, in the title question, is a homonym of *their*, which is more relevant to the theme of Judy Blume's novel. Despite beginning her prayers with a question, Margaret never really doubts the existence of God. She's simply calling God's attention to the fact that she's ready to talk. True, at one point Margaret turns away from God, but she returns when she gets her first period. She says, "I know you're there God. I know you wouldn't have missed this for anything!"

But Margaret does question how the people around her relate to religion. Her parents have opted out of the discussion, but Sylvia, Margaret's adored paternal grandmother, is elated when Margaret attends a temple service with her. Margaret is interested, but she's dismayed when she realizes that Grandma Sylvia wants her to commit to Judaism. "As long as she loves me and I love her, what difference does religion make?" Margaret asks. Similarly, when her mother's long-estranged parents visit, they're shocked and upset that Margaret hasn't been raised as a Christian. Margaret also attends services with friends belonging to different religions. Each visit resembles a first date, with Margaret wondering whether she's found a match. These experiences give rise to Margaret's real question: "Are you *their* God?" The book ends without an answer, but the reader knows that Margaret's conversations with God will continue.

One point about punctuation: in a situation grammarians call "direct address," the name of the person spoken to should be separated from the rest of the sentence by commas. No comma precedes *God* in Blume's sentence. This omission could reflect Margaret's faulty writing skills, but she makes no similar mistakes when addressing other characters. By removing the comma, Blume forces the reader to run *there* and *God* together, a situation in which *their* makes more sense.

REAL, BUT UNANSWERED

Anyone who ponders life's most important mysteries comes up with real but ultimately unanswered and perhaps unanswerable questions. When Bob Dylan sings

> How many roads must a man walk down
> Before you call him a man?

he concludes that the answer is "blowin' in the wind," a phrase that is also the title of the song. Besides this question about the relationship between experience and maturity, Dylan also asks about war, injustice, and indifference. Every line opens a new area of thought, but nothing is resolved. Perhaps nothing could be, given that Dylan questions the meaning of life and the motives for human behavior.

——————

Another unanswerable question: In Harry Bauld's poem "Myopia and the Sick Child," the speaker asks:

> How can I be anyone's father?

Those with *myopia* see clearly whatever is near; everything at a distance is blurred. Through the "unground lens" of the window by the child's bed, the speaker watches "clouds flee" his son's fever across an "El Greco sky," which is as distorted as the father's myopic vision is. The physical echoes the emotional here. What parent can focus on anything beyond a child's illness? What parent can clearly see beyond the present moment, to protect a child from future threats? And what parent hasn't wanted to preserve some bit of self despite a child's needs? It's not surprising that nature itself, in the form of clouds, is "escaping" and that the speaker harbors a wish to do so also. Although his glasses are "at hand," he doesn't want "to recognize anything anymore." But escape, like control, is not really an option for the speaker. Parenthood is a life-sentence to helplessness, whether a child is sick or not.

————

Nor can the question "Could Time End?" be answered. That's the title of an article by George Musser in which he explains various theories about the nature of time. Taken together, these theories add up to "yes and no," which is not coincidentally the subtitle of the article. I can't claim to understand every nuance of the theories Musser explains so well, but I do grasp that "Could Time End?" is inseparable from "Did Time Begin?" and that both questions involve the Big Bang, Einstein's theory of relativity, quantum gravity, and other scientific concepts I will not enumerate. To ask another question (and answer it): How many people eagerly pick up an article about quantum gravity—or quantum anything? Probably not as many as those who wish to read "Could Time End?"

————

Edna St. Vincent Millay focuses on a pair of lovers in her poem "Thursday," in which the speaker asks:

> And if I loved you Wednesday,
> Well, what is that to you?

Millay doesn't reveal the partner's response, and the question itself is open to more than one interpretation. The first line contains *if*, which may create a hypothetical question that protects the speaker from the vulnerability of candidly expressed love. The second line suggests defiance: *what is that to you?* may be another way of declaring "none of your business!" As a true question, the words demand an accounting: What did the speaker's actions or feelings on Wednesday mean to *you*? The demand is never satisfied because right after this question comes the speaker's declaration: "I do not love you Thursday." Ouch. Will the relationship work out? Another unanswered question, but I imagine most readers would say *no*.

QUESTIONS ANSWERED

Most authors do supply answers to the questions they pose. Beryl Markham, in her memoir *West with the Night*, asks

> What does a fall of rain, a single fall of rain, mean in anybody's life?

The context for Markham's query is a drought that drives her away from the family home in Kenya. She directs the reader's attention to "a seed in the palm of a farmer's hand" that "holds three lives—its own, that of the man who may feed on its increase, and that of the man who lives by its culture." When seeds die "on all the farms around Njoro, on the low fields, on the slopes of the hills, on the square plots carved out of the forests, on the great farms and on the farms built with no more than a plough and a hope," culture and community die. That is one answer to Markham's question.

But she has a more specific answer, one she could not have given when the drought began. She understands only much later, as an adult. Because there is no fall of rain, Markham and her father lose the family's land and business; her father emigrates to Peru to seek work, and she moves to a new area with all she owns: two saddlebags and one horse. By asking, not telling, what a single fall of rain means, Markham forces readers to involve themselves emotionally. They can't see the drought simply as "a single line (on a lesser page)" in a newspaper report.

———

Shakespeare's *The Merchant of Venice* both displays and partially rebuts the prejudices of its time. Nowhere is this more obvious than in Shylock's anguished questions:

Hath

not a Jew eyes? . . .

If you prick us, do we not bleed?

if you tickle us, do we not laugh?

Shylock, a Jew and the merchant of the title, has lent money to a Christian, Antonio, with "a pound of flesh" as security. Shylock's questions emphasize his humanity, his absolute equality to the Christians who deny him his dignity. But these questions, among others, come in the context of Shylock's determination to take Antonio's flesh if Antonio defaults on a loan. Shylock notes that the flesh will "feed" his revenge, and, he adds, "The villainy you / teach me, I will execute. . . ." Shylock's questions have obvious answers, but the audience's response to this character is far more complex.

———

An extremely simple Shakespearean question begins Sonnet 18:

Shall I compare thee to a summer's day?

What can a lover say but "Yes, please do!" The sonnet brims with the sort of compliment anyone would like to hear, especially the Bard's promise of immortality: "So long as men can breathe or eyes can see, / So long lives this, and this gives life to thee."

———

Not so romantic is Junior, the young narrator of Sherman Alexie's *The Absolutely True Diary of a Part-Time Indian*, who speaks directly to the reader with a mixture of self-deprecation and snark. Junior imagines the reader asking him this question:

Okay, okay, Mr. Hunger Artist, Mr. Mouth-Full-of-Words, Mr. Woe-Is-Me, Mr. Secret Recipe, what is the worst thing about being poor?

This question comes after Junior has explained that his parents can't always afford to buy food. But being hungry isn't too bad, he says, because food eventually arrives and tastes even better to a starving boy. The answer to the narrator's question is as devastating to the reader as the event is to Junior. Oscar, his dog, is sick and obviously suffering. Junior's father takes Oscar outside and shoots him. Junior understands that his father has no choice, because, he notes bitterly, bullets cost only two cents and veterinary care hundreds of dollars. And that is "the worst thing about being poor."

———

A few more questions:

Emphasizing theme:

> If Winter comes, can Spring be far behind?
>> —Percy Bysshe Shelley, "Ode to the West Wind"

> What is patriotism but the love of the good things we ate in our childhood?
>> —Lin Yutang, *The Importance of Living*

Argument:

> I have ploughed and planted, and gathered into barns, and no man could head me! And ain't I a woman?
>> —Sojourner Truth (civil rights activist, nineteenth century)

> You are correct but why no question of it?
>> —Toni Morrison, *A Mercy*

Humor:

Isn't it a bit unnerving that doctors call what they do "practice"?
—George Carlin (comedian)

In case you hadn't noticed
it has somehow become uncool
to sound like you know what you're talking about?
—Taylor Mali, "Totally Like Whatever, You Know?"

PROFESSOR CRAWLEY: What does an accomplished entomologist with a doctorate and twenty years of experience do when the university cuts all his funding?
RAJESH: Ask uncomfortable rhetorical questions to people?
—*The Big Bang Theory*

Foreshadowing plot:

She asked them in the cornfield between a work song, rumbling in the back of a buggy on the way to town: gray eyes, scar across the back of her right hand from a burn, maybe went by the name of Mabel, maybe not?
—Colson Whitehead, *The Underground Railroad*

What could there be about a shadow that was so terrible that she knew that there had never been before or ever would be again, anything that would chill her with a fear that was beyond shuddering, beyond crying or screaming, beyond the possibility of comfort?
—Madeleine L'Engle, *A Wrinkle in Time*

Character development:

What had brought her to say that: "We are in the hands of the Lord"? she wondered.

—Virginia Woolf, *To the Lighthouse*

"Let me see: that would be four thousand miles down, I think—" (for, you see, Alice had learnt several things of this sort in her lessons in the schoolroom, and though this was not a *very* good opportunity for showing off her knowledge, as there was no one to listen to her, still it was good practice to say it over) "—yes, that's about the right distance—but then I wonder what Latitude and Longitude I've got to?"

—Lewis Carroll, *Alice's Adventures in Wonderland*

FOR THE WRITER

Are you interested in incorporating more questions in your writing? Do I even need to ask? These exercises may spark some ideas.

BIG, WIDE, DEEP

Search for fundamental questions. Avoid clichés such as "What is the meaning of life?" Aim for one in each category; I've provided examples to get you started:

Philosophy
Does objective reality exist, or is everything affected by perception?

Arts
Why do standards of beauty change?

A WHAT POINT?

In the sixteenth century, Henry Denham, an English printer, introduced the "percontation point," a sort of backwards question mark.

The percontation point was meant to signal a question that wasn't truly a request for information, but rather an attempt to create drama, to nudge the audience to a specific line of thought, or to give the questioner a chance to leap in with a prepared response. In other words, a rhetorical question. The percontation point never found wide acceptance and died out a few centuries ago. Recently, some people have tried to resurrect and rename it as an "irony mark" to precede a question with some snark in it.

Human Nature
Can optimism be taught?

Politics
What is the relationship of rights to responsibility?

Science
Is a foolproof experiment possible?

Now outline a situation or describe a context in which the question should be asked. If you have the time and energy, attempt an answer.

WHO WANTS TO KNOW?

Select characters from a film, show, or book. (You can also make up your own characters for this exercise.) List some defining traits or memorable events or actions associated with each character. Now come up with a set of questions your characters might ask, consistent with their personality and situation. If you wish, expand the question into a scene. Your goal is to formulate questions that emphasize what you already know and perhaps extrapolate from that into new areas. For example, if the character is old, what would he or she have asked as a young person? How about a youngster? What question would the character pose twenty years down the road?

DISCOVERY

I once overheard this remark: "I wanted to be a scientist, but everything has already been discovered." I was too shy to leap into the conversation. So, you do what I did not. Think of questions—in science or other fields such as history or geography—that need answers. Draw from your own expertise or ask experts in various fields. What questions would they most like to answer?

LEDE WORK

A *lede* (not *lead*) is the opening paragraph of a news story or article. Find some stories with boring ledes (not a tough task, I'm sorry to say). Create an alternative by starting with a question. Go for the intriguing, not the obvious. In an article about the stock market, for instance, avoid asking "What factors influence investors?" Instead, begin with "Are shareholders more apt to buy shares in a company that's been in the news, even for negative reasons?" Your question should be answered somewhere in the article you've selected, though not necessarily in the lede. Bonus points: Write a transition between the lede and the rest of the opening paragraph. Or, rewrite the entire lede, ending with a transition that sets up the next paragraph.

PART II DICTION

VALUABLE VERBS

Dean lounged to the pitching mound.

—Red Smith, "Dizzy Dean's Day"

ind a crowded area and people-watch for a moment. What is everyone doing? Jot down some notes. Chances are you'll write mostly
verbs, the part of speech designated for human actions, even those
appearing as motionless as thinking or dreaming. Now evaluate your
verbs. Did the woman with the red scarf *walk* around a couple obviously
in the first throes of love? Maybe, but there are many ways to walk. If she
"stomped around" or "skirted" them, she may be jealous. If she "edged
around" them, she may be showing respect for the bubble they're in. Did
she "parade"? Perhaps she's feeling defiantly superior to the smitten pair.
All these verbs move the woman from one spot to another, but the alternatives carry an extra dose of meaning. When writers carefully select a
verb, they subtly shape the sentence, illuminating character, establishing
a theme, or emphasizing plotlines.

Walter "Red" Smith, who called himself "just a bum trying to make
a living running a typewriter," was a master at choosing the right verb
to express the motions and emotions of sports. The featured sentence
comes from a 1934 column in the *St. Louis Star*. Dizzy Dean, a pitcher
for the St. Louis Cardinals, had dominated opponents all season, but the
team as a whole had an uneven record. Now Dean was about to pitch the

last inning of the crucial game, one that would decide the winner of the National League baseball championship. In his piece, Smith describes the screaming fans, who "were there to see Dizzy come to glory."

In Red Smith's portrayal, Dizzy Dean himself was not screaming. He was confident and calm, unlike his manager, Frank Frisch. Smith describes Frisch as so worn out and bedraggled after his team won the game that "you could have planted petunias in the loam on his face." Frisch showed up for the postgame interview with his shirt hanging over his thighs and his unbelted pants around his ankles. (Fortunately, it was a radio interview.) Dizzy Dean, on the other hand, was fully dressed, "scrubbed and combed and natty," waiting for his turn at the microphone.

Smith's verb, *lounged*, is both unusual and entirely appropriate. *Lounge* is "move lazily, stopping now and then," "rest or relax," or "pass time without purpose." None of these definitions fit what you'd expect to see from a pitcher going from the team bench to his workplace— the batter's box in an earlier sentence and the pitcher's mound in this one. Whatever Dean really felt during this important game, no one will ever know. But his body language, in Smith's words, is eloquent: Dean appears comfortable, even nerveless. How much less the plain-vanilla verb *went* would have conveyed! Other choices, such as *ran* or *trekked*, would have undermined Smith's point. *Lounged* highlights a key element of Dizzy Dean's personality, his ability to project and justify confidence.

BUILDING CHARACTER

Robert Caro, acclaimed biographer of President Lyndon Johnson, speaks of searching for what Flaubert calls *le mot juste*—the precise word to fit the intended meaning. Caro's verbs illustrate how successful his searches are. Here's a sentence from *The Passage of Power* describing Johnson when he learned that opponents were attempting to overturn a bill he had championed:

"I hope that [bill] gets *murdered*," he snarled, and, sitting in the Oval Office, he kept telephoning senator after senator, cajoling, bullying, threatening, charming, long after he had the majority, to make the vote overwhelming enough to ensure the lesson was clear.

Murdered, snarled, cajoling, bullying, threatening, charming: with these verb forms, Caro illustrates how competitive and ruthless Johnson could be.

———

In fiction, too, verbs flesh out character. This sentence from Hugh Walpole's novel *The Captives* describes a rebellious young woman in a tightly structured society:

> She hesitated, clinging to a draper's shop; then, suddenly catching sight of the pillar-box a few yards down the street, she let herself go, had a momentary sensation of swimming in a sea desperately crowded with other bodies, fought against the fierce gaze of lights that beat straight upon her eyes, found the box, slipped in the letter, and then, almost at once, was back in her quiet quarters again.

The young woman in this sentence, Maggie, has been living in her aunts' house. Walpole describes her as under pressure to conform to their beliefs but determined "to lead her own life, to earn her own living, to fight for herself." The letter Maggie is mailing in *the pillar-box* seeks help from a friend to escape her aunts' supervision. Walpole's verbs illustrate the struggle: Maggie *hesitated, clinging* not just to a shop but to society's norms. Then she *let herself go*, literally from the shop but, in effect, from others' expectations. It's not easy for her (*fought, beat*), but she persists (*found, slipped*) and succeeds.

———

No one is better than Shakespeare at creating memorable characters, and verb choice is part of his toolkit. Here's a line from the title character of *King Lear*:

The thunder would not peace at my bidding.

As a verb, *peace* means "to calm or quiet." Earlier in the play, the elderly Lear relinquished his throne in a desire for *peace* (a noun) while expecting to retain power (*bidding*). By the time he makes this statement, Lear has lost everything, including the arrogance that allowed him to be shocked when nature would not obey him. Ironically, the realization that he cannot *peace* nature prepares the way for reconciliation—*peace*—with his faithful daughter, Cordelia.

———

Another Shakespearean title character, Hamlet, says

If you find him not within this month, you shall nose him as you go up the
stairs into the lobby.

Hamlet is referring to the body of Polonius, whom he has killed. The rhythm of the line would remain the same with a more common verb, such as *smell*. But Hamlet is preoccupied with the body and its functions. He agonizes over his mother's physical relationship with his stepfather, and in one of his soliloquies, he wishes that his own "too too solid flesh / would melt." (In some texts, "sullied" replaces "solid," but the effect is the same.) Thus *nose* fits the character Shakespeare created.

Nosy also describes Polonius's character, given that he sends a servant to spy on his son, secretly watches his daughter's encounter with Hamlet, and dies while hiding behind a tapestry where he can listen to Hamlet's conversation with the queen. Modern readers perceive the irony—a *nosy* man who may be *nosed*—but *nosy* came into the language after Shakespeare's death.

UNDERLINING THEMES

In addition to illuminating character, verbs may emphasize themes. Colson Whitehead underscores the structural racism endured by blacks and Native Americans with this sentence from his novel *The Underground Railroad*:

> White men squabbled before judges over claims to this or that tract hundreds of miles away that had been carved up on a map.

Fighting over land ownership may seem a weighty matter, but Whitehead employs *squabble* to reduce such lawsuits between *white men* to petty arguments. *Squabble* means "quarrel noisily over a trivial matter." In the agricultural economy of the early nineteenth century, working the land is definitely not trivial. Whitehead continues: "Slaves fought with equal fervor over their tiny parcels," the strips of land between cabins where many planted yams and other vegetables. But the *white men* of Whitehead's sentence are distant from the land they're claiming. To them, land is an investment, not a place to live and grow food for their families, as it is for the people whom *white men* claimed as property.

Whitehead's second verb reinforces the theme. The land *had been carved up* on a map. It's no more real to the disputing claimants than the piece of paper the map was drawn on. Furthermore, as one character reflects, "The land she tilled and worked had been Indian land." She and other enslaved workers are, she says, "[s]tolen bodies working stolen land." The passive voice of *had been carved* emphasizes Whitehead's point: *white men* deemed blacks and Native Americans less than human. Things could be done to these groups without penalty, their bodies *carved up* by whips or their lives ended for any reason or for no reason at all. The passive verb shows how whites distance themselves from responsibility. They don't *carve*. The land *had been carved up*.

———

Ta-Nehisi Coates, in *Between the World and Me*, writes:

> How, specifically, did Europe underdevelop Africa?

Underdeveloped, a passive verb form, is commonly used as a description. You've probably read about *underdeveloped* countries or regions. But that usage omits the responsibility that Coates ascribes to *Europe* with his active verb *underdevelop.*

———

Sheri Fink also selects verb forms to reinforce a theme. Fink's *Five Days at Memorial* is an account of the life-and-death decisions hospital personnel in New Orleans made after a catastrophic storm, Hurricane Katrina. In this sentence she describes the hospital before the storm:

> For nearly eighty years the steel and concrete hospital, armored in reddish-brown tapestry brick blazoned with gray stone and towering over the neighborhood near Claiborne and Napoleon Avenues, had defended those inside it against every punch the Gulf's weather systems had thrown.

Fink emphasizes a common attitude in the city prior to Hurricane Katrina: New Orleans had withstood the forces of nature before (*every punch the Gulf's weather systems had thrown*). The verb *had thrown* and the reference to *punch* liken the storm to a boxing match—a sporting event with a winner and a loser but seldom a fatal situation. Memorial *had defended* patients before, so people expected it to do so again. In fact, nonpatients sought refuge there as the hurricane approached.

Fink presents the building as a physical testament to confidence. It's *armored* and *towering*, even *blazoned* in *tapestry brick*—references to medieval castles where people sheltered from invading armies. But the confidence is misplaced. People die after Katrina hits, and some are hastened to their deaths because the hospital lacks the supplies and personnel needed to save them. Fink's harrowing book ends with a discussion of more recent deadly storms. Lack of preparation and overconfidence have led to more fatalities, making the confident attitude projected in the featured sentence even more ironic.

———

One more example, from Ian Frazier's *New Yorker* article "Fish Out of Water":

> The invasion of Asian carp into the waters of the South and the Midwest differs from other ongoing environmental problems in that it slaps you in the head.

The carp, Frazier reports, "leap from the water, sometimes rocketing fifteen feet into the air" when they're frightened. They hit nearby boaters with some force. It may look comical, but this invasive species poses a threat to the ecosystem of rivers and lakes and, by extension, to the fishing industry. Thus Frazier's verb, *slaps*, implies a double dose of harm.

FORESHADOWING

Have you ever finished a book and realized that the author had planted clues to the ending along the way? Madeleine L'Engle's *A Wrinkle in Time* hints at the plot in the very first scene:

> The furnace purred like a great, sleepy animal; the lights glowed with steady radiance; outside, alone in the dark, the wind still battered against the house, but the angry power that had frightened Meg while she was alone in the attic was subdued by the familiar comfort of the kitchen.

Meg goes on to confront more than one "angry power" after she discovers that her family has already been *battered*. Spoiler alert: Meg's enemies are eventually *subdued*. L'Engle's contrast between the house and the outside world (in this case, worlds!) relies on verbs. Inside: *purred, glowed, subdued*. Outside: *battered, frightened*.

‹

———

Readers of J. K. Rowling's *Harry Potter* books know that what appears to be a random element in an early book will have great significance in the concluding volume. Here's a sentence from *Harry Potter and the Goblet of Fire*, the fourth installment of the series:

> The golden thread connecting Harry and Voldemort splintered, though the wands remained connected, a thousand more beams arced high over Harry and Voldemort, crisscrossing all around them, until they were enclosed in a golden, dome-shaped web, a cage of light, beyond which the Death Eaters circled like jackals, their cries strangely muffled now.

Rowling's verb forms—*splintered, connected, crisscrossing*—hint at how she will tie various parts of the story together. Voldemort's attempt to attain immortality involves *splintering*, he and Harry are *connected*, and various characters seem to *crisscross* from one side of the epic struggle to the other.

———

One last sentence, from "Waste MGMT" by Evan Schwartz, an article about space junk that appeared in *Wired*:

> From his office at NASA's Johnson Space Center in Houston, he [Eric Christiansen] directs a team that studies what happens when orbiting objects get whacked, slammed, pierced, and pummeled.

We can only hope that *whacked, slammed, pierced*, and *pummeled* don't foreshadow what will happen to us when old satellites and rockets hit Earth, a fate Eric Christiansen and his team are trying to prevent.

FOR THE WRITER

Changing verbs is a relatively simple way to improve your writing. Two cautions: take care not to overuse unusual verbs. After a single paragraph in which characters *strut, stagger, promenade,* and *tread,* your readers will yearn for something simple, like *go.* Also, be sure you understand not just the definition but also the emotions and opinions associated with a word. There's a world of difference between *grasp* and *embrace,* for example, despite the fact that they're both synonyms of *hold.*

SAY WHAT YOU MEAN

Watch a scene from a film. Select verbs that suit the content and tone of various lines of dialogue—*declared, whispered, hinted, shouted, screamed,* and so forth. They all mean *said* but give extra information about the mood, purpose, or personality of the person speaking. Note: This exercise may be beneficial to your mental health if you adapt it to your relatives' comments during a holiday dinner. Silently selecting verbs for a crazy cousin or an eccentric parent keeps you occupied and out of the fray. This I know from experience.

CHAIR

What are you sitting on? Take a good look and describe it in five or six sentences. Read what you wrote, underlining all forms of the verb *be* and *have.* Rewrite the sentences, avoiding these two verbs. For example:

Original: There is a gentle curve on the back of the chair that is a good support for my back. The chair has a shiny polished surface.

Rewrite: The back of the chair curves gently, supporting my back. The polished surface shines.

The rewritten sentences don't rise to Pulitzer Prize level, for sure, but they're more interesting and more concise than the originals.

COFFEE

Create a character. Imagine the character drinking a cup of coffee, and then write that moment as a scene from a short story. Your goal is to present a vivid glimpse of the character's personality displayed through this ordinary action. Pay special attention to the verb forms in your scene. Ask yourself what each reveals about the character. If you wish, expand your scene with dialogue, thoughts, and physical description. Who knows, you may end up with the basis for a story.

TONE

The people of the village began to gather in the square, between the post office and the bank, around ten o'clock; in some towns there were so many people that the lottery took two days and had to be started on June 26th, but in this village, where there were only about three hundred people, the whole lottery took less than two hours, so it could begin at ten o'clock in the morning and still be through in time to allow the villagers to get home for noon dinner.

—Shirley Jackson, "The Lottery"

Because the human voice can carry happiness, nostalgia, regret, sarcasm, and a host of other tones, hearing is the easiest way to identify a speaker's attitude. Without spoken cues, readers "hear" an internal narrative, inferring tone from details omitted or highlighted, word choice, and sentence structure. They don't generally set out to identify tone, but on a subconscious level, readers react to it.

Not always correctly, of course. When Shirley Jackson's short story "The Lottery" was first published, people often asked the location of this event and whether they could attend. Given that the story describes a ritual stoning held annually in a small town, such a misreading is chilling. Jackson's sense of horror toward the violence she describes was lost on those readers, and their response proves the author's point: violence is so common in American life that it seems ordinary. More than seventy years after its publication, the story is unfortunately still relevant.

"The Lottery" begins on the morning of a "full-summer day." As they *gather*, the men are "speaking of planting and rain, tractors and taxes," and the women are gossiping. Mrs. Hutchison arrives late, explaining that she "clean forgot what day it was." Mr. Summers, who conducts the lottery as one of his "civic activities," performs the same function at "square dances, the teen club, and the Halloween program." Had Jackson given these details and nothing more, readers would likely picture a neighborly scene in a neighborly town—as American as apple pie.

Jackson subverts that image. The lottery requires the head of every family to draw a slip of paper from "a black wooden box." Mr. Hutchison's has a dot. Mr. and Mrs. Hutchison and their three children now draw from a set of five slips. The mother gets the dot. Despite her protests, almost immediately the "first stone lands on the side of her head" and "then they were upon her." Jackson's detached tone intensifies the horror and creates irony.

Take a closer look at the featured sentence. The villagers are *in the square, between the post office and the bank,* centers of communal life. The lottery is also a communal act. Every resident is present, except for one with a broken leg. Between lotteries, citizens take turns caring for the box. It spent "one year in Mr. Graves's barn and another year underfoot in the post office," and "sometimes it was set on a shelf in the Martin grocery." Further, in a town this small (*only about three hundred people*), everybody knows one another. As Mr. Summers calls the roll, people offer information about others—which households have no male head, how old some children are, and so forth. The lottery will also, Jackson is careful to state, *be through in time to allow the villagers to get home for noon dinner.* How thoughtful to schedule human sacrifice so that eating schedules aren't disrupted.

Jackson plays off readers' expectations of small-town friendliness and loving family ties. Mrs. Delacroix "laughed softly" and chatted with Mrs. Hutchison as the latter rushed in. Yet after Mrs. Hutchison draws the fatal paper, Mrs. Delacroix selects "a stone so large she had to pick it up with both hands." The Hutchisons show no rancor toward each other before Mr. Hutchison draws the ticket—and no concern for each other or for their children during the second drawing. The four safe Hutchisons participate in the stoning, even the youngest, who has been given "a few pebbles." These neighbors and this family are ready to murder one of their own.

Much can be written about the nuances of Jackson's story, and much has. "The Lottery" alludes to ancient harvest sacrifices, the Bible, and theological disputes in colonial America. Jackson herself said that she wanted to shock people by depicting the "pointless violence and general inhumanity in their own lives." She succeeded.

MATCHING TONE AND AUDIENCE

Pick up a novel by Ian Fleming and you expect a spy-about-town tale related in an ominous "what will happen next?" tone. And in the majority of his books you get exactly that, because Fleming is most famous for adult thrillers featuring "Bond, James Bond," the British operative who is "licensed to kill" criminal masterminds intent on destroying the world as we know it. One Fleming novel, though, is different. Fleming wrote *Chitty-Chitty-Bang-Bang* for his son Caspar. Change in audience, change in tone.

Some elements of the Bond series are present in *Chitty-Chitty-Bang-Bang* (heroes and villains, danger and escape), but this is a more innocent fantasy than the Bond books. The title character is a magical car owned by an eccentric family, the Potts. The father is an inventor:

> Commander Pott's inventions were sometimes dull things like collapsible coat hangers, sometimes useless things like edible phonograph records, and sometimes clever things that just, only just, wouldn't work, like cubical potatoes—easy to slice and pack and peel but expensive to grow, each in its little iron box—and so on.

Can you read that sentence without smiling? Probably not. Fleming's tone in this novel is affectionate and humorous. Young readers grasp the silliness—*cubical potatoes!*—and appreciate Fleming's assumption that they're in on the joke. Though danger threatens (near-drowning, gangsters, kidnapping), Fleming's tone is always light. Chitty-Chitty-Bang-Bang, the car named for the sounds it makes, never fails to rescue the Potts, who in turn forestall the gangsters' crimes. There's even a chocolate reward at the end.

_____

Another fantastic means of transportation is the *Nautilus*, a submarine that sails *Twenty Thousand Leagues Under the Sea*, which is both the distance traveled and the title of Jules Verne's novel. It's a work of science fiction—no vessel like the *Nautilus* was possible in the mid-nineteenth-century setting—but Verne also takes a stand on contemporary political movements and advocates for preservation of the marine environment. He wants his audience to take the ideas in his novel seriously while they enjoy the fictional journey. His tone is that of a scientist or a journalist observing objectively along with the "isn't this exciting!" edge of an adventure novel. Both are on display in this sentence:

> I was observing the sea in these conditions, in which even the largest fish were no more than barely perceptible shadows, when without warning the Nautilus was lit by a brilliant illumination.

The narrator is Professor Pierre Aronnax, a marine biologist. When Aronnax's vessel is attacked, he and two others are captured. On the *Nautilus*, they meet Captain Nemo, a mysterious figure who's given up life on land. Aronnax is fascinated by the wonders he sees through the *Nautilus*'s observation window—the Antarctic ice shelf, coral reefs, and, in the quoted sentence, the mass of phosphorescent creatures responsible for *a brilliant illumination*. Verne conveys the marvels of the sea's depths, where *even the largest fish were no more than barely perceptible shadows*. The phrase *without warning* maintains the adventure-novel slant, as does a visit to the imaginary lost city of Atlantis.

_____

Zora Neale Hurston trained as an anthropologist; one of her field studies focused on African American communities in Florida. Writing during the Harlem Renaissance, Hurston knew that many of her readers would be unfamiliar with the culture and traditions of those towns. She employed both anthropology and artistry to create characters that engage interest and follow believable story arcs. Her 1937 novel, *Their Eyes Were Watching God*, serves as a window into the society she studied as well as an examination of the growth of one individual.

The novel begins as the protagonist, Janie Crawford, walks back into town, alone and silent, years after she left with her lover. The towns-people gossip, somewhat pleased with what they assume is her failure. Hurston writes:

> Now, women forget all those things they don't want to remem-ber, and remember everything they don't want to forget.

This is another way of saying that Janie will tell her own story. It won't be the whole story: she will *forget all those things* she doesn't *want to remember.* But she will tell *everything* she doesn't *want to forget.* And there's a lot to say: an early marriage to Logan Killicks, a man she doesn't love but who, her grandmother believes, can give Janie a secure life. To Logan, Janie is a convenience, someone who will work hard and tend to his needs. Convinced there's more to life than servi-tude, Janie runs away with Joe Starks, an ambitious fellow who soon becomes the mayor of the African American town of Eatonville, Flor-ida. To Joe, Janie is a possession he can show off to residents. After Joe's death, Janie leaves home with Tea Cake Woods, a man she's attracted to. To Tea Cake, Janie is a passionate partner. He doesn't always treat her well, but he sacrifices his life to save her. Tea Cake's death brings Janie back to Eatonville and those gossipy neighbors, not as a failure but as a mature woman.

Janie's three relationships are akin to the growth rings of a tree. Janie makes mistakes, but Hurston's tone is steadfastly supportive and affec-tionate. Early in the novel she describes Janie as having "glossy leaves and bursting buds," wanting to "struggle with life" even though "it eluded her." When Janie returns to Eatonville, she sees her life like "a great tree in leaf with the things suffered, things enjoyed, things done and undone." The reader wants to believe that Janie will *remember every-thing she doesn't want to forget,* clear-eyed and strong, because Hurston has nurtured that hope. She's brought the reader into Janie's world and made an indelible impression.

NONFICTION WITH AN ATTITUDE

Relaying information is a subjective process. Selecting, emphasizing or downplaying, and framing facts all play a role in establishing tone, as do diction and sentence structure. Here are a few examples of nonfiction sentences with distinct tones:

Self-mocking

Mindy Kaling uses a hip, ironic tone in her memoir, *Is Everyone Hanging Out Without Me?* In a section entitled "I Get to See the Lakers All the Time," she measures how famous she'd like to be by referring to a professional basketball game:

> I don't need to have Jack Nicholson seats or whatever—honestly, who needs to live in constant peril of a sweaty, 7-foot-tall, 240-pound guy falling on you?—but I'd love to be so famous that people who do have amazing tickets would be psyched to have me come with them.

As a comedian, screenwriter, and actor, Kaling already *is* that famous, whether she sits courtside or not.

Disapproving, ironic

Ring Lardner is most famous for his short stories, but he spent many years as a journalist. Here he comments on Prohibition, the ban on alcohol created by the Eighteenth Amendment to the US Constitution in 1919:

> Congressman Volstead of the lowest house yesterday issued a proclamation declaring this Sunday a legal holiday as it is the 4th, or glass wedding anniversary of the date when his act pre-

venting the sale or manufacture of liquor went into such good and lasting effect.

Even without the next sentence ("Everything will be closed but the saloons"), it's easy to perceive Lardner's disapproval. He calls the House of Representatives *the lowest*. Also, contemporary readers knew that the ban was widely flouted, far from a *good and lasting effect.* Labeling the proposed holiday as the *glass wedding anniversary* is particularly clever. For anyone not familiar with the custom, every anniversary is assigned an official gift category (silver for the 25th, gold for the 50th, for example). *Glass* breaks. So did Prohibition, when the Twenty-first Amendment was ratified in 1933.

Grieving
In her memoir about growing up in Kenya, *West with the Night*, author Beryl Markham visits her dog's grave:

> How completely ended!—for Buller too, bearing the scars of all his battles, holding still in his great dead heart the sealed memory of his own joys and mine, the smells he knew, the paths, the little games, those vanquished warthogs, the soundless stalking of a leopard's paws—he too had lived a life and it was ended.

Markham's love for Buller permeates this sentence.

Admiring
Sportswriter W. C. Heinz described an upcoming event this way:

> Starting tomorrow night and continuing at least two nights a week for the next three weeks a young woman named Marjorie Clair Brashun will engage in a campaign of assaulting other young women in many living rooms—even bar rooms—in this section of the country.

Heinz goes on to explain that "Miss Brashun" is "the most popular participant in a sporting enterprise known as the Roller Derby," in which five-member teams skate around a circular track, crashing into opposing players in order to clear a path for their own teammates. With *a campaign of assaulting other young women*, Heinz calls attention to the sport's rough tactics. He admires Brashun's toughness and her skill at what he calls "a combination of six-day bicycle racing and professional wrestling."

Indignant

In his famous "Cross of Gold" speech, orator William Jennings Bryan rails against those who oppose changing the gold standard for United States currency:

> We have petitioned, and our petitions have been scorned; we have entreated, and our entreaties have been disregarded; we have begged, and they have mocked when our calamity came.

The *calamity* is a financial crisis, the Panic of 1893. Though Bryan's crusade was unsuccessful, his speech became a classic, not only for his words but also for his fiery delivery.

Alarmed

In "Imagining the Post-Antibiotics Future," Maryn McKenna recounts the death of her great-uncle from an infection that penicillin could have cured, had the drug been discovered five years earlier:

> In Joe's story I see what life might become if we did not have antibiotics anymore.

By recounting the swift, fatal path of a young man's illness, McKenna makes her readers care. By invoking *what life might become*, she raises alarm. Her description of life without effective antibiotics is harrowing—

no cancer treatment or organ transplants that rely on immunosuppressants, death from a simple scratch, no implantable medical devices that attract bacteria, and fatal tattoos. McKenna's words are simple and straightforward, her tone serious. She doesn't need fireworks to induce fear; the facts she presents are scary enough.

FOR THE WRITER

If you have an attitude toward your subject, you have a tone. Whether your tone comes across as confusing or clarifying depends on how well you express that attitude.

ARGUMENT

Standard school assignments call for a defined idea (thesis) that the writer proves. You've probably written dozens of such pieces. Did you realize, as you worked on them, that your tone can help or hurt your case? Come across as condescending, and readers walk away. Argue too stridently, and the same thing happens, unless you undermine that reaction with self-mockery.

Take a look at essays, letters, or online comments. Or read some of your own writing. Identify the tone and select a sentence that exemplifies it. Now take a shot at changing the tone. For example:

ORIGINAL: Unless we severely curtail carbon emissions, the planet is doomed. (desperate)

REVISION: Every step to curtail carbon emissions has an impact on climate change. (hopeful)

Note: You don't have to agree with the statements, original or revised. Just practice tone-switching.

INCIDENT REPORT

Choose an ordinary event (blowing out candles on a birthday cake, buying a car, lacing up a shoe, and so forth). Report it in several tones: admiring, nostalgic, regretful, angry . . . you get the idea. For example:

> Jean yanked her sneaker laces as if they were strangling her worst enemy. (angry, aggressive)

> Jean pulled the left lace of the sneaker and paused for a moment, reviewing her race strategy, before she tugged the other one. (thoughtful, calm)

For the ambitious: Place the incident in context by writing a story.

MIXING IT UP

Life's not simple, and neither, most of the time, is our attitude toward it. Reflect this reality through a change in tone. (You may need several sentences for this one.) A few possible switches:

> defiant → resigned
> approving → disapproving
> uncaring → sympathetic
> whimsical → serious

An example:

> That road should be repaired immediately. Wait, you can't work at night! No one on the block will be able to sleep with all that noise.

WORD SHIFTS

Love loves to love love.

—James Joyce, *Ulysses*

Empires of chocolate candy, diamond rings, and pop songs support the idea that love is a force to be reckoned with. Who would question its power? James Joyce, for one, albeit from the viewpoint of a disturbing character in *Ulysses*, Joyce's novel that, when it was published in 1922, cracked open the traditional narrative style and introduced an entirely new way to present characters, through their thoughts.

One of the best works of the experimental Modernist movement, *Ulysses* traces the path of Leopold Bloom, a Jew, through the course of a June day in Dublin. Chapters correspond roughly to the adventures of Ulysses, the main character in Homer's epic poem *The Odyssey*. *Love loves to love love* comes from a chapter modeled on Ulysses's encounter with a Cyclops. Homer's one-eyed monster captures Ulysses (called Odysseus in the Greek version) on his journey home from the Trojan War. Ulysses cleverly outwits the monster with, fittingly, wordplay.

In the featured sentence Joyce writes a form of the word *love* four times. But Joyce isn't simply repeating himself. Instead, he subtly changes the definition and function of the word each time he uses it. The base word links ideas; the changes reveal varied perspectives. The featured sentence is typical of Joyce: he was fascinated by wordplay, puns, and language in all its forms. In fact, for his last novel, *Finnegans Wake*, Joyce coined numerous words and arranged them in unique ways. Many deem *Finnegans Wake* unreadable; *Ulysses* is not easy either, but it's more accessible than the later book and rewards careful attention.

For convenience, I'll refer to the man who says the featured sentence as "the narrator," despite the fact that the chapter has several narrators, including one dubbed "the citizen," and it's not clear which one actually says *Love loves to love love*. Regardless of the speaker's identity, the implications of the statement are the same. In the Cyclops chapter, the narrator is figuratively one-eyed; he sees life from a single, extremely narrow, prejudiced point of view. Bloom, on the other hand, is open to alternative ideas.

When Bloom is told that Jews should fight injustice, he responds that "insult and hatred" aren't "life for men and women" and that love is "the opposite of hatred." The narrator ridicules Bloom's ideas and launches into an anti-Semitic rant.

Love is a complicated topic in this novel, as it is in life. Elsewhere in *Ulysses* Joyce refers to the distinction between love as a sincere wish for the well-being of another person and love as a selfish desire for one's own pleasure. The latter definition is relevant to the Cyclops chapter because also at the pub is Hugh Boylan, who is having an affair with Bloom's wife, Molly.

Which love is the narrator talking about? Here's one possibility:

Love [the emotion as the narrator understands it] loves [likes to an extreme degree] to love [to feel positively toward] love [the emotion again].

And another:

Love [a shortened form of *lover*] loves [enjoys] to love [make love to] love [the person desired].

And still another:

Love [the ideal form of this emotion] loves [has intense, positive feelings for] to love [to wish for the well-being of] love [the person cared for].

Perhaps more important than nailing down a specific interpretation is to listen to the statement. With four *loves* in a five-word stretch, Joyce's sentence invites a singsong voice and resembles a jingle or a nursery rhyme. Because the sentence sounds ridiculous, by extension so does *love*. On the other hand, read in a solemn tone, this sentence comes across as cryptic and profound. You wouldn't be surprised to find it on a refrigerator magnet. And *Love loves to love love* does indeed appear on one! It's worth noting that "ridiculous" and "profound" are both descriptions that have been applied to love in real life.

After his initial statement, the narrator adds examples:

Jumbo, the elephant, loves Alice, the elephant. Old Mr Verschoyle with the ear trumpet loves old Mrs Verschoyle with the turned-in eye. The man in the brown macintosh loves a lady who is dead. His Majesty the King loves Her Majesty the Queen. Mrs Norman W. Tupper loves officer Taylor. You love a certain person. And this person loves that other person because everybody loves somebody but God loves everybody.

This chain of love appears to go only one way. Although some couples are mentioned, there's no way to tell whether love is reciprocal. Old Mr Verschoyle loves Mrs Verschoyle, for example, but does she love him? Overall, the narrator's depiction of love appears to mock Bloom's claim of love's power. How can love be a life force if it's reduced to a futile, unfulfilled yearning? Or, given the presence of Boylan in the pub, a betrayal? Joyce raises these questions, but he doesn't answer them.

MORE LITERARY SHIFTS

Love overwhelms the featured sentence, as does *mock* in these lines from Shakespeare's *Henry V*:

> ... for many a thousand widows
> Shall this his mock mock out of their dear husbands,
> Mock mothers from their sons, mock castles down,
> And some are yet ungotten and unborn
> That shall have cause to curse the Dauphin's scorn.

Mock has two meanings here. The first (*his mock*) refers to an act of disrespect. England's King Henry, somewhat wild in his youth, has claimed power over French lands. The Dauphin, heir to the French throne, denies the claims and sends Henry a box of tennis balls. This gift is meant to insult Henry; you're still a boy playing games, it implies. The next three instances of *mock* are different. They may be defined as "bring to a state or condition through mockery." The Dauphin's gesture will create *a thousand widows ... mock out of their dear husbands.* It will also *mock mothers from their sons* (cause mothers to lose their sons), and *mock castles down* (reduce castles to rubble). Shakespeare pounds the audience with this word to show that Henry sees one act (the Dauphin's insult) as inextricable from the other (war and the suffering it brings).

––––––––

Moving from the Elizabethan era to the twentieth century: The narrator of "The Lost Salt Gift of Blood," a short story by Alistair MacLeod, visits a small town in Newfoundland. He watches young boys fishing for trout and debates whether to leave or to accomplish the purpose of his visit, which is to meet his son. MacLeod purposely withholds information; only gradually does the reader find out that the boy has been living with his maternal grandparents and that his mother is dead. The narrator goes to their house and shares a quiet meal with the family. Afterward, the boy does his homework, the grandmother knits, and the grandfather invites the narrator to drink and to play checkers in another room. The narrator thinks that

> It is difficult to talk at times, with or without liquor; difficult to achieve the actual act of saying.

Actual act is a potent phrase, well suited to the characters' temperaments. *Actual* is a description, defined as "arising from action" or "real and carried out." An *act* is "a deed" or "something done." By doubling up on the base word *act*, MacLeod underscores that the grandfather and the narrator are afraid to *act*. They can barely manage to discuss what they must resolve: whether or not the boy should stay with his grandparents or move to the American Midwest with his father. Yet they must *achieve the actual act of saying* because the boy's future depends on their doing so. And, eventually, they do.

————

A few other word shifts drawn from literature:

> . . . she now mourned someone who even before his death had made her a mourner.
> —Bernard Malamud, *The Natural*

> She's missing among the missing in Cambridge.
> —Gish Jen, *Mona in the Promised Land*

> Diamond me no diamonds, prize me no prizes.
> —Alfred Lord Tennyson, "Lancelot and Elaine"

> Ah! He [Death] strikes all things all alike,
> But bargains: Those he will not strike.
> —Walter Savage Landor, "Age"

> The signora at every grimace and at every bow smiled a little smile and bowed a little bow.
> —Anthony Trollope, *Barchester Towers*

> To England I will steal
> And there I'll steal.
> —William Shakespeare, *Henry V*

With eager feeding food doth choke the feeder.

—William Shakespeare, *Richard II*

POLITICAL SHIFTS

Politicians are often shifty. (I refer to their rhetoric, not to their political stances or actions. I'll let you decide whether this description applies to more than parts of speech.) A good example is Franklin Delano Roosevelt, who became president in 1933, when the Great Depression was intensifying. About a quarter of working-age Americans had no jobs, and nearly half of the nation's banks had failed. Early in his inaugural address, Roosevelt declared:

> So, first of all, let me assert my firm belief that the only thing we have to fear is fear itself—nameless, unreasoning, unjustified terror which paralyzes needed efforts to convert retreat into advance.

Both *fear*s play an important role in this sentence. In the first instance, *have to fear* means "must fear," with *fear* as an action. In the second instance, *fear* is an emotion: *nameless, unreasoning, unjustified terror.* Roosevelt uses the word twice to acknowledge that action and emotion appear inseparable. But they are not. People can't control what they feel, but they can control how they act. Roosevelt hints at what he really needs from his audience, support for the actions he will take as president.

These actions were many and varied, beginning with a four-day "bank holiday," a forced closure so that depositors had a chance to overcome *fear. Fear* was not the only reason banks were failing in 1933, but it certainly contributed to the disaster. The mere rumor that a bank was about to close could set off a panicked rush to withdraw money, further weakening the bank and making its collapse more likely. Thus *fear* of failure became failure because of *fear.*

———

On the other side of the Atlantic, a British aristocrat, Lord Acton, made this point in a letter:

Power tends to corrupt, and absolute power corrupts absolutely.

Often misquoted and shortened, Lord Acton's remark was itself a restatement of ideas expressed by many earlier writers. Apparently, the temptation to link dictatorship (*absolute power*) with moral bankruptcy (*corrupts absolutely*) has always been difficult to resist.

———

Another political quotation, also with word shifts:

Your argument is sound, nothing but sound.

This sentence is attributed to Benjamin Franklin, though whether or not these are truly his words is debatable. That's fitting, given that this "compliment" is about the quality of a debate. The first *sound* is a description meaning "free from error, well founded." The second *sound* is a noun meaning "noise." If you're debating, you have to hope that the judge stops after the description, well before the noun appears.

———

Franklin also shifted words at the Constitutional Convention of 1787. When Alexander Hamilton pleaded for a unanimous vote by saying that the delegates must "all hang together," Franklin replied:

We must indeed all hang together, or, most assuredly, we shall all hang separately.

Hang together means "agree unanimously." *Hang separately* refers to execution by hanging—a real possibility for these men if the British ever regained control over their former colony.

———

One shifty sentence did not originate in politics but is applied increasingly often to political investigations or accusations:

There is no there there.
—Gertrude Stein, *The Autobiography of Alice B. Toklas*

Stein's meaning: She returned to California to visit her childhood home, only to discover it had been torn down. Current meaning: My attorney assures me that the charges have no merit.

MUSICAL SHIFTS

With their connection to sound, song lyrics attract wordplay. Take the early Beatles tune "Please Please Me." The song is addressed to a girl by a lover who doesn't "want to sound complaining." The first *please* is a courtesy word, what parents teach their children to say when making a request. The second is the command form of the verb *to please*, meaning "give pleasure," implying, of course, sex. In formal English you'd place a comma after the first *please*, but rock music and formal English don't often mesh. As an experienced teacher, I can't help picturing the lover as an overeager student. In that scenario, with a comma before *me*, the lover, like the student, would be waving one arm and begging. "Don't choose someone else! *Please please,* [choose] *me.*"

———

Tim McGraw's "Where the Green Grass Grows" begins with the singer on the road and unhappy about it. He complains about the monotony and the loneliness of a long drive:

And there's bars on the corner and bars on my heart.

The *bars* (where liquor is served) and *bars* (jailing his heart) have more than sound in common. The singer longs to leave both behind and live "where the green grass grows," raising both corn and kids there.

———

Stevie Wonder's song "Love's in Need of Love Today" envisions *love* almost as a bank account that must be refilled. The first *love*, a universal emotion, needs the second—good deeds and good will—to nurture it.

———

Singer Billy Ocean had a hit with "When the Going Gets Tough, the Tough Get Going," a title based on a popular saying attributed to football coach Knute Rockne and, by others, to Joseph Kennedy, the patriarch of the Kennedy family. The line (not the song) inspired journalist Hunter S. Thompson to remark, "When the going gets weird, the weird turn pro." I can only imagine what sort of song that line would be in.

FOR THE WRITER

Adopt a word family (a base word plus all its forms and definitions) and give it a home in your writing. These prompts will get you started.

THE *-ER* ROOM

Write down a few verbs (action words) and add *-er* to the end. Compose a sentence with the pairs you've created. An example:

groan, groaner: "I hate when you *groan*," *groaned* the *groaner* in a painfully loud voice.

Good verbs for this exercise include *kiss, scream, paint, build, light,* and *rent.* I'm sure you can think of many more.

DOUBLE MEANINGS

Find some words with more than one definition. Insert them into a sentence or two, using more than one definition. For example:

> Kate glanced at the puckered lips of her would-be *kisser.* "You expect me to *kiss* you!" she exclaimed as she punched him right in the *kisser.*

In case you're not familiar with the term, *kisser* is a slang term for the mouth.

A few pairs to spark your imagination:

> *duck*—a bird; to dip one's head or body, usually to avoid injury or to avoid being seen

> *bus*—public transportation; to remove dirty dishes from a table, especially in a restaurant

> *tender*—flexible and soft; painful to the touch; showing care and concern; offer as payment

> *figure*—a number; body shape; to think, as in *figure out*

SHOPPING CART

Browse an online shopping site or walk through a store. Look for brand names derived from English words (the laundry detergent *Tide,* for example). Compose an advertisement, with visuals if you're so inclined, to sell the product. For instance:

> SETTING: A construction site.

> ACTION: Child walks through a bucket of tar, a paint tray, and a slab of wet cement. Stains result.

SLOGAN: Until the perfect child is invented, *Tide* will *tide* you over.

COMPOUNDS

Compounds are two separate words that, when combined, form a word with a different meaning. *Base* and *ball* become *baseball*, for example. Write a sentence using the separate components of the compound and, if you can, incorporate the compound word as well. Here are two:

> Every *baseball* team needs a *base* where players feel at home and where fans can have a *ball* watching them play.

> My son's wife just finished law school, so now I have a daughter-in-law in law.

Okay, so they're not Pulitzer Prize material. You'll do better! Try these, and any other words that come to mind: *firefly, makeup, milkshake, backpack, notebook,* and *doorknob*.

COINAGE

I trusted myself back into the store.
—Maya Angelou, *I Know Why the Caged Bird Sings*

In Lewis Carroll's *Through the Looking-Glass*, a somewhat grouchy Humpty Dumpty declares, "When *I* use a word, it means just what I choose it to mean—neither more nor less." Humpty Dumpty's emphasis on *I* implies that only he can create, combine, and repurpose words. In the non-Carroll world, France maintains an academy to decide whether a coined word is acceptable or not, as do some other countries. With no official governing body, English relies on dictionaries to give the stamp of approval.

In fact, the authority of an academy or a dictionary—or Humpty Dumpty, for that matter—is an illusion. In language, power belongs to the masses. Only when enough people understand and use a word does it become part of the language. Once it's in the common vocabulary, of course, a coined word is no longer a coinage; it's just a word.

But is it a good word? Anyone can coin, but only the best writers manipulate language to add resonance to a theme. Maya Angelou is one of those writers.

In the first volume of her autobiography, *I Know Why the Caged Bird Sings*, Angelou wrenches a verb, *trust*, from its standard meaning. The most common definition of *trust* is "have faith in the reliability or truth of" or "allow someone to take care of a valuable person or object." In Angelou's sentence, the narrator (Angelou herself, called Marguerite in this portion of the book) is a traumatized little girl. After spending her early childhood in her grandmother's house, Marguerite and her brother move to their mother's home in St. Louis. There her mother's boyfriend rapes Marguerite. When she is hospitalized for injuries he inflicted, she gives his name to the authorities. He is arrested and killed in an "accident" likely engineered by her outraged relatives. With a child's logic, she believes her words caused his death and opts to stop talking altogether. Marguerite returns to her grandmother's house in the small community of Stamps, Arkansas, to recover.

The featured sentence comes from a scene in which Marguerite's grandmother has asked her to carry groceries for Mrs. Flowers, a woman Marguerite views as an elegant aristocrat. The awesome responsibility of choosing clothing to accompany Mrs. Flowers weighs heavily on the child, who considers and discards several dresses before returning to her grandmother's store, where Mrs. Flowers is waiting for her.

Angelou layers meaning into her verb. On the simplest level, Marguerite must *trust* that she's chosen the correct outfit. She rejects a church dress as sacrilegious; Mrs. Flowers is not God. She tosses a house dress aside because it's too casual. Plus, she reasons, her grandmother would not have asked her to change out of one clean outfit into another. Finally, Marguerite settles on a school dress. She must *trust* that she's chosen correctly.

The narrator must also *trust* herself to behave properly in a situation that is entirely alien to her. She's never been to Mrs. Flowers's home, and the woman's speech and manners seem different from—and, in Marguerite's opinion, far superior to—her family's. She knows that any infraction will shame both herself and her loving but exceedingly strict grandmother.

The most important layer of meaning is that the narrator's trauma occurred just after she moved to a new household in an unfamiliar setting. Marguerite must *trust* that a visit to Mrs. Flowers's home will not be dangerous. The verb that moves her from a safe space (the family's living quarters) to a public area (the *store*) reflects the first step in her recovery. *Trust* is what she must do in order to go with Mrs. Flowers and, ultimately, what she must do in order to heal. She begins to visit Mrs. Flowers weekly, slowly regaining her voice and reclaiming her sense of self.

SLIPPERY PARTS OF SPEECH

Maya Angelou redefines; other authors coin by sliding words into a different category, making a descriptive word into a noun or a verb, for instance. Here, baseball player Phil Rizzuto explains why he failed to tag a runner, leading to five runs for the opposing team:

I was nonchalanting it.

In common usage, *nonchalant* is a description meaning "casually calm, unconcerned, not displaying anxiety or interest." Rizzuto sends it into his sentence as a verb—an expression of action or, in this case, inaction. He held on to the ball too long and lost track of the game, *nonchalanting* his way into a costly error.

———

Samuel Beckett morphs a verb into a noun in his novel *Murphy*:

A foot from his ear the telephone burst into its rail.

Rail as a noun is "a type of bird" or "a bar," the sort you might find in a fence or under a locomotive. The verb *rail* means "to scold or to shout at." In Beckett's sentence, *rail* appears as a noun. The telephone's ring—*its rail*—disturbs the commitment-averse Murphy, who experiences the sound as a rant from an authority figure.

———

In *How the García Girls Lost Their Accents*, Julia Alvarez turns adjectives, *singsong* and *blah*, into verbs:

"I do, I do," she singsang.

He hemmed, he hawed, he guffawed. Finally he blahhed . . .

Both coined words indicate something of the character they're attached to. *Singsang* comes from a character who struggles to speak. She sounds artificial, for good reason. The *he* of the second sentence needs no explanation. Everyone knows someone whose mannerisms take the place of substance.

————

Shakespeare was one of the most productive coiners, though recent scholarship credits others with the first use of many words once thought to be his inventions. He was particularly adept at changing the part of speech of existing words. Take *drug*, for example. Originally a noun naming any substance used in pharmacy, chemistry, or industry, *drug* becomes a verb in this sentence from *Macbeth*:

> I have drugg'd their possets,
> That Death and Nature do contend about them,
> Whether they live or die.

These are Lady Macbeth's words, spoken while her husband is murdering King Duncan. Up to this point, Lady Macbeth has been all action. She has overcome her husband's initial reluctance to kill the king, planned the crime, and carried out the first step when she *drugg'd* (drugged) the king's guards by giving them a nearly lethal dose of sleeping potion. How fitting to assign an action verb to her! Later she will falter and go mad with guilt, but here her words reflect her determination to do something—anything—to increase her husband's (and therefore her own) power.

————

Moving from Shakespeare to another sort of classic: In the 1966 hit song "These Boots Are Made for Walkin'," the singer berates a lover:

Yeah, you keep lyin' when you oughta be truthin'.

Lyin' (lying) is a conventional verb form, but *truthin'* isn't. Nor is the slightly longer form, *truthing. Telling the truth* fits nicely with the conventions of English, but not with the rhythm or tone of the song. Coinage to the rescue!

———

Nonfiction writers also coin. Here's a phrase from Ernest Hemingway's 1935 account of a safari, *Green Hills of Africa*, in which he describes an interchange with a Masai man who doesn't speak English:

Me, dictionary-ing heavily . . .

Hemingway's usage of *dictionary-ing* is literal and specific, describing himself as he thumbs through the book urgently, seeking words to ask the African guide about hunting. But *dictionary-ing* also supports a key theme of the work. Woven through accounts of tracking and shooting are long discussions of literature and nineteenth-century American writers such as Twain, Emerson, and Thoreau. Hemingway comments frequently on his own work and "the feeling [that] comes when you write well and truly of something and know impersonally you have written in that way and . . . you know its value absolutely." In this and other remarks he defines his role as a writer and his place in the American literary tradition—and what is a dictionary but a collection of definitions?

———

In her novel *White Teeth*, Zadie Smith doesn't just reinforce a character trait by changing a part of speech, as Hemingway does. In her sentence, the trait not only defines but actually becomes the character:

In North London, where councillors once voted to change the name of the area to *Nirvana*, it is not unusual to walk the streets and be suddenly confronted by sage words from the chalk-faced, blue-lipped or eyebrowless.

Even comic-strip characters shift parts of speech—and deplore the practice as they do so. Calvin (of Bill Watterson's *Calvin and Hobbes*) remarks:

Verbing weirds language.

I add more optimistically, maybe verbing, like other shifts in usage, makes language grow.

BRAVE NEW WORDS

If you're inventing a world, you're in need of new words to name its features. Aldous Huxley, in his 1931 novel, *Brave New World*, coined terms to describe a society in which the state controls and dehumanizes its citizens, who are genetically altered, indoctrinated, and rendered docile with a tranquilizing drug. Many of Huxley's inventions change the meaning of a standard word or allude to a person or practice:

freemartin (in the real world, a sterile calf; in the novel, a sterile woman)

Malthusian drill (Huxley's term for birth control, a reference to Thomas Malthus, an economist who warned against overpopulation)

A.F. (an abbreviation for "After Ford," a reference to Henry Ford, who automated the manufacturing process)

decanting (in the real world, pouring from one container into another; in the novel, birth)

Though Huxley doesn't explain Malthus's theories or describe Ford's assembly lines, the coined words emphasize Huxley's distaste for conformity and genetic manipulation—important themes in the novel. One of Huxley's coinages, *decanting*, is particularly clever. There are no families in Huxley's *Brave New World*. Embryos grow in a laboratory setting, in bottles. Huxley's coinage for the birth process moves the full-grown baby out of the embryo bottle to another container—the regulated, artificial world of the title. Underlining the point is another play on words. *Cant* is "a standardized set of ideas or language that has lost meaning through mindless repetition." It may also be defined as "hypocritical speech, often on the subject of religion or politics." Both definitions fit the "brave new world" of the title.

———

Another world-maker, J. K. Rowling, selected bits of Latin and Greek and added a huge dose of her own imagination to coin hundreds of terms for the *Harry Potter* series. A few:

dementors (punishing beings who pull hope and joy from their victims)

merchieftainess (a female leader of underwater creatures)

disaparate (disappear from one location and reappear in another)

Some of Rowling's coinages are simply amusing. I dare you to say *niffler* without a smile! Others have meaning packed within. *Death Eater* (a follower of the evil Lord Voldemort) is a case in point. Most people fear death, so initially a creature that "eats death" may seem appealing. But Voldemort's quest for immortality causes others to die; he feeds on their deaths as he grows stronger. By splitting his soul so that he cannot be killed, Voldemort loses his humanity. With this coinage, Rowling emphasizes that death is what makes us cherish life—a critical idea that her hero, Harry, grasps.

—————

On a lighter note, Craig Taylor coined a word for his *New York Times* review of *The Patch*:

> Here is the seventh collection of essays by John McPhee, his 33rd book and perhaps his eleventy-billionth word of published prose.

Two real numbers (*seventh* and *33rd*) give context to *eleventy-billionth* and emphasize McPhee's long and distinguished career as a nonfiction author.

—————

Henry James, in a letter to a friend, coined a word that perhaps may also be applied to John McPhee:

> I have many irons on the fire, and am bursting with writableness.

Writable is a word, but adding the noun suffix -*ness* is James's invention. Like all coined words, it captures attention—not enough to enter the common language, but sometimes the goal is a unique usage that the reader admires for its cleverness.

—————

Not all of Lewis Carroll's coined words have made it into the dictionary, but they're fun all the same—so much so that they've decorated a thousand coffee mugs and T-shirts:

> The hurrier I go, the behinder I get.
> Curiouser and curiouser!

One Carroll coinage, *chortle*, did fill a need and does appear in the dictionary. The sound existed before Carroll named it (just listen to any tickled baby), but there was no *chortle* until Carroll combined *chuckle* and *snort*.

ELEVATING IMPORTANCE

Some words, such as *nothing*, can be dismissive. Imagine that answer to a typical parental question, "What are you doing today?" and you see my point. Insert *the* or *that*, however, and the meaning changes:

> I remember being amazed that death could so easily rise up
> from the nothing of a boyish afternoon, billow up like a fog.
> —Ta-Nehisi Coates, *Between the World and Me*

> He [Lyndon Johnson] had had three years of that nothing; to
> stay as Vice President might mean five more years of it.
> —Robert Caro, *The Passage of Power*

In each sentence, *nothing* takes on importance because of its modifier. Coates's *the nothing of a boyish afternoon* shows the end of innocence, the very last moment when "nothing happened" was the norm. Caro emphasizes Johnson's frustration with the relatively powerless role he held as vice president during John Kennedy's presidency.

———

Elsewhere is another vague word, but it too can gain significance:

> For those of us who had an elsewhere in our blood, some foreign
> origin, we had richer colors and ancient callings to hear.
> —Guy Gunaratne, *In Our Mad and Furious City*

Gunaratne follows this sentence with "Fight with, more likely, and fight for, a push-pull of ancestry and meaning." *Elsewhere* isn't just "somewhere that's not here" in Gunaratne's novel; it's a defining trait of his

BACK TO THE MINT

Re-coining a coinage: That's what columnist Herb Caen of the *San Francisco Chronicle* did when he added the suffix *-nik* to *beat*. This happened in the 1950s, when the United States and the Soviet Union were the world's primary superpowers and bitter enemies. The Cold War was at its height, as was the fear of communist infiltration and subversion of American society. The Soviet Union had just launched a pair of satellites, *Sputnik I* and *Sputnik II*, putting it ahead of the United States in the space race.

To backtrack: writer Jack Kerouac coined *beat* to describe his group of friends, who defied what they saw as the rigid rules of society. At various times Kerouac defined *beat* as "weary," "beaten down," or "beatific." To him, the *Beats* were a rebellious but angelic set of artists, writers, and musicians.

Caen, clearly not a fan of the group, wrote:

Look magazine, preparing a picture spread on S.F.'s Beat Generation (oh, no, not AGAIN!), hosted a party in a No. Beach [North Beach] house for 50 Beatniks, and by the time word got around the sour grapevine, over 250 bearded cats and kits were on hand, slopping up Mike Cowles' free booze.

For those unfamiliar with 1950s slang, *cat* and *kit* are male and female *Beats*. By adding a Russian suffix to Kerouac's coinage, Caen associated the group with anti-Americanism. Kerouac was so irritated that he confronted Caen and asked him to stop using the word *beatnik*. Furthermore, when Kerouac and his wife divorced, he demanded that *beatnik* not be allowed in court documents because, he said, "In conventional society the term *beatnik* is a term of disfavor, conjuring up images of unwashed, bearded persons." Neither plea kept *beatnik* out of the language, and arguably Caen's term is more familiar than the original coinage.

characters. They aren't from London, the "mad and furious city" of the title, and the *elsewhere* in them strongly influences their identity and fate.

FOR THE WRITER

Minting shiny new words can be fun. Perhaps these suggestions will help you get started.

REPURPOSE

This challenge comes from the *Washington Post*, which sponsors an annual redefinition contest. Select a word that exists, but change its meaning. Some past winners of the *Post*'s contest:

abdication—giving up on ever having a flat stomach
tumbling—a belly-button ring
coffee—a person who's coughed on
flabbergasted—appalled about the amount of weight you've gained

Notice that part of each word already has a definition. The new meaning of *abdication* riffs on the original, "ceding power or responsibility," and *abs*, a shortened version of "abdominal muscles." *Tumbling* plays with *tummy* and *bling*, the slang term for jewelry. The suffix *-ee* indicates a receiver, in this case the receiver of a cough, hopefully not phlegm-filled. *Flab* is slang for "fat," and *gast* is a play on "aghast" (horrified).

Flip or scroll through the dictionary and see what new definitions you can create. Then write a sentence for your coined terms. Extend the exercise, if you wish, by creating a scene that depends on the same ideas expressed by your word.

FILLING A NEED

Identify something that has no name and create one for it. Start with food: What would you call these?

> the crumbs at the bottom of a bag of potato chips or a box of cereal
> what sticks to the knife when you cut a cake
> a chewy bit of crust
> vegetables that have cooked too long

Move on to sports:

> a football player's big toe
> the first string to break on a tennis racket
> a lost golf ball
> the bottom of a basketball net

Try entertainment:

> four hours at the video game console
> a song dropped from a playlist
> an actor learning lines
> audience members who skip out on the credits at the end of a film

These are only a few suggestions. Once you start coining, it's hard to stop. To make the task harder, and potentially come away with something valuable, write sentences or a scene containing your coinage.

CHARACTER BUILDING

Select a character from a novel, play, film, or television show. Or invent a character. In one column, list words that describe the character. In another column, turn the descriptions into actions. For example, a ballet dancer is *graceful* (description) and *graces* (action) across the stage. A toddler can be *stubborn* (description), one who *stubborns* her parents into giving her what she wants. If you like, write a scene in which your character displays the qualities you've assigned, employing the word you coined. Careful: overuse ruins the novelty, so place your invention in just one sentence.

NEW NEWS

Select a news story and identify key events. Rewrite the story, or just its headline, with a coinage that reflects the most significant aspect. A stalemate over health care legislation, for instance, might be entitled "Congress Sicktalks Without Result." An article about a hurricane may state that the storm was "windwet" while the people in it huddled, "feareyed but hopeful" that they would survive.

PART III SOUND

ONOMATOPOEIA

I think I can—I think I can—I think I can—I think I can—I think I can—I think I can—I think I can—I think I can—I think I can.
—Watty Piper, *The Little Engine That Could*

Imagine cave dwellers huddled near a fire when language was in its infancy. They must have used sound effects: a *swoosh* for the spear flying toward a bison, a *neigh* marking the presence of a horse—perhaps even the *smack* of a kiss. Fashioning a word that sounds like what it means has a very long history—a history that repeats itself in every toddler learning a first language and in anyone struggling to acquire a second or a third. When a standard word fails to appear, a soundalike gets the job done. If you don't know how to say, "I drove over a nail," pointing to the car and saying *pop-hiss* is a good alternative. The technical term for soundalike words is *onomatopoeia*. I'm stretching it to cover a whole statement, because the overall sound of a sentence may fit the meaning very well.

Eventually, many soundalike words find their way into the dictionary, but not all. I doubt you'll find anything in the dictionary from Don Martin of *Mad* magazine, a cartoonist whose captions are legendary. Two of my favorite "Martin-isms" are *argle glargle glorgle gluk* (mouthwash in use) and *kachugh chuh* (a train starting up). With onomatopoeia, Martin adds sound to his cartoon panels and creates a better story.

So does "Watty Piper," the pseudonym of Arnold Plunk, one of the publishers of the 1930 edition of *The Little Engine That Could*. This classic children's story existed long before "Piper" wrote it down, and many other versions have followed. If you've had the pleasure of reading *The Little Engine That Could* to a small child, followed by the dubious pleasure of rereading it to the same child nineteen more times, you know that the featured sentence comes at the climactic moment, when the "Little Blue Engine" strains to pull boxcars of toys and food to the "good little boys and girls" on the other side of the mountain. Will she make it? Will the children be left toyless and hungry? There's no suspense for an adult reader, but the target audience hasn't lived long enough to be complacent. Besides, the kids like the sound. They can hear the overtaxed locomotive and can share its struggles.

I think I can is more than engine noise. It's an affirmation: "Yes, I can face a challenge. Yes, I'll try. Yes, I know I may fail." A young audience always needs that message, and so did adult readers when Watty Piper's book was published. To those dealing with the Great Depression and the hopelessness it bred, *I think I can* must have been comforting.

The punctuation and repetition of the featured sentence enhance its effect. All those dashes add hesitancy. Saying the same thing nine times—nine!—underlines how hard the task is. And the task is not just to climb the mountain with a train in tow. It's to believe that the mountain *can* be climbed. If you've ever given yourself a pep talk, you know that one encouraging comment is not enough.

The individual words are carefully chosen also. Each is a single syllable, with three sharp sounds (*I, I, can*) interrupted by one soft sound (*think*). The sharps are stabs of effort, the soft a pause to gather strength. Taken together, and repeated, they signal extreme effort.

Piper omits one word from the sentence—*that*—thus giving the personal pronoun *I* more prominence. The "Little Blue Engine" takes responsibility when other, bigger engines decline. Achievement enhances self-confidence, and *I* represents the self.

MOVING SOUND

The featured sentence isn't the only one to capture sound in *The Little Engine That Could*. Just before it comes this line: "Puff, puff, chug, chug, went the Little Blue Engine." *Puff* and *chug* are fairly standard in train stories. Zora Neale Hurston is even more inventive:

> Suddenly he was conscious of a great rumbling at hand and the train schickalacked up to the station and stopped.

This sentence from her novel *Jonah's Gourd Vine* captures a moment when a young man encounters a locomotive for the first time. Naturally, he lacks words for it. Hurston's coinage, *schickalacked*, emphasizes the novelty even as it echoes the sound of the movement it represents.

––––––

Cars and trucks are the noisemakers in this sentence from *Durango Street* by Frank Bonham:

> Stretched out on his cot, he listened sleepily to the diesels blatting by, the cars passing with a rising and falling whoosh.

––––––

And boats in this one, from Samuel Taylor Coleridge's "The Rime of the Ancient Mariner":

> The furrow followed free . . .

Say it aloud to hear how the words capture the sound of water rushing past a ship.

Even horsepower is noisy. Listen to the animal's hooves in Alfred Noyes's poem "The Highwayman":

Over the cobbles he clattered and clashed in the dark inn-yard.

Later, the sound of the same hooves is represented by "*Tlot-tlot*, in the frosty silence! *Tlot-tlot*, in the echoing night!"

One more horse, in this line from William Butler Yeats's poem "Easter 1916":

A shadow of cloud on the stream . . .
And a horse plashes within it . . .

Plash is "break the water surface with a splashing sound." Yeats could have chosen *splashes*, but he selected the less common word, perhaps for dramatic effect.

ADVERTISING SOUNDS

The attraction of onomatopoeia hasn't escaped the advertising industry. Campaigns to encourage seatbelt usage have featured these slogans:

Clunk click, every trip. (UK)
Click, clack, front and back. (Australia)
Click it or ticket. (US)

MUSICAL NOTES

Who can write about music without onomatopoeia? Listen to the feet (yes, feet) of a piano player in Langston Hughes's poem "The Weary Blues":

Thump, thump, thump, went his foot on the floor.

For years I read this line with equal spacing between words. Then I heard a jazz musician recite it differently: "Thump [pause] thumpthump." The pianist in the poem is playing "a drowsy syncopated tune," which the jazz musician's reading matches. His was much better than my evenly spaced version.

———

In *The Song of the Lark* by Willa Cather, a musician named "Spanish Johnny" entertains the crowd in a saloon:

He would go on [singing] until he had no voice left, until he wheezed and rasped.

This character is ill and exhausted, which Cather conveys with *wheezed and rasped.*

———

Poet Carl Sandburg also visits a bar in his poem "Honky Tonk in Cleveland, Ohio":

It's a jazz affair, drum crashes and cornet razzes.

———

Lawrence Durrell in his memoir *Bitter Lemons* describes a flute:

It was obviously being played by someone with an imperfect command over it; it squeaked and yipped, started a line again, only to founder once more in squeals.

Durrell apparently had bad luck with music; elsewhere in *Bitter Lemons,* Durrell hears a mandolin's "whimper" and "whining."

––––––––

A character in Lisa Chen's story "Night Beat" plays a phonograph record, not an instrument. As the needle hits the vinyl, she hears:

A pop and a hiss before the tom-tom of the bass.

––––––––

Edgar Allan Poe, in his poem "The Bells," describes a variety of rings. Some are pleasant:

How they tinkle, tinkle, tinkle,
In the icy air of night!

and some are not:

How they clang, and clash, and roar!

Regardless, all are examples of what Poe calls "tintinnabulation," a word for bell sounds that is itself an example of onomatopoeia.

VOICE TO THE VOICELESS

The natural world attracts onomatopoeia. How else can its sounds be conveyed? Listen to the animal kingdom:

Ernest started trumpeting, and cracked his manger,
Leonard started roaring, and shivered in his stall,

James gave the huffle of a snail in danger
And nobody heard him at all.

In these lines from A. A. Milne's *When We Were Very Young*, Ernest is
an elephant, Leonard a lion, and James a snail. *Trumpeting* and *roaring*
are common descriptions of the sounds elephants and lions make, but
not the snail's *huffle*. As snails lack vocal cords, it's not surprising that
nobody heard poor James.

––––––

Even more traditional is "Old MacDonald Had a Farm," the venerable
children's song, and its cow:

With a moo-moo here, and a moo-moo there . . .

The cow's *moo-moo* is joined by the pig's "snort" or "oink" (depending
on the version), the sheep's "baa," the chicken's "cluck," and the duck's
"quack." Quite a symphony, that farm.

––––––

Tennyson evokes a rural scene in "Come Down O Maid":

. . . the moan of doves in immemorial elms,
And murmuring of innumerable bees.

––––––

Of a character in *For Whom the Bell Tolls*, Ernest Hemingway writes:

He saw nothing and heard nothing but he could feel his heart
pounding and then he heard the clack on stone and the leaping
dropping clicks of a small rock falling.

———

Similar sounds, but with a twist, appear in Robert Frost's poem "Birches":

They [ice-covered birches] click upon themselves . . .

Later, a breeze causes "cracks and crazes" in the ice, a compact image that evokes both the sight and sound of cracking ice.

———

So does this one by Emily Dickinson:

I heard a Fly buzz when I died

———

Ogden Nash writes about the dead, too, specifically the title characters of his poem "Fossils," who have

no drums or saxophone
But just the clatter of their bones.

———

Flowers lack sound, but their names don't. Kate Daniels's haunting narrative poem "In the Marvelous Dimension" follows several people trapped on a California highway after an earthquake. Through his shattered windshield, one speaker can see only a single flower and says:

Until then, I'd never liked
petunias, their heavy stems,

the peculiar spittooning sound
of their name.

A *spittoon* is a receptacle for chewed tobacco—and, with its forward thrust of air from the first two letters, a good fit for *petunias*.

MACHINE LANGUAGE

Machines, except those with artificial intelligence, can't talk, but many are noisy and thus a fine target for onomatopoeia. Take this description of the simplest machine, a poorly maintained well, that appears in T. H. White's novel *The Sword in the Stone*:

> "Clank, Clank, Clank," said the chain, until the bucket hit the lip of the well, and "Oh, drat the whole thing," said the old gentleman.

————

Barely audible, according to a character in *The Dresser* by Ronald Harwood, is the staged storm in *King Lear*. The fan and gears creating the sound of wind and rain are not acceptable to the lead actor:

> I ask for cataracts and hurricanes and I am given trickles and whistles.

————

Speaking of rain, E. L. Doctorow observes in "All the Time in the World":

> It might be just a few drops, but out floop the umbrellas.

———

Unacceptably loud are the tools Lawrence Durrell describes in *Bitter Lemons*:

> A circular saw moaned and gnashed all day in one of the shacks under the ministrations of two handsome Turkish youths with green headbands and dilapidated clothes; a machine for making cement blocks performed its slow but punctual evacuations, accompanied by a seductive crunch.

———

The time-traveler in Stephen King's *11/22/63* reports:

> I could hear the thunder of the dyers and dryers, the *shat-HOOSH, shat-HOOSH* of the huge weaving flats that had once filled the second floor.

———

More melodious is the human hand, portrayed in this sentence from James Joyce's *Ulysses*:

> I was beginning to yawn with nerves thinking he was trying to make a fool of me when I knew his tattarrattat at the door.

Joyce's coinage, *tattarrattat*, is a palindrome. It reads the same from right to left or from left to right. It's also a fair imitation of the sound of knocking.

———

Pity the poor fellow waking to this noise, as described by Richard Wright in *Native Son*:

Brrrrrrriiiiiiiiiiiiiiiiiiiinng! An alarm clock clanged in the dark and silent room.

———

Now listen to the gamblers in Rod Serling's "The Fever," who are playing the slot machines:

There was a continuous clack, clack, clack of lever, then a click, click, click of tumblers coming up.

and hoping for

. . . a metallic poof sometimes followed by the clatter of silver dollars coming down through the funnel to land with a happy smash in the coin receptacle at the bottom of the machine.

FOR THE WRITER

Writing soundalikes can be great fun, whether you select standard words or make up your own. These exercises may fine-tune your ear for onomatopoeia.

FOOD FIGHT

What does dinner sound like? Invite friends and family to share a meal and listen—not just to what they say, but to the sounds they make. You may hear a *gulp* or a polite *burp* or even a *belch* or two. Write a paragraph describing the event, employing as many soundalikes as possible. Tip: Not many people want to read about their ingestion and digestion. Keep your words to yourself, or disguise the identities and occasion that inspired you.

FORECASTING

Watch video reports of hurricanes, tornados, blizzards, and other extreme weather events. Ignore the bedraggled reporters gamely clutching soggy microphones. Instead, note the rain, the wind, the snow, or anything else Mother Nature is hurling at the world. Now write it! Comparisons are fine, but strive for soundalikes: *shushes, susurration,* and *patpatpat,* for example.

CONCERT-ING

Attend a concert if you can, or listen to a recording. Deconstruct what you hear and write about it. Many standard words to describe music exist, but you can always fashion a few more. To the *plunk* of a piano key, add the *donk* of an emphatic note. To the *screech* of a misplayed violin note, add *yrrkk.* Isolate each instrument or try to convey the sound of the entire orchestra or band—a much harder task.

AT THE RACES

NASCAR races, not horses! Open your ears to the car's acceleration at the start of a lap and the changes you hear as the pack hits a turn or slows when the finish line appears in the rearview mirror. Once again, mix standard words (*purr, roar*) and your own creations (*rrrriiiiptptpt* or *vreech,* for example).

MATCHING SOUNDS

Soul I say, even if the dead cannot tell us
about the bristles of God's beard because God has no face,
soul I say, to name the smoke-beings flung in constellations
across the night sky of this city and cities to come.
                    —Martín Espada, "Alabanza: In Praise of Local 100"

O n a recent visit to the library I noticed a sign affixed to a low door-
way: "Duck or Bump." In that same library I read about a company describing itself as a "female film force." The ideas carried by
these phrases are not particularly memorable, yet I remember them. By
matching "uh" sounds in *duck* and *bump* and beginning three words
with *f*, the writers upped the odds that their words would remain with
me. Matching sounds—not just end-of-the-line rhymes but sounds
within lines—is a technique as old as literature itself. Were this simply a
mnemonic device, it would not have endured from the wax- through to
the electronic-tablet era. What else can matching sounds accomplish? A
pleasing impression, for one. Also, similar sounds create links in meaning, whether the words are read aloud or silently. This sort of rhyming
does its work under the radar (sonar?). It's often created unconsciously,
too. As the Duchess in Lewis Carroll's *Alice's Adventures in Wonderland* explains, "Take care of the sense, and the sounds will take care
of themselves."

Martín Espada does not let the sounds in his poems "take care of
themselves." He reads aloud as he writes, deliberately choosing words to
please his mind and ear. The featured sentence is excerpted from "Ala-

banza: In Praise of Local 100," a moving tribute to forty-three restaurant workers who died in the North Tower of the World Trade Center in 2001. They were members of the Hotel and Restaurant Employees Union, and most were immigrants—from *"Ecuador, México, República Dominicana, / Haiti, Yemen, Ghana, Bangladesh."*

With small details—a tattoo, a favored song, a baseball cap—Espada makes these men and women come alive. He orders us to praise them, using that word as well as its Spanish equivalent, *alabanza*. The poem celebrates their ordinary actions on September 11th—arriving at work, turning on a radio, cracking eggs, stacking cans. Then Espada turns to the "thunder wilder than thunder" of the plane's strike. Lastly, he imagines the spirits of the dead.

The featured sentence follows a reference to "a cook's soul." In that context, it's a defiant assertion: yes, the cook had a *soul*. The speaker is so vehement that *soul I say* appears twice. The linked *s* sounds (*soul*, *say*) add another meaning: the *soul* has a *say*, a voice unextinguished by death. The *soul* has another sort of *say*, also: a vote on what happens next.

Espada follows this sentence with a reference to "Manhattan and Kabul," one attacked on September 11th and the other in the ensuing war. The dead from both places mingle as *smoke-beings*, and they share music. The *s* of *soul* and *say* is not exactly the same as the *sm* combination in *smoke*. That's appropriate, because the speaker is alive, and the *smoke-beings* are not. They're both human, but in different forms.

The vowels in Espada's sentence don't match, but many are long. *Soul I say*, for example, has a long *o*, *i*, and *a*. *Smoke-beings* has two, *o* and *e*. There are others: <u>e</u>ven, b<u>ea</u>rd, f<u>a</u>ce, n<u>a</u>me, n<u>i</u>ght, sk<u>y</u>. By nanoseconds, a long vowel is audible for more time than a short vowel. A long vowel can thus, ever so subtly, keep listeners' attention on the word it appears in. I don't want to overinterpret this aspect of the sentence, but I venture to say *beard*, *face*, and *name* evoke the mistaken belief that terrorists can be identified by physical appearance or national origin. *Sky*, of course, is where the attackers' plane flew.

Espada places three sound-pairs in this sentence, perhaps an unconscious reference to the setting of the poem (the Twin Towers). In addition to *soul I say,* the lines include two near-matches: *God's/God* and *city/ cities.* Espada writes that *the dead cannot tell us / about the bristles of God's beard.* That's the sort of detail important only to someone bypassing the core meaning of faith and religion, focusing on a twig while missing the forest. Espada counters with *God has no face.* No outward sign reveals the deity—just as no outward sign reveals a terrorist. Moving on to the last pair: the deaths of "Local 100" members occurred in one *city,* New York. But in death, *smoke-beings* are *flung in constellations across the night sky of . . . cities to come.* Espada correctly anticipates the rebuilding of one ruined *city,* with hope that *cities to come* will welcome these souls and give *alabanza,* or "praise," to those who light their skies. With *cities to come,* Espada also predicts more death by violence. Sadly, his 2002 statement has proved accurate.

MORE MATCHES, MOSTLY VOWELS

Poetry is a natural place to search for sound effects, but prose writers also work with sound. Lewis Thomas, physician and philosopher, describes the English language in his essay "On Speaking of Speaking":

> It suits every need that I can think of: flexibility, clarity, subtlety
> of metaphor, ambiguity wherever ambiguity is needed (which
> is more often than is generally acknowledged), and most of all
> changeability.

Thomas goes on to speculate that language is created by children playing together and exchanging sounds until they eventually codify a way to communicate. A striking aspect of his sentence is the matching *-ity* sound in the qualities he cites, not surprising because that suffix marks an abstract noun. (Only *subtlety* breaks the pattern, by replacing *i* with *e,* but the sound is similar.) Stringing these *-ity* words together gives them equal importance; *flexibility* is as necessary as *clarity,* for instance. Thus, Thomas implies, new words are welcome because, I'd add, they're a *necessity.*

———

Also playing with short *i* sounds is Tom Hawkins, who writes in "Putting a Child to Bed":

> She noticed the imaginary hamster grew just a little bit as he held
> it there for her examination.

She is a mother, *he* her nine-year-old son, who's asked his mother for a pet and is stretching his fingers to show how small (and therefore how little trouble) the hamster would be. As he pleads his case, the mother pays close attention, an attitude emphasized by matching short-*i* sounds (*noticed, little bit, examination*). The mother isn't convinced and postpones a decision, the love between the two obvious despite their disagreement on the merits of a hamster in the house.

———

One more short *i*, from *The Nero Wolfe Cookbook* by mystery author Rex Stout:

> Clean it and split it and wipe it off with a damp cloth.

The *it* is a "well-fed turkey, 10-weeks old" that the reader has been instructed to "procure." The cadence of this instruction, with repeated *it*s and one *split*, creates a sense of simplicity. How appropriate for a sentence supposedly written by Stout's detective, a gourmet who almost never leaves his house and who most likely would delegate the procuring to an employee. Simplicity is easy when you have minions.

———

From short- to long-*i*: William Blake describes a tiger (spelled "tyger" in his poem) with several memorable images. Here's one:

In what distant deeps or skies
Burnt the fire of thine eyes?

Skies, fire, thine eyes: exotic (*skies* are far away, as are *distant deeps*) and dangerous (*fire of thine eyes*).

———

Sandra Cisneros, in her novel *The House on Mango Street*, also plays with long vowels, specifically the long-*e* sound. The narrator remarks:

Keep, keep, keep, trees say when I sleep. They teach.

What do *they teach*? Perseverance. "Four grew despite concrete," she adds, and their survival inspires her. The matching long-*e* sounds of *keep, sleep,* and *teach* come across as advice that the *trees* (with another long-*e*) give. The sounds resemble a chant, almost a spell, exactly the sort of magic a youngster might turn to.

———

Comedian Dick Gregory unites long-*a* words in his autobiography:

I never learned hate at home, or shame.

He continues, "I had to go to school for that." The context is a humiliating incident during which a teacher says publicly that the class is "collecting money for you and your kind"—that is, poor people. Adding to his distress, she points out that he has no father. *Hate* and *shame* go together in his sentence, as they do in life. The *h* sound also repeats (*hate, home*) but in disunion, because *never* negates the connection. Gregory's *home* may have been poor, but neither *hate* nor *shame* is there.

———

This melodious catchphrase, probably apocryphal, concerns the "Black Sox" baseball scandal of 1919:

> Say it ain't so, Joe.

Joe was "Shoeless Joe" Jackson, an outstanding hitter who was accused, along with eight other players, of accepting money to play poorly in the World Series. The line, reportedly from a young fan, resonates with two long-*a* sounds (*say, ain't*) and two long-*o*'s (*so, Joe*).

———

Last, neither long nor short, is this repetition of the "ooh" sound:

> Bang, zoom, to the moon, Alice!

That's a nonserious threat from Ralph Kramden to his wife, Alice, of *The Honeymooners*, the legendary television sitcom.

ON TO CONSONANTS

Also linking ideas are repeated consonant sounds, such as the *st-* in this sentence from Gish Jen's *Typical American*:

> Still he studied.

These three words appear in the middle of a paragraph about a married couple emigrating to America. The wife notices physical details (also with matching consonants): how the sea "sang and spit" and how islands emerged from the horizon with "brown, bristled backs." She's anchored in the present moment. The husband is determined to read, to prepare himself for a new career and life. He is *still*, or motionless. He also *still . . . studied*; he won't stop. Their attitudes divide them, but the matching sounds describing each unite them.

———

The narrator of Mary Gaitskill's "Today I'm Yours" unexpectedly meets a former lover. She explains:

> I dreamed of Dani only once that I can remember, but it was a deep, delicious dream, like a maze made of diaphanous silk, or a room of hidden chambers, each chamber nested inside the previous one—except that according to the inverse law of the dream, each inner chamber was bigger, not smaller, than the last.

The linked consonants (*deep, delicious, dream, diaphanous,* and *maze made*) reveal the narrator's feelings for *Dani*. There's attraction (*deep,*

THE SOUND OF SONGS

Simon and Garfunkel's hit "The Sound of Silence" is only one of many song titles relying on repeated consonant sounds. Here is a selection, each with one or more artists who performed the song:

"Bye Bye Baby" (Bay City Rollers)
"Dancing in the Dark" (Bruce Springsteen)
"Let Love In" (Goo Goo Dolls)
"Jumpin' Jack Flash" (Rolling Stones)
"Lay Lady Lay" (Bob Dylan)
"September Song" (JP Cooper)
"Delta Dawn" (Tanya Tucker)
"Poor People of Paris" (Les Baxter)
"Sunshine Superman" (Donovan)

delicious, diaphanous), but it's complicated and probably impossible (*dream, maze made*).

————

Another dream, much less complex, appears in Beatrix Potter's *The Tale of the Flopsy Bunnies*. The little ones are tired and so

> The little rabbits smiled sweetly in their sleep under the shower of grass; they did not awake because the lettuces had been so soporific.

With *smiled, sweetly, sleep, shower, so,* and *soporific,* young readers may find themselves lulled also—until Mr. McGregor pops the bunnies in a sack. Danger threatens, but the animals escape with no more damage than one thump with a rotted vegetable, which hit the youngest and "rather hurt."

————

Rocky Balboa, hero of the *Rocky* films, might have counseled the rabbit this way:

> Nobody is gonna hit as hard as life, but it ain't how hard you can hit.

He adds that what's important is to "keep moving forward." All those *h* sounds in Rocky's sentence (*how,* plus a doubled *hit* and *hard*) give a sense of breathlessness, appropriate for the long-suffering, exhausted fighter.

————

On the other side of the Atlantic is Virginia Woolf, who often roamed London, observing with a writer's eye. In this sentence she describes the docks, where cargo from the British Empire is unloaded:

Here growls and grumbles that rough city song that has called ships from the sea and brought them to lie captive beneath its warehouses.

The scene is *rough*, with the hard sounds (and meaning) of *growls and grumbles*. But Woolf romanticizes the docks, giving softer *s* sounds to her sentence: *city song*, *sea*, plus the near match of *ships*.

———

William Wordsworth turns to the soft, repeated *s* for the first line (and title) of a poem expressing grief on the death of a loved one:

A slumber did my spirit steal . . .

———

Anne Bradstreet also considers mortality in "To My Dear and Loving Husband":

Then while we live, in love lets so persever,
That when we live no more, we may live ever.

Live, love, lets (modern writers would insert an apostrophe or write "let us"). Bradstreet's *l* words are shorthand for "seize the day." She's not advocating hedonism, however. Their faithful love will be their salvation and they will *live ever.*

———

One more love, for Christopher Smart's cat Jeoffrey, which he praises:

For at the first glance of the glory of God in the East he worships in
    his way
For is this done by wreathing his body seven times round with ele-
    gant quickness.

Smart gives sixty or so more examples of Jeoffrey's excellence, many with matching consonant sounds. Here he associates *glance*, *glory*, and *God*. The last word, *God*, deviates from the *gl-* pattern, but only a little. Anyone living with a cat understands why Smart makes this link. Cats do seem to believe that they're akin to deities.

FOR THE WRITER

Kids fiddle with sounds just for the fun of it. Recapture your inner child through these exercises.

PLAYING WITH MATCHES

Below are a few pairs of words with matching vowel sounds. Tweak the pairs until they fit into a sentence. Turn it up a notch: Turn the pair into triplets, quadruplets, or as many *-lets* as you wish. Note: If you add more matching words, concentrate on sound, not spelling (*lotto* and *wash*). An example with a short *e*:

> Step away from the window so I can place my bet before the race begins.

Pairs: *ray* and *day*, *tee* and *believe*, *why* and *sigh*, *although* and *borrow*, *you* and *unite*, *qualm* and *Mom*, *with* and *bliss*.

PLAYING WITH MATCHES, PART 2

Quite a few common expressions, such as "tip of the tongue," contain matching consonant sounds. Perhaps that makes them easier to remember, or perhaps they satisfy a need for pattern. Either way, brainstorm until you have a list of catchphrases with repeating consonants. For the energetic: create new expressions that could conceivably catch on. (Notice all those *c*-sounds? Maybe *CCCO* will become the texting version of "could conceivably catch on," a way to label the next meme.)

SUPPORTIVE SOUND

Throughout this chapter I've related sound to meaning. Time for you to do the same. Select a sentence from something you've already written, or write a new sentence. Choose words that have matching vowel or consonant sounds, taking care that your matches bolster the meaning or fit the context.

REPETITION

But then they danced down the streets like dingledodies, and I shambled after as I've been doing all my life after people who interest me, because the only people for me are the mad ones, the ones who are mad to live, mad to talk, mad to be saved, desirous of everything at the same time, the ones who never yawn or say a commonplace thing, but burn, burn, burn like fabulous yellow roman candles exploding like spiders across the stars and in the middle you see the blue centerlight pop and everybody goes "Awww!"

—Jack Kerouac, *On the Road*

How many real or would-be rebels have made Jack Kerouac's words their anthem? I've known many, and my guess is that you have, too. The featured sentence appears in *On the Road*, a fictionalized version of several trips Kerouac took with his friends, during which the travelers fight and reconcile, meet and discard sexual partners, drink and take drugs, and discuss every topic intensely. In short, they do what Kerouac says the *mad ones* do. Kerouac employs repetition in this sentence for the same reason many other authors do: to emphasize and unite ideas.

Usually, when I see this sentence on a poster or embroidered on a flag (and, yes, I've seen it in both spots), only the middle appears. The common version begins after *because* and stops after *roman candles*. That's fitting, because once the fireworks end, aspiring rebels become bored, and boredom is the last thing Jack Kerouac represents in the public imagination. Instead, he's the hero who embarks on a journey of adventure and self-discovery, the rebel who hates the conformity of the 1950s, the best of the *mad ones* who *burn, burn, burn* with creative fire.

The complete version of the sentence adds nuance to this image. Kerouac's narrator (called Sal Paradise in the novel and a stand-in for

Kerouac) separates himself from the *mad ones*. They are the ones who *dance down the streets like dingledodies*. (Don't look for *dingledodies* in a standard dictionary. Kerouac coined the word.) Sal *shambled after*. *Shamble* is "walk awkwardly or unsteadily," a gait common in the fast-growing teen years. And what is adolescence if not a nest for rebellion? The *mad ones* may be *the only people* for Sal, but in his own estimation, he stands apart. Did Kerouac know that he was describing Sal (and therefore himself) as a writer? Sal, who *shambled after*, was observing. It's what *I've been doing all my life*, he says.

The legend is that Kerouac wrote *On the Road* in a three-week burst, typing on a continuous "scroll" he'd made by taping long sheets of paper to each other. In those precomputer days, he would have had to pause at the end of each page to insert a new sheet into the typewriter, and he didn't want to break the flow of creative energy even for a moment. Or so he said. In fact, he'd worked on an initial draft for years before the three-week typing spree began, and he spent several more years editing. The final version differs little from the scroll, but Kerouac was a writer, not a force of nature. Thought and care went into *On the Road*.

Now to the first repetition:

mad ones
mad to live
mad to talk
mad to be saved

Mad means "insane, delusional" or "angry, violent." It also applies to infatuation; if you're *mad about* or *mad for* something, you think of little else. The word may also be used as an intensifier: *mad afraid*, for example, conveys extreme fear. By repeating *mad*, Kerouac links the three activities to the group he designates as the *mad ones*: *to live, to talk, to be saved*. The first two imply independence. Barring outside interference, the *mad ones* control how *to live* and *to talk*. But the third, *to be saved*, implies dependency. Grammatically, it's a passive verb, with the subject receiving, not performing, the action. The salvation the *mad ones* seek must come from someone or something else. Viewed in that light, the road trips sound like desperate searches.

Impossibility joins desperation in the next portion of the sentence:

> desirous of everything at the same time
> the ones who never yawn or say a commonplace thing

As the Rolling Stones put it a couple of decades later, you can't always get what you want, and *everything at the same time* is a nonstarter. Even discounting the *yawn* reference (is there anyone who *never* yawns?), everyone says *a commonplace thing* sometimes. And Kerouac, the observer whose alter ego *shambled after* his friends, knows it.

Now to the second repetition: *burn, burn, burn*. The verb refers to fire, of course, but figuratively it's often used for passion. A hint of violence lies within *burn*, just as it does within *mad*. Kerouac's narrator is attracted to fireworks that light up the sky, but the moment of glory is fleeting. As *everyone goes Awww!* at the *blue centerlight*, the firework burns out.

It's *mad* to think you can have it all, do nothing normal, and go out in a blaze of glory that will amaze those around you. There's more than a hint of anger—of being *mad*—here, too. The world isn't what Sal Paradise (or Jack Kerouac) wants it to be, nor can he *be saved* by going on the road.

Kerouac's sentence doesn't need repetition to convey the basic idea. Written this way

> But then they danced down the streets like dingledodies, and I shambled after as I've been doing all my life after people who interest me, because the only people for me are the ones who are mad to live, to talk, to be saved, desirous of everything at the same time, the ones who never yawn or say a commonplace thing, but burn like fabulous yellow roman candles exploding like spiders across the stars and in the middle you see the blue centerlight pop and everybody goes "Awww!"

the content remains the same, but not the tone. By inserting extra *mad*s and *burn*s, Kerouac's sentence attains the passion he admires.

GOING DEEPER

Bob Dylan said of *On the Road*, "It changed my life like it changed everyone else's." Many of Dylan's songs echo Kerouac's themes. Some, like this line from "I Shall Be Released," employ repetition:

Any day now, any day now,
I shall be released.

On the surface, the words come from someone in jail who's resentful of those who imprisoned him. The prisoner hears a man protesting innocence and weeping. The repeated phrase, *any day now, any day now*, expresses both a desire for freedom and an attempt to comfort. This is how a parent speaks to an impatient child, with repeated words that offer hope. The song's meaning goes deeper than a prisoner's lament, however. Anyone yearning to escape life's burdens—to die—might say the same words to stave off despair.

––––––––

A different Dylan, Dylan Thomas, chose a strict poetic form for "Do Not Go Gentle into That Good Night." The poem is a villanelle, which requires two refrains (repeated lines) in specific places. But Thomas goes beyond the requirements of the form by embedding repetition within one refrain:

Rage, rage against the dying of the light.

Thomas claimed that the poem was about his father's growing blindness, but most readers see "Do Not Go Gentle into That Good Night" as a poem about death. Perhaps Thomas himself might have been blind to the references to death he embedded in the poem ("at their end," "last wave," "grieved," "grave men," and so forth). Either way, Thomas wields repetition like a hammer. *Rage, rage* is pure emotion, not logic. Had the poet's father attempted to *rage* against either blindness or death, he would not have succeeded. Little wonder the poem sounds like a scream of *rage*.

———

Ani DiFranco, in her song "Back Back Back," also contemplates the nature of rage and its consequences:

Back back back in the back of your mind
Are you learning an angry language?

DiFranco addresses a nameless boy, telling him about "nursing homes" where "old old old people" are "scowling away at nothing." Nurturing a negative emotion makes it grow and intensify, she explains. If the boy wants a "comfortable chair" to sit on "in the middle of yourself," he must "practice happiness" before it's too late to change.

DiFranco's repetition reaches into the unconscious. A single *back* might refer to an unexpressed thought, but four *back*s in a nine-word line go further. The boy *learning an angry language* may not be aware of what's happening *back back back in the back* of his mind, but it's happening nonetheless. The song also brings in a spiritual dimension, whatever is in *back back back in the back* of existence. DiFranco pleads with the boy to "renovate" his "soul" because he's "gonna be housebound there" someday.

———

Another sort of reckoning comes after war. As long as there have been soldiers, there have been veterans struggling to make sense of their experience. Repetition is an appropriate tool for this task: A single strike seldom determines the outcome of a battle, nor can one insight bring peace of mind. In *Bloods*, Wallace Terry's oral history of African Americans who served in Vietnam, Harold "Lightbulb" Bryant explains that after returning home he spoke with many chaplains and preachers, asking for "a satisfactory explanation of what happened overseas." And every year he reads the Bible, "cover to cover," "looking for the explanation." But, he explains:

I can't find it. I can't find it.

The impact of that line—technically two sentences but inseparable in meaning—is stunning, as much a product of Bryant's desperation as Terry's art. Oral historians always deal with the false starts, backtracks, and repetition that clutter human speech. In most circumstances, though, an oral historian edits the narrative to represent what's been said, but more cleanly and concisely. Terry's decision to include this repetition is a wise one, laying bare Bryant's fruitless search for meaning.

———

Also voiceless is the woman Frederick Douglass refers to in his autobiography:

She was nevertheless left a slave—a slave for life—a slave in the hands of strangers; and in their hands she saw her children, her grandchildren, and her great-grandchildren, divided, like so many sheep, without being gratified with the small privilege of a single word, as to their or her own destiny.

Three times Douglass writes *slave*, first simply and then adding words to be sure that the reader understands the horror of her state: *a slave for life* and *a slave in the hands of strangers.* He also repeats *children*, extending the word through generations, from the mother to her *great-grandchildren.* She can protect no one, including herself. Each repetition is a step on the path to more agony.

———

Now, some comedy, specifically the famous "dead parrot" sketch by the comedy troupe Monty Python. A pet-shop clerk insists that the parrot a customer just bought is "resting." The customer rants for several minutes. This sentence is one of the best:

> He's kicked the bucket, he's shuffled off his mortal coil, run down
> the curtain and joined the bleedin' choir invisible!

No word repeats, but the meaning does. Each statement is a euphemism for death, including the last sentence: "THIS IS AN EX-PARROT!" By saying the same thing in different ways, the writer shows that there is no way to convince the clerk that the customer has a legitimate complaint.

WHAT YOU SEE IS WHAT YOU GET

You don't always have to dig into a text to see the effects of repetition. Staying on the surface—mostly—are these sentences. The repeated words may cause a smile, elicit a surge of pride, or accomplish other goals:

Perspective

> In times like these, it is helpful to remember that there have
> always been times like these.
> > —Paul Harvey (radio commentator)

Opinion

> A hundred times have I thought New York is a catastrophe, and
> fifty times: It is a beautiful catastrophe.
> > —Le Corbusier, *When Cathedrals Were White*

Inspiration

... we shall fight on the beaches, we shall fight on the landing grounds, we shall fight in the fields and in the streets, we shall fight in the hills; we shall never surrender. . . .

—Winston Churchill

Information

If instead, you had started reviewing your Amazon purchases, built a reputation as a reliable reviewer, secured an invite to the Vine program, kept your head down, filed your assignments and avoided the occasional purges of reviewers, your take-home total might today exceed that number [the amount a cash investment in Amazon would have netted], although in somewhat less liquid form: five vacuums here; 14 hard drives there; some laptops and cellphones' Bluetooth speakers, and headphones, and headsets, and, well, pretty much anything with Bluetooth, so much Bluetooth, mouthful after mouthful of blue teeth.

—John Herman, "Free Stuff, But It Comes at a Price"

Definition

Motivation is the art of getting people to do what you want them to because they want to do it.

—Dwight D. Eisenhower (president of
the United States, 1953–61)

Despair

> You cannot, sir, take from me any thing that I will
> more willingly part withal:
> except my life, except my life, except my life.
>
> —Shakespeare, *Hamlet*

Advice

> Believe not all you can hear, tell not all you believe.
>
> —Native American proverb

FOR THE WRITER

No one wants to read a great two-page essay that's ten pages long. (Trust me on this: I've graded thousands of them.) The writers quoted in this chapter use repetition wisely. One principle to keep in mind as you experiment with repetition: repeat yourself only when you know why you're doing so.

FULL CIRCLE

Experiment with beginning and ending a sentence with the same word, with, of course, one or two others in the middle. For example, here's why you should put your cash into a bank account instead of under the mattress:

> Money grows money.

If you're stuck, one of these words may spark an idea: *friends, enemies, poverty, wealth, my boss/teacher/parent* (select one), *summer.*

TO . . . TO

This one is a variation of "Full Circle." Select an infinitive (*to* plus a verb). Begin and end a sentence with one, adding your own words of wisdom to the middle. For instance:

To have a life, don't waste time planning to have a life.

You may disagree with the sentiment. No matter! Just try the pattern. A few infinitives to get you going:

to be successful, to dance, to ensure, to end, to advance, to change

Now try the *to* exercise with a noun—a person, place, or thing. Here's one:

To Mary, the perfect present was what Edward gave to everyone but to Mary.

I don't know the relationship between Mary and Edward, who are both characters I've just now made up. But wouldn't it be fun to explore? In fact, once you've written your own "to . . . to" sentence, fashion a scene around it. Who knows, you may have just begun a novel.

CLIMBING

Think of a sentence that's a staircase, with the edge of each step formed by a repeated word or phrase. The actual steps—where you place your foot—are made from added words. What's important here is to climb, to take the reader with you to a conclusion that has more significance than the words preceding it. Here's an example:

After the house shuddered, after the cracks split the street in half, after the chimney teetered like a child's tower of blocks and landed on what had been my lawn, the warning siren blew.

Notice that each "step" is slightly longer than the one before, but the "landing" is short and simple. In this example, length creates the climb, but you can also climb by raising the significance level of each step. You might move from the first glance to the date to meet-the-parents night to . . . well, you know where this staircase leads. Because everyone is familiar with this particular climb, your challenge is to find an original path.

The staircase sentence is also good for argument. Think of phrases beginning with "for this reason" that lead to an inescapable conclusion. One more variation is accusation: *he has . . .* or *she has . . .* are good beginnings for a multipart indictment.

SELF-TALK

Do you talk to yourself, silently or otherwise? Most people do, especially when their confidence level ebbs or when they're trying to come to terms with the unexpected. In these situations, repetition mirrors how people process reality. One self-affirmation or explanation is seldom enough.

Create a character who needs a pep talk or a reality check. Toss a phrase representing the character's thoughts in the middle of an account of the situation, and then repeat the phrase. In this sentence, George has a job interview:

> "Good tie, best suit, hand-sewn briefcase, impeccable résumé—they'll hire me, they'll hire me," George muttered as he left the house.

Are you as ambitious as George? If so, expand the sentence into a story.

PART IV CONNECTION/ COMPARISON

FIRST PERSON

If you really want to hear about it, the first thing you'll probably want to know is where I was born, and what my lousy childhood was like, and how my parents were occupied and all before they had me, and all that David Copperfield kind of crap, but I don't feel like going into it.

—J. D. Salinger, *The Catcher in the Rye*

It says something about the human ego that expressing the *I* or *we* point of view is known as "first person." For who could be more important? Not *you* (second person) or *he, she,* and *they* (third person). Placing ourselves first is natural, both in life and in writing. That said, some spots for first person are less obvious than others. Authors of autobiography and memoir easily land in first person. So do some writers recounting events they witnessed or participated in, even when their primary purpose is to transmit facts. Many fiction writers and poets also select first-person viewpoint. Why? Perhaps to help readers connect more viscerally to a character or to give them the advantage of knowing more than a clueless or deluded narrator. And, most important, an individual's voice conveys personality and attitude.

Take Holden Caulfield, for example, the narrator of *The Catcher in the Rye*, the source of the featured sentence. Holden is always confused, at times wistful, and often bitter. The featured sentence is his declaration of war. In it, Holden reacts to his own assumptions: that *you* are making a demand (*to hear about it*) and that *you* think Holden's childhood was *lousy*. Because Holden narrates his story from some sort of mental institution, his words evoke psychology. Holden, and readers, picture a therapist who wants *to hear about* Holden's youth, which must have been *lousy* enough to cause problems. But he's no *David Copperfield*, enduring poverty and mistreatment like the title character of Dickens's novel. Instead, he's from a wealthy family with disappointed but reasonable parents. Not that everything has been easy: Holden's brother Allie is dead, and Holden has just been expelled from a fourth school. The novel takes place in the days following the expulsion.

To some readers, Holden is an idealistic rebel; to others, he's a cynic. To my mind, he's both. Holden is sarcastic and judgmental not because he feels superior but because he wants childhood to last, and it never does. He demands purity, condemning "phonies" right and left, even though he says that he's "the most terrific liar you ever saw in your life." But Holden's lies are a defense. By not putting his real self out there, he protects it. Amid the sarcasm, first person gives readers a glimpse of Holden's underlying grief. In the featured sentence, *really* is almost plaintive. Holden would like a human connection, but only if *you really want to hear about it*. Because he expects phoniness or rejection, he *doesn't feel like going into it*.

That last pronoun has more than one meaning. *It* is what happened just before and after the expulsion. But *it* is also adulthood. Holden admires children, and when he visits his little sister he tells her that he keeps "picturing all these little kids playing some game in this big field of rye." They're near a cliff, and Holden's job, as the only "big" person, is to "catch everybody if they start to go over"—into danger, into adulthood. Holden, of course, is already there, and he knows it: he uses the past tense (*what my lousy childhood was like*). First person increases the odds that readers will sympathize with this character, because the loss of innocence is usually a tragedy.

———

Usually, but not always, particularly when a character's "innocence" is a way of ignoring others' lives. Clarice Lispector's novel *The Passion According to G.H.* is narrated by a wealthy woman identified only by the initials on her luggage (G.H.). Her thoughts are tumbled and relentlessly introspective as she describes the events of the previous day. As translated by Idra Novey, G.H. says:

> Yesterday morning—when I left the living room to enter the maid's room—nothing led me to suspect that I was a step away from discovering an empire.

An empire is grand and expansive, not what you'd expect to find in *the maid's room* of an apartment in Rio de Janeiro. It's bare (the maid quit the day before), with a charcoal sketch on one wall. G.H. realizes that she's the woman in the sketch and that the maid hated her. G.H.'s world now begins to open up. Previously she viewed her servant as an anonymous, interchangeable part of the household's regimen. G.H. can't even remember her name. In the vacant room, though, the maid becomes real to her. This is a rather obvious point about the class divide, but Lispector isn't content to rest there.

When the narrator looks in the maid's empty wardrobe, a cockroach crawls out. G.H. slams the door, catching the roach in the frame. As she watches it die and eventually eats it (yes, eats it), G.H. thinks about the nature of identity: of the maid, of herself, and of the roach. She realizes that she has been no more than an accumulation of others' opinions of her. *Nothing led* [her] *to suspect* what she now recognizes: she's connected to all life, even to the cockroach. In that sense she's part of another *empire*, one that is nonhuman or, rather, not exclusively human. This sparks her spiritual awakening, which could not have happened had she not *left the living room*—that is, the life she'd been living until *yesterday.*

First-person point of view makes readers active participants in G.H.'s struggle to understand, although this isn't a "how I found myself" uplifting text. The opening sentence of the novel, "I'm searching, I'm searching," is true at the end of the story as well. Like G.H., readers are *a step away from discovering an empire.* They just have to take that step.

THE INSIDE STORY

The unnamed teenage narrator of Walter Dean Myers's story "Big Joe's Funeral" is just as philosophical as G.H., albeit in very different circumstances. He lives in New York City. This sentence about his home block captures the character's voice perfectly:

> I'm not saying that 145th is weird or anything like that, but it's, like, intense.

How *intense*? Well, the story's title character decides to cash out his insurance policy early so he can arrange a satisfying funeral for himself, which, he explains, he couldn't enjoy if the wake and burial were held after his death. Big Joe invites the neighborhood, lies down in a casket in his best clothes, and after a stirring ceremony, sits up and parties enthusiastically with his friends . . . until the cops show up to search for nonexistent drugs, having been called by his prospective and reluctant stepdaughter. More happens, all narrated in a dry, almost world-weary tone. The narrator shrugs when the police approach ("They got dogs on the street that have heard the sirens so many times they can imitate them perfectly") but occasionally reveals anxiety ("I knew that Big Joe was alive but I didn't know what I would do if he suddenly sat up").

The first-person point of view lets readers see 145th Street, which is also the title of the short story collection, through an insider's eyes. He knows his neighborhood, and readers most likely don't. It's easy to accept him as a qualified guide and commentator. His experiences are different, perhaps, from those of many readers, but his reactions aren't. The night of the comic funeral, for example, the narrator wakes to a commotion on the street. He can't laugh it off because he sees two kids crying after their father has been arrested for beating their mother. The narrator remarks, "It's almost as if the block is reminding itself that life is hard, and you have to take it seriously." Seriously enough to relish your own funeral.

———

Nick Carraway, the first-person narrator of F. Scott Fitzgerald's *The Great Gatsby*, is also a guide, one of the more famous in American literature. Through his eyes, readers see the excesses of the Jazz Age, the lives of the rich and unhappy, and the perils of the American dream of constant possibility and reinvention. Nick describes himself as someone too willing to listen to others and imagine their lives. While this habit subjects him to many boring conversations, he says, it also gives him access to secrets. He learns of affairs, discontent, illegal activities, and obsessive love.

Nick is in the story, but the story isn't about him. It's about Gatsby, whose identity unfolds slowly. As Nick learns more of Gatsby's secrets, so do readers. As Nick's feelings for Gatsby evolve, so do the readers'. At the beginning of the novel, Nick, looking back at his relationship with Gatsby, states:

No, Gatsby turned out all right at the end; it is what preyed on Gatsby, what foul dust floated in the wake of his dreams that temporarily closed out my interest in the abortive sorrows and short-winded elations of men.

No is often the beginning of a counterargument. What's being countered is readers' probable dislike of Gatsby, a shady businessman who ostentatiously displays his wealth. Nick himself says that Gatsby "represented everything for which I have an unaffected scorn." Such a confession makes Nick's approval (*Gatsby turned out all right*) more convincing.

But readers must still decide how much trust to place in Nick. He uses extreme terms: *foul dust, abortive sorrows*, and *short-winded elations*. These expressions hint at what he will relate: the *dust* of death, not a clean but a *foul* death; *abortive sorrows*, suffering that teaches nothing; and *short-winded elations*, temporary pleasures. In his sentence, Nick has set up two sides, not yet naming those he compares to Gatsby. He's also pushed readers toward Gatsby, because it's natural to root for someone with *dreams*. There's irony in Nick's statement, too, though readers don't appreciate it until they learn, *at the end*, of Gatsby's murder and nearly mournerless funeral. How has that *turned out all right*?

Nick's first-person narration at first glance seems almost journalistic, overflowing with objective detail. He downplays his own emotions and analyzes the feelings of other characters. Little by little, though, Nick's judgments add up to a complete and believable portrait of Gatsby as a tragically misguided man. By the time Nick realizes how much he cares about Gatsby—and how little others do—readers are ready, as Nick is, to grieve.

IN AND OUT

First-person point of view is often split. Readers see through the narrator's eyes, but they also see through the narrator, detecting biases and flaws the narrator isn't aware of. For example, in "A Hanukkah Eve in Warsaw," Isaac Bashevis Singer lets children (his intended readers for this story) experience a special day in a young boy's life. The narrator, whose name isn't revealed, chafes at his mother's protective actions. He explains that she's "a worrier" because she grew up in a small town and "provincial people imagined all kinds of danger in a big city." Then he adds,

> I had come to Warsaw when I was three and I considered myself
> a city boy.

Important fact: The narrator is six years old. Readers, but not the little boy, understand that he's overestimated his ability to navigate Warsaw. So when the boy sets out to walk home alone from religious instruction, he's confident, but readers are wary. Sure enough, the boy loses his way. A series of small adventures and big plans ensue. He's rescued from the path of a trolley, impulsively claims to be an orphan to avoid facing his parents' disapproval, and seeks out the house of a little girl he'd like to marry someday—and to run away with immediately. The scheme unravels, and his mother brings the boy home. His father bestows Hanukkah presents as the family sits down to a joyful holiday meal.

Singer's choice of first person puts readers outside the action. Unlike the narrator, they grasp the impossibility of a six-year-old's traveling from Poland to Berlin without adult help. In case anyone misses that point, Singer has a little girl (the invited companion) ask questions: "What will we eat?" and "Where will we sleep?" The narrator "had completely forgotten that a person had to eat" and has no plans for lodging.

Yet first person places readers inside the child's world, too. Even as they smile at his naivete, they cheer him on. He's honest about his faults, or at least those he perceives. He's curious and wants to know "how high is the moon and what happens up in the stars," among many other things. Readers recognize themselves in the little boy's emotions, especially when he explains, "I wanted to turn back to where I had come from, but apparently I only strayed farther away." Who hasn't wished at some point, as the narrator does, to "grow up faster" and be "through with being a child" while still receiving the attention of loving parents?

———

Like Singer, Eudora Welty creates a narrator who lacks self-awareness. Unlike Singer, Welty gives "Sister," the narrator of "Why I Live at the P.O.," no sense of her own shortcomings. Though she begins by claiming that her sister, Stella-Rondo, broke up Sister's romance with Mr. Whittaker with the lie that Sister was "one-sided," Sister actually *is* one-sided. Perhaps not physically (Welty doesn't address this point) but certainly in her opinions. Sister knows she's right in every sibling interaction. Readers aren't so sure. Clearly, some of her grievances are justified. Also clearly, some are not. Consider this complaint:

> There I was over the hot stove, trying to stretch two chickens over five people and a completely unexpected child in the bargain, without one moment's notice.

The occasion necessitating *two chickens* is the arrival of Stella-Rondo, who left the year before with Mr. Whittaker and has now returned with a *completely unexpected* two-year-old she claims is adopted. Sister's not convinced, and on this point she and readers likely agree. But Sister's also angry at the attention Stella-Rondo receives from the family, while Sister herself gets (in her opinion) not *one moment's notice*. Like an un-prodigal child, she's not celebrated. Instead, she's cooking.

Further, Sister avoids an open discussion of Stella-Rondo's real offense. Sister never goes into the implications of a two-year-old off-spring of a one-year marriage. Readers, but not Sister, infer that Mr. Whittaker and Stella-Rondo were a couple while Sister thought she was dating him. Now that's something to talk about! Instead of dealing with this important issue, Sister piles up a list of petty offenses, *stretching* more than chickens: Stella-Rondo was born on Sister's birthday, she received a valuable necklace as a gift and lost it, and she's "spoiled." Sister loses readers' sympathy when she prepares to live at the China Grove "P.O.," the smallest post office in the state of Mississippi. She snatches a house plant, grabs her mother's sewing machine because Sister "helped pay the most," and takes a radio, a calendar, a ukulele, and many more items with her.

Sister's first-person voice is petulant (and hilarious). Everything is an exaggeration, an accusation, a condemnation. By the time the argument ends with Sister's move to the P.O., readers have no reason to accept her assertion that if Stella-Rondo ever tried to explain what happened with Mr. Whittaker, Sister would put her fingers in her ears and "refuse to listen." If only for the gossip, it's a sure bet that Sister would be all ears.

ON THE SCENE

Traditionally, reporters are taught to present facts objectively, leaving themselves out of the picture. Complete objectivity is, of course, impossible. First-person nonfiction is unabashedly subjective. The *I* or *we* may be a signal to readers: opinion here! First-person reporting also gives readers a surrogate: *I* am there, so *you* readers are, too. First person establishes authority: *I* know what *I'm* talking about because *I did* or *spoke to* or *saw* or *was*.

—————

John McPhee is an adept nonfiction writer, whether he explains and describes in third person (talking about the subject) or inserts himself into the scene with first-person point of view. In "Under the Snow," McPhee spends a day with wildlife biologists who protect bears in Pennsylvania. Before he gets to the bears, though, McPhee devotes a paragraph to the behavior of his third and fourth daughters when they were infants. Young McPhee number three would stick to his shoulder "like velvet," but the fourth squirmed so much that holding her posed "a risk both to her and to the shoulder." He explains:

> These memories came very much alive some months ago when—one after another—I had bear cubs under my vest.

With this sentence, McPhee gives readers a reason to care about bears and their survival. They're babies! True, they're wild animals ("If you have an enemy, give him a bear cub," says a wildlife expert), but McPhee puts readers on the scene with him as the cubs cry and tremble in the cold. He piles fact upon fact: how many offspring are born, how orphaned cubs are fostered, where bears hibernate, and much more. His reactions thread through the data. Along with the initial comparison to human infants, first person keeps readers involved. McPhee is a trustworthy source because he was there. By the time he describes driving home, readers understand why he can't stop thinking about "the covered entrance in the Pennsylvania hillside" and "the thought of what was up there under the snow."

—————

Like John McPhee, Rebecca Traister also inserts herself into her nonfiction exploration of American culture. In *Good and Mad: The Revo-*

lutionary Power of Women's Anger, Traister examines how female anger has been perceived, condemned or praised, and expressed at various points in the nation's history. She writes:

> What I have glimpsed, in the moments when I have let myself give voice to the deep, rich, curdled fury that for years I tried to pretty up and make easier on everyone's stomach, is that for all the care we take to bottle it up, rage can be a powerful tonic.

The *powerful tonic* sets up her primary thesis, that women's anger has frequently been channeled into activism. Traister weaves her own, first-person observations into extensive historical research and numerous interviews. She doesn't pretend to be neutral (she won't *pretty up* her *deep, rich, curdled fury*) and thus respects her readers' ability to evaluate her conclusions. She presents her own experiences as her credentials; she understands what others are saying or what she has discovered in her research through the lens of her personal history. It's not an easy task (there are only *moments when I have let myself give voice*), but for her, it's essential.

FOR THE WRITER

I imagine you've often written from the first-person point of view, in personal letters or posts or other formats. Try moving into unexplored territory—first-person expressions of character, data, or ideas.

SNAPSHOT

Who are you? You're in the "For the Writer" section, so I assume that label applies to you. Create a one-sentence, first-person statement about yourself as a writer. To inspire you, here are two examples:

Roy Blount Jr.: I have written some of the clumsiest, most clogged-yet-vagrant, hobbledehoyish, hitch-slipping sentences ever conceived by the human mind.

Virginia Woolf: I like sentences that don't budge though armies cross them.

DATA FLIP

Surf the internet or peruse the paper until you find an article providing information without a first-person point of view. Select a few sentences. Before you alter them, examine them for assumptions and clues to the writer's state of mind. Now rewrite the sentences, this time openly revealing the writer's stance. Here's an example:

THIRD-PERSON POINT OF VIEW: The new tax takes effect in 2025, giving struggling florists a temporary reprieve before they regroup.

CLUES TO THE WRITER'S OPINION: "struggling" (assesses financial status), "temporary reprieve" (sounds like a stay of execution), "regroup" (assumes they must change the business model).

FIRST-PERSON VERSION: I can't see how florists can continue the same business practices after the new tax takes effect in 2025. I imagine most will stay open, after a period of adjustment.

Before you leave this exercise, decide which version you like better. First person isn't inherently superior; it's just different.

TRUST ME . . . NOT

I once had a neighbor explain to me, at length, how sensitive she was to everyone's needs. This monologue occurred at three in the morning, when she woke me to pick up a spare set of keys. On a work night! With my baby in the next room! Nice lady, really, but not as sensitive as she thought. Have some fun creating characters who are blind to some aspect of themselves. Decide what the character believes, and then subvert it with the character's own words. Write a sentence and, if you have the energy, expand the sentence into a scene.

SECOND PERSON

She will say thanks honey when you come slowly, slowly around the corner in your slippers and robe, into the living room with Grandma's old used-to-be-salad-bowl piled high.
—Lorrie Moore, "A Kid's Guide to Divorce"

You, the second-person point of view, is a risky choice for fiction writers. It has a tendency to send readers screaming into the night, book not in hand. In fact, one critic, in a positive review of a second-person novel, urged readers to resist the impulse to "set the book aside immediately, preferably with tongs," because the content would reward their patience.

Knowing that second person may alienate readers, why do writers—albeit only a few—choose this point of view? Some, such as self-help authors, need second person because they're speaking directly to readers, coaching them through various challenges. Others embrace *you* in order to invite readers into the narrative; egotism and courtesy make it hard to ignore someone who's directly addressing *you*. Still other writers use *you* to represent a character's internal dialogue. If you've ever argued with or berated yourself, you know that second-person point of view suits that conversation perfectly. *You* may also represent a dream state, when the conscious and subconscious exist in uneasy equilibrium.

The featured sentence comes from Lorrie Moore's collection of short stories *Self-Help*. Moore doesn't parody that genre. Instead, she plays with its conventions—notably second person—as her protagonists navigate love affairs, quarrels, and, in the featured sentence, divorce. The story follows two characters, a mother and a child, from the early evening through the child's bedtime. The gender of the child is never identified, another advantage of *you*. Some readers assume the child is a daughter, perhaps because the author is female or because readers apply gender stereotypes to the child's actions, such as dancing around the room or snuggling next to the mother. When I assign this story to students, I find that boys tend to assume the child is a son and girls, a daughter—a testament to the power of *you* to entangle readers in the character's life.

In the featured sentence, *she* is the mother. The child and *she* are watching television and eating popcorn from the *used-to-be-salad-bowl*. There's some conversation about the show, a pretend quarrel ("Act hurt. . . . Your mom will try to pep you up"), and a question from the mom about "what you did." The child doesn't answer, but when the mother asks again, "hesitantly like she always does," *you* "leave out the part about the lady and the part about the beer" and offer a few neutral bits of information ("a new silver dart-board" and "a pretty funny story about this guy named Hudson"). At this point readers understand, if they hadn't grasped the scenario already, that the child has just returned from a weekend visit with the father.

Sometimes the second-person sentences in this story are commands ("Look straight ahead"). Sometimes they're narration in future tense ("Your mother will look disappointed"). The commands and future tense fit the guidebook format the title refers to. The sentences tell *you* what to do, what will happen next, and how *you* should respond to each event. The second-person viewpoint also creates a separation. The events are happening to *you*, a less intimate stance than a first-person *I* narration. But it's a small separation, matching *you*, the small child. Third-person viewpoint would create a bigger gap.

Moore's word choice and descriptive details add shades of meaning. The child selects a *used-to-be-salad-bowl*. The marriage, and the child's place in that family, *used to be* but now are not. *You* moves *slowly, slowly around the corner. Around the corner* fits the child's manipulation; *you* asks for things normally forbidden (soda, a scary program) or pretends to be hurt. *You* is also protective, evaluating the mother's moods, trying to distract her during tense moments and move her *slowly, slowly* to a better frame of mind. At one point, for example, the mother says, "Men can be so dense and frustrating," ostensibly about a film but more plausibly about her ex-husband, and the child does a silly dance. The pair are in *the living room*, another phrase with double meaning. *The living room* is a natural physical space for a television, but it's also the space *you* and the mother have carved out for *living* after divorce.

––––––

The self-help facade also appears in Mohsin Hamid's *How to Get Filthy Rich in Rising Asia.* The novel traces the protagonist's life from a village childhood in an unnamed South Asian country through life in a big city; to the founding, success, and failure of a business empire; and then to old age and peaceful death. Entwined with the story of *you* is that of *your* love, a "pretty girl," whose path has a different trajectory that at intervals intersects with *yours.* By never naming *you* or the girl, Hamid makes the details of their lives emblematic of something larger; their successes and failures, both personal and financial, are those of their society. Hamid also inserts the voice of the supposed self-help writer:

> You read a self-help book so someone who isn't yourself can help you, that someone being the author.

This comment appears in the first chapter, but its full significance arrives in the last, when happiness for *you* and the pretty girl comes from companionship. They live together as friends, a situation that permits *someone who isn't yourself* to *help you.*

TALKING TO YOURSELF AND YOURSELVES

Jay McInerney's novel *Bright Lights, Big City* takes readers into the mind of a young man who loses his job and wife, parties desperately, and finally comes to terms with the emotions he's been fleeing. The novel is written from the second-person point of view, but at one point, McInerney twists second- and third-person narration into a knot:

> You thought of yourself in the third person: *He arrived for his first interview in a navy-blue blazer.*

This is how *you* imagines his future biography, which will chronicle his rise from the fact-checking department of an important magazine to his rightful place as a writer of literary renown. But there is no biographer; *he* and *you* come from the same mind and reflect the fact that *you* is a divided self. *You* constantly makes resolutions and breaks them: "*Go home. Cut your losses. Stay. Go for it.* You are a republic of voices tonight." *You* darts one way and then another, like an animal in a cage desperate to find a way out. What *you* needs is a way in, though, to the grief of his mother's death. This finally happens outside a bakery, where *you* begs for a fresh roll. *Roll, role*: McInerney's choice of this homonym isn't coincidental. The novel ends with the realization that "[y]ou will have to learn everything all over again" and embrace a new role or, more accurately, an old, more authentic one.

––––––––

Ernest Hemingway, working as a journalist, chose second person to describe a luge, the tiny sled familiar to modern viewers of the Winter Olympics but entirely new to most newspaper readers in the early twentieth century. In his article he emphasizes how fast the luge moves over ice and explains how body movements are the only means of steering. Then he takes readers on a ride:

> You are sitting absolutely unsupported, only ten inches above the ice, and the road is feeding past you like a film.

Though the ostensible purpose of Hemingway's article is to give information about the luge—a purpose fulfilled, by the way—Hemingway also props up his own ego. "Look what you did! See how brave you are!" he seems to say, talking to himself more than to the reader.

———————

Tom Robbins's *you* is Gwen, the protagonist of *Half Asleep in Frog Pajamas*. The narrative traces *you*, a commodities broker, from Friday afternoon on "the worst day of your life" through the weekend. The stock market is bouncing up and down like a ping-pong ball and *you* worries that a definitive crash will ruin her career. *You*, who's bought a Porsche and is about to close on a luxury condo, remarks:

> How typical of your luck that when you finally arrived in a position to poach your golden eggs, the goose had a hysterectomy.

You can easily repel readers with the self-pity and materialism of statements like the one above. But, as with McInerney's protagonist, Robbins's *you* has an unmet need. The second-person *you* reels readers in and helps them relate to Gwen's state of mind. The job has become her life, and when it's about to implode, so is Gwen.

———————

Kwame Alexander's *you* is more likable, as twelve-year-olds generally are. The novel, written in verse, is *Booked*, and the boy talking to himself is Nick, given to daydreaming during English class and fantasizing about scoring the winning goal of a soccer game. There are bullies, too, and parents with marital problems. The icing on the cake? *You* must read the entire dictionary, per Dad's orders. But *you* and best friend Coby are determined:

> Ninth grade is five months from now
> when you and Coby have vowed
> to have a girlfriend or die.

How can any reader not root for *you* to succeed?

———

Vendela Vida shapes *you* into multiple identities, all attached to the same woman, in her novel *The Diver's Clothes Lie Empty. You* first appears on a plane to Morocco, upset and fearful—and nameless to the reader. At the hotel, *you* loses focus for a moment, long enough for a backpack with her computer, passport, and wallet to disappear. The police return a different backpack with someone else's passport and credit cards. At this point, *you* has a choice: explain that there's a mistake or co-opt the other woman's identity. Here second person hits readers hard. "Don't do it!" is a natural response, because most people would tell the truth and go to the American embassy for help. But *you* accepts the backpack and checks into a luxury hotel with the other woman's identity documents. There, readers begin to grasp the reason for this choice:

> You dive from the edge of the pool where it says NO DIVING, and swim underwater to the other side, not once coming up for air.

You is on the edge, literally of the pool but on the edge of a breakdown, too. *You* is contrary: *NO DIVING* is an invitation for *you* to dive. *You* acts without thinking, diving in and *not once coming up for air.*

Soon another choice appears. A film crew needs *you* to stand in for a famous actress. Once again, "Don't do it" comes to mind, but with less force. This deep in complications, *you* has fewer options. *You* sheds and accepts new identities several more times, and each switch is easier for *you* and readers to accept. Underlying these misadventures is a terrible secret, which the author reveals gradually. By the end, *you* is liberated from her baggage (the backpack, the past, the old self) and ready for still another identity.

YOU, DREAMING

Have you ever recounted a dream? Or listened to someone else describing one? A surprising number of people turn to second person for this task. Maybe the divided self is responsible: *you* are talking about *you*, the narrator in the waking world coexisting with the *you* of REM sleep. Or perhaps second person is a defense against the reality that a dream reveals—hidden desire, hurt, or guilt.

———

In Nathaniel Hawthorne's story "The Haunted Mind," second-person narration is a way to examine the nature of dreaming itself:

> . . . you find yourself, for a single instant, wide awake in that realm of illusions, whither sleep has been the passport, and behold its ghostly inhabitants and wondrous scenery, with a perception of their strangeness, such as you never attain while the dream is undisturbed.

This desirable, *wondrous* state, with "the mind's eye half shut" and where "the business of life does not intrude," gives way to memories, regret, and guilt. But there's hope, too—images of "sunny trees," a rainbow, and "the unbroken sheet of snow." Just as Hawthorne's *you* slips into deep sleep, *you* wishes that the last moment of life, "the final change," will be as peaceful.

———

Annie Dillard, in *Pilgrim at Tinker Creek*, recounts a year of discovery during which she minutely examines nature. At one point she describes the moment of waking, when fragments of dreams linger:

> You remember pressure, and a curved sleep you rested against, soft, like a scallop in its shell.

Dillard explains, "We wake, if we ever wake at all, to mystery, rumors of death, beauty, violence. . . ."

———

All those elements are present in Nicholas Christopher's *Desperate Characters: A Novella in Verse*. The poem is a nod to dreams, or more accurately, to comic nightmares. It begins:

> Here you are in Hollywood
> on an empty stomach in an unlit room.

Christopher thrusts the reader into the most unreal of worlds: *Hollywood*. He plays off the conventions of film noir with the reference to *an unlit room*. Odd characters appear (a bodyguard, a teenage widow, Rocco the Human Cannonball, Romanian opera singers, Thomas Jefferson's ghost), and as the title suggests, they're desperate. The plot loops along, but, as in a dream, what happens isn't always coherent. That's the point. With second person, Christopher makes the reader participate in the protagonist's reality. Like *you*, the reader can't quite grasp what's really happening and what's only a dream. Nor can the reader take an objective stance to judge whether *your* account is accurate. *Desperate Characters* is great fun, but it poses a serious question: how can *you*—any *you*—understand reality?

———

Italo Calvino inserts dreams into *If on a winter's night a traveler*, but the book in its entirety is more dreamlike than any specifically acknowledged dream. It begins:

> You are about to begin reading Italo Calvino's new novel, *If on a winter's night a traveler*.

Immediately, readers recognize themselves as *you*, part of the novel they're about to read. Not just one novel, actually, but a whole bookshelf. But none of the novels within *If on a winter's night a traveler* are complete. *You* begin to read one after another. All break off abruptly, and *you* return several times to the bookshop to complain. The plot—plots!—can't be summarized because Calvino breaks apart the usual structure of beginning-middle-end. He involves *you* in this destruction and makes readers become partners of the author. Which is exactly what readers are, just as novels, like dreams, are fantasy worlds where scenes abruptly begin and end, shift, and reconfigure themselves.

COMMANDING PRESENCE

Speaking to someone, such as *you*, is what English teachers call "direct address." When that speech is an order, *you* is understood. Nike's slogan, for example, is a command to *you*, an order to "Just do it." (*Just do* what? I'm sure the company would say this command applies to a sports goal, but to my mind what the expression really means is "Just buy our stuff.")

––––––––

Literature is filled with commands:

Call me Ishmael.

—Herman Melville, *Moby-Dick*

. . . oh, romantic reader, forgive me for telling the plain truth!

—Charlotte Brontë, *Jane Eyre*

move & roll on to this poem
do not resist this poem

—Ishmael Reed, "Beware: Do Not Read This Poem"

Take, if you must, this little bag of dreams;
unloose the cord, and they will wrap you round.

—William Butler Yeats, "Fergus and the Druid"

As are songs:

> So don't look now, I'm shining like
> fireworks over your sad, empty town.
>
> —Taylor Swift, "Dear John"

Regardless of genre, the goal is the same: to engage *you* fully.

FOR THE WRITER

You should try second-person narration. These prompts may help you start.

SELF-HELPLESS

Pick a self-help book—any self-help book. Select a sentence with the second-person point of view. Parody it. Make it as ridiculous as possible. For example:

> ORIGINAL, FROM A BOOK ON RELIEVING STRESS: Imagine you are resting in a field of soft grass, clouds drifting above you, carrying your cares away.
> PARODY: Imagine you are resting in a tub of soft concrete, mobsters bent over you, waiting for the concrete to solidify.

WHO ARE *YOU*?

The *you* point of view inevitably creates a split. In second person, a real or implied speaker addresses *you*, giving a command or making a comment, arguing or narrating. Explore that split. Write several second-person sentences. Identify the "speaker" and the "spoken to." A couple of sentences should involve two people (a command sentence is good for this), and a couple should reflect a single, conflicted self. Once you've identified the speaker and the spoken to, describe each. For example:

TWO SEPARATE PEOPLE: Take out the trash, honey, because it's your turn.

SPEAKER: Cody, who has a cosmic scorecard of chores and whose goal in life is to keep the score tied.

SPOKEN TO: Jackie, who hasn't noticed that (A) there's trash and (B) there's a curb and (C) A has to go to B twice a week.

ONE, CONFLICTED PERSON: You pick up the can in a silence much heavier than the trash, remembering that without Jackie's rent you'll have to move.

SPEAKER: Cody's long-suffering, angry, and misunderstood self.

SPOKEN TO: Cody's practical side.

ONE TWO THREE

Select a second-person sentence from the examples in this chapter or from another source. Change the point of view to first (*I, we*) or third (*he, she, it, they*). Examine the results. What's gained? What's lost? Now go the other way. Select a first- or third-person sentence and change it to second person. Same questions: What have you gained and lost from the switch?

CONTRAST

That's one small step for a man, one giant leap for mankind.
—Neil Armstrong, First Words on the Moon

Contrast focuses on difference. Put two things together, and you immediately notice how they vary. Perhaps this ability was hardwired into the brain long ago; distinguishing between a berry that nourishes you and one that kills you is rather important to a hunter-gatherer. And even when no lives are at stake and the variation between two elements is subtle, your perception of each element changes, simply because they're together. Writers know and exploit this quality.

Neil Armstrong, not known primarily for his writing ability, was nevertheless skilled with words. On July 20, 1969, his foot made contact with the surface of the moon—the first human foot ever to do so. Stepping on the moon was extraordinary. Nearly as extraordinary was that more than 500 million people around the world watched it happen in a live broadcast. Armstrong claimed that he hadn't decided what to say until he was descending the ladder of the lunar module. I doubt that's entirely true, as he knew that his words would be historic. The featured sentence is the first uttered by a human being who was neither on Earth nor in a spacecraft.

What the world heard, though, was not exactly what Armstrong said. A burst of static or Armstrong's own nervousness obliterated the *a*, and his phrase came across as *one small step for man*. Whether Armstrong said *a* or not, his intention was clear. He wanted to contrast his individual deed, walking on the moon, with the collective accomplishments of human beings throughout history.

In Armstrong's sentence, these contrasting elements dominate:

one small step for a man
one giant leap for mankind

The contraction *that's* (short for *that is*) introduces and unites both elements. The common words, *one* and *for*, also link them, as does the grammatical structure of each:

number—description—noun-phrase

Within likeness, though, lies difference:

small → *giant*
step → *leap*
a man → *mankind*

You don't have to be a rocket scientist—or an English teacher—to detect the pattern. *Giant* is bigger than *small*, a *leap* takes you farther than a *step*, and *mankind*, the species, is immense compared to the tiny fragment of life that is *a man*. (In 1969, feminism was gaining strength, but *mankind* was still considered a universal term encompassing both men and women.) How wise of Armstrong to emphasize growth at this historic moment! Human beings have gazed at the moon for as long as they've had eyes. Every scientific discovery and technological advance added to the body of knowledge, which grew until it was big enough to support the Apollo space missions. Armstrong's *giant leap* was powered by multitudes.

The preposition, *for*, is also significant. Armstrong could have said *from* and still created a contrast between *a man* and *mankind*. But *from* would emphasize the source, what comes *from a man* and *from mankind*. *For* highlights the receiver. You do something *for* another or *for* yourself. In the first phrase, the *step* is *for a man*, the individual who was Neil Armstrong. Being first on the moon brought him fame and some fortune, but Armstrong wasn't after glory. Throughout his life he reached for the highest level of every endeavor: as an Eagle Scout, a decorated veteran, and a test pilot. Proving that he was capable of these achievements was a benefit *for* him. The second phrase is *for mankind*. Here the benefit *for* all of us is discovery, the knowledge acquired on the moon and during the process of planning the voyage. For both *a man* and *mankind*, the ultimate benefit is the thrill of proving that human beings can strive and, at times, succeed.

CONTRASTING DESCRIPTIONS

Closer to earth than Armstrong, but still in the air, is boxer Muhammed Ali's description of his fighting style:

> Float like a butterfly, sting like a bee.

Ali, nicknamed "The Greatest" with some justification, was twenty-two years old when he made this remark, just before beating Sonny Liston to become heavyweight champion of the world. He was known, as his comment implies, for quick footwork and stealthy punches. He was also famous for his bravado, claiming to be so fast that he could "turn off the light switch" in his hotel room and be "in bed before the room was dark."

Ali's sentence, like Armstrong's, places two elements next to each other. A *butterfly* isn't a threat; it's one of the few insects that appeal to nearly everyone. It's light, a creature of the air that flutters in unexpected directions. A *bee*, on the other hand, isn't cuddly. A *bee sting* hurts—a lot! The anticipation is enough to make a bee's target fearful, which, by the way, was the goal of Ali's prefight remarks. The contrast between *a butterfly* and *a bee* is stark: Each brings a quality that the other lacks (unpredictable movement from the *butterfly*, painful jab from the *bee*). Together they create a greater threat.

———————

But not as great of a threat as that posed by the Vogons in Douglas Adams's *The Hitchhiker's Guide to the Galaxy*. Earth is slated for demolition because it's in the path of "a hyperspatial express route." As the contractor prepares to vaporize the planet, people stare at the sky, where

> The ships hung in the sky in much the same way that bricks don't.

Adams's sentence contrasts *ships* and *bricks* and gives a nod to the proverbial "ton of bricks" that is about to kill everyone on the planet except Arthur Dent, who escapes. People watching the sky can't quite believe what they are seeing. Enormous, heavy spaceships are, after all, a surprise. They shouldn't be able to hover *in the sky*, nor should the Earth end this way. But in Adams's novel, that's what happens. Adams isn't truly contrasting *ships* and *bricks*; he's contrasting what people think is possible and what actually occurs.

———————

The end of the world—the current social-media world—is the topic of this sentence from Roger McNamee, interviewed by a reporter from the *Claremont Courier*:

> The punch line of the book is that I'm actually very optimistic because the human beings formerly known as users have far more power to effect change than they realize.

McNamee, once Mark Zuckerberg's mentor and an early investor in Facebook, is dismayed at Facebook's effect on privacy, politics, and pretty much everything else. The expression *human beings formerly known as users* contrasts what now exists (*users*) and what might be reclaimed (our identity as *human beings*). As McNamee defines them, *users* are subject to invasion of privacy. Facebook and other social-media sites collect, sell, and exploit their personal data in ways most *users* aren't aware of. He favors laws to protect privacy and curb abuse of our information and urges everyone to "deny them [social media] the same attention we've given them in the past, to deny them the ability to play with our emotions." Of course, in framing the implied question (do you want to be a *user* or a *human being*?), McNamee sets up the answer (*human being*), which sets up his thesis, the need to change ourselves and wrest power from social media.

A few more descriptive contrasts:

> In America there are two classes of travel—first class and with children.
>
> —Robert Benchley (humorist)

> A good education is usually harmful to a dancer. A good calf is better than a good head.
>
> —Agnes de Mille, *Dance to the Piper*

> The mother looked young and the daughter looked old; the mother's complexion was pink, and the daughter's was yellow; the mother set up for frivolity, and the daughter for theology.
>
> —Charles Dickens, *Great Expectations*

> Serenity now, insanity later!
>
> —*Seinfeld* episode

> Happy families are all alike; every unhappy family is unhappy in its own way.
>
> —Leo Tolstoy, *Anna Karenina*

Old elephants limp off to the hills to die; old Americans go out
to the highway and drive themselves to death with huge cars.
—Hunter S. Thompson, *Fear and Loathing in Las Vegas*

BY DEFINITION

To see what is, examine what is not. That, in essence, is definition by contrast. The advantage of this technique is that it provides an entire worldview, because the defined word comes with context. Take *history*. In his
essay collection *Bad Mouth*, Robert Adams supplies this definition:

History does not unfold: it piles up.

Two views of human events reside in this sentence. The first sees *history* as a ribbon, unspooling fresh new lengths. In the second, *history* is
baggage, or maybe landfill. You may push the *pile* away, but that doesn't
make it disappear. The *pile* of events grows until it either topples or
uplifts. The first verb, *unfold*, seems less connected to human agency.
Events *unfold* as a surprise, and whoever is responsible for them hovers
in the background. The second verb, *pile*, also declines to identify history makers, but somehow they're more present. No one has to deal with
a ribbon; *piles* eventually require attention.

———

And what about art? Ansel Adams said:

You don't take a photograph, you make it.

These few words say a lot about photography and about art in general.
Even a faithful recorder of a scene—in Adams's case, a camera—involves
subject selection, focus, editing, and many other choices. The result isn't
a slice of reality. It's an artwork. By contrasting *take* (a spontaneous
action) with *make* (purposeful creation), Ansel Adams defines his art.

———

And Oliver Wendell Holmes defines life:

> It is painting a picture, not doing a sum.

Holmes could have skipped the contrast, letting the reader imagine what life as a painted picture implies—details added slowly, each changing the image slightly, the whole emerging gradually. By contrasting *painting a picture* with *doing a sum*, Holmes implicitly disparages the pursuit of wealth, honors, and accomplishments. The contrast favors the arts (*painting*) over logic (math). To Holmes, life doesn't make sense as a set of numbers; there's no answer to calculate. There is a *picture* to appreciate.

———

Activist Betty Friedan, whose book *The Feminine Mystique* ignited second-wave feminism in the United States in the 1960s, explains:

> This is not a bedroom war. This is a political movement.

By refusing to reduce feminism to individual quarrels or restrict it to private life, Friedan challenged feminists to work for structural change. Contrasting *political movement* with *bedroom war* acknowledges a limited view of feminism and then simply and forcefully dismisses it. Friedan's statement is akin to a declaration of war.

———

Dorothy Canfield-Fisher in *Her Son's Wife* also creates a definition with contrast:

> A mother is not a person to lean on but a person to make leaning unnecessary.

Canfield-Fisher wrote this in 1926, but it's just as relevant today. Maybe more so, given the ubiquity of helicopter and snowplowing parents.

———————

Also on the topic of children and adults is this sentence from Fran Liebowitz, who claims that kids ask better questions than their elders:

> "May I have a cookie?" "Why is the sky blue?" and "What does a cow say?" are far more likely to elicit a cheerful response than "Where's your manuscript?" "Why haven't you called?" and "Who's your lawyer?"

———————

Last, a comment from Johann Wolfgang von Goethe:

> Love is an ideal thing, marriage a real thing.

Which anyone who's ever argued about whose turn it is to do the laundry already knows.

AM TOO! AM NOT!

Contrast also sharpens self-definition. In 1983, after more than twenty years of writing and performing music, Joan Baez remarked:

> When somebody says to me—which they do like every five years—"How does it feel to be over the hill," my response is, "I'm just heading up the mountain."

She was right. Her most recent album, *Whistle Down the Wind*, came out in 2018. Do the math to see how far from being *over the hill* Baez was when she made her statement.

————

Author Zora Neale Hurston dealt with assumptions, too, in her essay "How It Feels to Be Colored Me":

> I do not weep at the world—I am too busy sharpening my oyster knife.

For Hurston, lamenting injustice (*weep*) wasn't a tempting option. Attacking it head-on (*knife*) was her preferred path. It's worth noting that oysters don't open easily. Force is necessary to sever the tough muscle that holds an oyster shell together. Adding *oyster* to *knife*—not to mention *sharpening*—underscores Hurston's determination and strength. Plus, an oyster may hold a pearl, the reward that follows the struggle.

————

E. B. White explained himself this way:

> I arise in the morning torn between a desire to improve (or save) the world and a desire to enjoy (or savor) the world.

He added dryly, "This makes it hard to plan the day." Parallel elements (*improve* and *enjoy, save* and *savor*) heighten the contrast and reveal White's conflicting impulses.

————

Rose Bird, chief justice of California for ten years, definitely favored the "save the world" option that E. B. White cited. Not everyone agreed with her notion of improvement, and her decisions often ignited controversy. Undeterred, Bird commented:

> It is easy to be popular. It is not easy to be just.

Not easy at all. Rose, the first woman on the court, was voted out of office in 1986.

––––––––

Jack London contrasts the life he doesn't want to live with the one he desires:

> I would rather be a superb meteor, every atom of me in magnificent glow, than a sleepy and permanent planet.

Perhaps his wish was fulfilled. During his short life (London died at the age of forty), he was an oyster pirate, a hobo, a workers' rights activist, and, of course, a writer. He searched for gold in the wilderness of northwest Canada, covered the Russo-Japanese war for a California paper, and wrote an eyewitness account of the 1906 San Francisco earthquake. More *magnificent glow* than *sleepy*, indeed.

––––––––

In the same vein, singer/songwriter Neil Young writes that

> It's better to burn out
> Than to fade away.

––––––––

And Helen Hayes, whose acting career spanned eight decades, agrees:

> If you rest, you rust.

––––––––

One more self-definition, as recounted in the hymn "Amazing Grace":

I once was lost, but now am found
'Twas blind but now I see.

The *I* in this sentence is John Newton, a slave trader who became an abolitionist and cleric. Amazing grace, without a doubt.

FAIR WARNING

"Or else" may be a villain's favorite line, but not only villains warn of consequences. By showing contrasting outcomes, advice givers nudge readers to one course of action.

———

It's not hard to identify the direction Derek Bok, former president of Harvard, favors:

If you think education is expensive, try ignorance.

Tuition and school taxes are easily computed, but how might the cost of *ignorance* be measured? Bok doesn't say, and he doesn't have to. The contrast pushes the reader to prioritize *education*, as he wishes.

———

Similarly, Margaret Chase Smith, who served first as a representative and then as a senator for the state of Maine from 1940 to 1972, reminds Americans that

Freedom unexercised may become freedom forfeited.

———

Fifty years earlier, activist Jane Addams, the pioneering social worker, said:

This is the penalty of a democracy,—that we are bound to move forward or retrograde together.

In both Smith's and Addams's sentences, the contrasting element (*freedom forfeited*, *retrograde*) makes the other choice desirable. Which is not to say that the proper choice is inevitable. As Alexander Pope notes:

To err is human; to forgive divine.

FOR THE WRITER

Adjust the contrast on anything with a screen (phone, tablet, computer, television) and you see instantly how strongly this quality affects perception. Try the same technique with words.

OBJECT LESSONS

Before you write, train your eye to notice contrast. Select two objects—flowers, shoes, combs, light bulbs, whatever. Look closely. Make a list of the ways in which the objects differ. Your left sneaker, for example, may have a raised bump that the "matching" sneaker lacks. Now insert the contrasting elements into a sentence. Working from the sneaker example, you might come up with something like this:

My left pinkie toe smashed into the chair leg and healed poorly, giving my left sneaker a bump where the right one was smooth.

Bonus question: Check out some of Andy Warhol's series, artworks depicting the same image many times, each with subtle differences of tone or line. Write what you see.

THEN AND NOW

You can do this one by scanning your own life, or you can direct your attention to someone else. Think of several ways to contrast qualities, beliefs, or emotions. Plug your ideas into this structure:

_____ used to be _____ but now _____

Don't limit yourself to the literal. Perhaps you used to be *shy* but now you're *outgoing*. Add imagination to those adjectives: you were *the Loch Ness Monster* (famously hard to spot) but now you're a *Forrest Gump* (friendly to all).

DEFINING MOMENT

Move away from the dictionary to create a definition of something abstract: maturity, hope, freedom, difference, and so forth. Create a contrast by defining something close in meaning to the original, but with enough variation to matter. An example:

A pessimist can't take "yes" for an answer, while a cynic believes every answer is a lie.

NEGATIVITY

Not all of us can always be Jackie Robinson—not even Jackie Robinson was always Jackie Robinson.

—Ta-Nehisi Coates, *Between the World and Me*

If internet memes are any indication, negativity is out of fashion. Variations of "think positive!" are all over the web, usually superimposed on a photo of a struggling baby animal. In writing, though, negativity has value—perhaps because a negative expression taps into the primal "no" from parents setting boundaries or because, used creatively, negativity attracts attention.

Ta-Nehisi Coates's masterful negative statement comes from *Between the World and Me*, an extended meditation on race and racism written in the form of a letter to his son. The featured sentence refers to Jack Roosevelt Robinson, who in 1947 became the first African American of the modern era to play major-league baseball. Robinson was not only an outstanding ballplayer but also a courageous man who challenged racism wherever he encountered it. And he encountered it everywhere: in the army, where he was court-martialed and eventually acquitted after refusing to leave a "white seat" and sit in the back of the bus; on the playing field, where he endured taunts and threats; and during road trips, where his white teammates were welcomed to hotels and restaurants that denied Robinson entry. His nonviolent response to racism earned him the respect of millions of Americans and turned the man into a symbol of principled resistance. Even now, people who break through a wall of segregation are dubbed "the Jackie Robinson" of their professions. Beneath the calm image that the public saw, however, was a real person living a real life—and not an easy one. Robinson bore the hate of those who wanted segregation as well as the hopes of those who strove for justice.

Ta-Nehisi Coates's sentence acknowledges Robinson's burden. The context: when Coates's son was five years old, a white woman pushed the little boy to hurry him along. Coates reacted with the anger "of any parent when a stranger lays a hand on the body of his or her child." But, he explains, the long history of white violence toward African Americans intensified his feelings. A crowd gathered, and Coates pushed a white man away. Realizing that he and his son were in danger, Coates controlled his emotions, took his son, and left. He tells this story to his son because, he writes, "You are human and you will make mistakes." His son won't always be a *Jackie Robinson*, a hero whose composure never cracks.

The featured sentence relies on two negative expressions:

Not all of us

not even

Not all of us draws a figurative boundary within the African American community, creating two groups—some who *can always be Jackie Robinson* and some who can't. With *not all*, Coates generously allows the possibility, albeit remote, that flawless heroes do exist. *Not even* creates another boundary, this time within Robinson himself, distinguishing between the man and his public image. Reinforcing Coates's point is the repetition of *Jackie Robinson*. The first and third instances refer to the persona Robinson created, the strong and stoic hero who rises above racism by denying its legitimacy. The second refers to the human being who has all the emotions and frailties of our species.

Compare Coates's sentence with this alternative:

Some of us lose our temper occasionally and make mistakes, even Jackie Robinson.

This positive statement comes across as a bromide, a smoothed-over declaration more suitable for a child's temper tantrum or a minor incident. Coates's version points to something much more serious. He tells his son that "the price of error is higher for you than for your countrymen" and cites several fatal responses to a perceived mistake by an African American male.

The two-part structure of the featured sentence matches the duality that Coates sees. His son is part of a group (*us*, African American males), but he is also a unique individual. The word *always* appears in both parts because, to Coates, these two identities are inextricably entwined. Furthermore, Coates uses a dash to connect two ideas, each of which could stand alone as a complete sentence. The strictest grammarians frown on a dash for this purpose, reserving it for an interruption or an unfinished thought. Here, both functions relate to Coates's point. His son will make mistakes, and Coates fears that those mistakes could interrupt the course of his son's life or even end it. Coates believes the pushing incident could have been fatal, had the crowd turned violent. Nor is the matter finished. Coates says that he still mulls over the events of that day, many years after the incident occurred.

His message is dire, but Coates's wording softens the tone. The reader can easily imagine a quiet conversation in which the father advises his son not to fault himself for imperfections, to forgive himself for not always being a hero like *Jackie Robinson*.

COMPARATIVELY NEGATIVE

Much like Coates, in his novel *The Road Home* Jim Harrison employs a negative statement to compare image and reality:

But I'm not Keats, she insisted, to which I answered, Neither is he, but aside from his work he is an accumulation of our opinions about him.

The first portion of this sentence is an understatement (who can equal Keats?) and the second an exaggeration. Keats was Keats, just as Jackie Robinson was Jackie Robinson. Neither was solely, or free of, "an accumulation of our opinions."

———

Another negative comparison is the first line of Shakespeare's Sonnet 130:

My mistress' eyes are nothing like the sun

The next eleven lines of the poem come across as the world's worst valentine: the *mistress* has wiry hair, no roses in her cheeks, and breath that "reeks." But the negative images are a buildup to the last two lines, when the speaker redeems himself by saying that his beloved is "as rare" as any "belied with false compare."

———

Still another comparison, this one from *The New Yorker* editor and writer Mary Norris:

Woolf did not know Greek the way bees do not know pollen.

Bees know pollen, of course, and Virginia Woolf knew classical Greek very well. Norris's negative verbs (*did not know, do not know*) form a startling image, mirroring her surprise on discovering this fact about Woolf.

———

In an article about a former ballerina who now coaches gymnastics, Carla Correa subtly compares her subject to others in the field:

Like any coach, Kondos Field may have her detractors, though they are not that easy to find.

Not that easy to find is an elegant way to say that just about everyone praises Kondos Field.

———

Now to the world of Disney: Belle, the "beauty" of *Beauty and the Beast,* sings about the "beast" she's falling in love with:

> True, that he's no Prince Charming,
> But there's something in him that I simply didn't see.

By going negative, Belle downplays the beast's ugliness.

DOUBLING THE NEGATIVE

In some languages, the more negative words you write, the more emphatic your denial. Formal English is different in that two negatives create a positive statement. But not all English is formal. Rapper Eminem turns to *ain't no* in his song "Not Afraid":

> . . . ain't no way I'm a let you stop me from causin' mayhem.

———

Bruce Springsteen's "The Rising" is a haunting tribute to first responders climbing floor after floor of the World Trade Center to rescue survivors:

> Can't see nothin' in front of me
> Can't see nothin' coming up behind
> I make my way through this darkness
> I can't feel nothin' but this chain that binds me

Can't . . . nothin' intensify the danger and confusion of the situation, as well as the devotion to duty (*this chain*) of the heroes.

———

Now to formal English. Some sentences, such as this one, intentionally double up negatives to create a positive:

> You are not one who eats and leaves nothing on his plate for children.
>
> —Wole Soyinka, *Death and the King's Horseman*

and some triple up:

> Is he not a man of complete virtue, who feels no discomposure though men may take no note of him?
>
> —Confucius, *Analects*

———

Further, the expression *not un-* _____ turns a negative into a positive, as in this sentence from Jonathan Swift's *A Tale of a Tub*:

> I am not unaware how the productions of the Grub Street brotherhood have of late years fallen under many prejudices.

Grub Street brotherhood refers to the media of Swift's time. *Not unaware* means "aware," with the double negative acknowledging an objection (don't you know that they're prejudiced?) and answering it in advance (yes, I do know).

———

Though this construction may be useful, it can also annoy the reader. In his essay "Politics and the English Language," George Orwell counsels against its usage:

One can cure oneself of the *not un-* formulation by memorizing this sentence: *A not unblack dog was chasing a not unsmall rabbit across a not ungreen field.*

MORE NEGATIVES

In addition to comparison, there are many other reasons to go negative. A few:

To call attention
In an essay about his hometown of Covington, Louisiana, Walker Percy explains why he lives there:

> The reason is not that it is a pleasant place but rather that it is a pleasant nonplace.

Walker defines a *nonplace* as one of two alternatives: an anonymous new environment or anywhere a writer can live without being overwhelmed by family history. Each is the geographic equivalent to a neutral color. *Nonplace* captures the reader's attention, as Percy intends.

To soften
Abigail Adams wrote this sentence in a letter to her husband, John Adams, while he and other delegates to the Continental Congress were formulating the principles of American government:

> I cannot say that I think you are very generous to the ladies; for, whilst you are proclaiming peace and good-will to men, emancipating all nations, you insist upon retaining an absolute power over wives.

Her objection is forceful, but the phrasing (*I cannot say that I think you are very generous*) is gentle. She can't rein in all her emotion, however: The verb *insist* has more than a bit of anger in it.

To emphasize

Musician Alicia Keys would probably have agreed with Abigail Adams about some aspects of male-female relationships. In "Girl on Fire," Keys's lyrics describe a woman who's "so bright she can burn your eyes." Keys sings,

> You can try but you'll never forget her name.

You can't get much more intense than *never forget*.

To understate

The flip side of emphasis, understatement, can make a point forcefully. Here's an example from Emperor Hirohito of Japan, in a speech conceding defeat in World War II:

> The war in the Pacific has not necessarily developed in Japan's favor.

Having just endured two atomic bomb blasts, Hirohito's audience no doubt agreed.

———

Another understatement comes from Principal Rooney, a character in *Ferris Bueller's Day Off*. The film recounts a day when the title character, yet again, cuts school in order to hang out with his friends:

> Ferris does not have what we consider to be an exemplary attendance record.

To focus on sound

The speaker in Tennyson's "Merlin and Vivien" pleads:

> Trust me not at all or all in all.

This simple but effective sentence plays with sound, repetition, and negativity.

———

So does President Ronald Reagan in his farewell address to the nation, which summed up the achievements of his administration:

> We made a difference. . . . All in all, not bad at all.

To define/exclude
Exclusion depends on negativity (what or who is not in the group) and defines what remains:

> [Dance] gives you nothing back, no manuscripts to store away, no paintings to show on walls and maybe hang in museums, no poems to be printed and sold, nothing but that single fleeting moment when you feel alive.
> —Merce Cunningham (choreographer and dancer)

> How vain it is to sit down to write when you have not stood up to live!
> —Henry David Thoreau, *A Year in Thoreau's Journal*

> No man but a blockhead ever wrote, except for money.
> —Samuel Johnson, quoted by his biographer James Boswell

To reveal character
This line from the title character of *Forrest Gump* summarizes his key traits:

> I'm not a smart man, but I know what love is.

———

Alice Walker, in "Fame," describes the protagonist by showing how others react to her:

> [The interview was a] gentle interrogation with no embarrassing questions, because Andrea Clement White was now old and had become an institution and there was never anyone in her presence who did not evince respect.

———

In the film *Juno*, the stepmother of an unmarried, pregnant teenager turns protective when she challenges a condescending medical technician who's performing an ultrasound on the girl:

> Well, my five-year-old daughter could do that and let me tell you, she's not the brightest bulb in the tanning bed.

To offer advice
By stating which sort of behavior is not acceptable, an advisor reinforces what is proper, as in this sentence from Abraham Lincoln:

> In times like the present, men should utter nothing for which they would not willingly be responsible through time and eternity.

The *times like the present* Lincoln refers to are the Civil War years. As president, Lincoln was commander in chief of the Union forces. His opponent, Robert E. Lee, also offered advice:

> Never do a wrong thing to make a friend or keep one.

———

One more bit of counsel from a politician:

> It is better to offer no excuse than a bad one.
>
> —George Washington

Mystery
Archibald MacLeish's poem "Ars Poetica" states:

> A poem should be equal to
> Not true.

And

> A poem should not mean
> But be.

These lines negate the possibility of a literal explanation for poetry. The two-word lines (*Not true, But be*) land like punches, leaving the reader wondering, as MacLeish intended, how to read a poem.

———

An element of mystery permeates these lines from the title character of Shakespeare's *King Lear*:

> I will have such revenges on you both,
> That all the world shall—I will do such things,—What they are, yet
>   I know not: but they shall be
> The terrors of the earth.

Lear's threat to his traitorous daughters is all the more ominous because of the negative core: *What they* [his vengeful actions] *are, yet I know not.* Anyone who's ever seen the standard horror-film scene—a creaking door opening as the camera cuts away—knows that the unknown can be more frightening than the explicit.

FOR THE WRITER

Negative statements appear in everyone's writing, but most have little artistic merit. The challenge is to create a few that enhance the effect you're striving for.

YOU: THE MOVIE

Who would play you in a film about your life? Formulate a negative expression for your answer. For example:

> I won't say no to Meryl Streep, because there's no character she can't embody.

If you wish, list some actors who aren't suitable and explain why, again with a negative statement such as this one:

> There's not enough makeup in the world to make Emma Stone unremarkable enough to play that part.

STREET TALK

The Rolling Stones can't get no satisfaction, but you can by writing some double-negative lines for characters likely to use them. You don't have to flesh out the character, but it helps to form a basic image before you create dialogue. Additional challenge: embed the dialogue in an action that also sheds light on the character's personality. For instance:

> "Ain't no way I'm falling for someone that cheap," she snapped as she turned and walked away. Roger gestured to the drink he'd bought her and asked the bartender for a refund.

PATTERNING

Choose one of the examples from this chapter and write a sentence that follows the same pattern. Merce Cunningham's definition of dance, for instance, lends itself to other creative activities:

> Writing poetry is a worthless endeavor, creating no material gain, attracting no enormous crowd of readers, and adding nothing to the world but beauty.

Shakespeare, George Washington, Alicia Keys—it doesn't matter who inspires you, as long as someone does.

REVISION

Pull out some writing you've already done. Underline a couple of descriptions. Recast the sentences they appear in, changing a positive to a negative. Here's what I mean:

> ORIGINAL: The light shone brightly on her tired face.
> REVISION: The light shone, not softly, on her not-so-fresh face.

It's likely that your revisions will vary in quality. Before you accept or reject any, ask yourself how each version affects your reader. Then decide which one best serves your purpose.

CREATIVE DESCRIPTIONS

The two-plied strands of your chromosomes have been spun by all thin-skinned creatures for all of time, and now they offer you no more bottomless thrill than the point-nosed plow of preparedness.
—Barbara Kingsolver, "Where It Begins"

It's a big world, and someone's got to describe it. Or, more accurately, everyone *wants* to describe it. But how? English has a huge trove of single-word descriptions. Nevertheless, writers—or, again more accurately, everyone—reaches for creative descriptions. One moment the choice is a simile ("sounding like a parrot with laryngitis"), another a metaphor ("New York City, the Mount Everest of traffic control"), another a significant detail ("thirty identical pairs of socks in his suitcase"). More important than its category is that a description resonate with meaning or provide a vivid image.

Barbara Kingsolver's sentence does both. First, it piques curiosity. The title of her essay, "Where It Begins," has already given rise to the question "where *what* begins?" The featured sentence sparks more questions: Those *two-plied strands of your chromosomes*—is this essay about the double helix of DNA? With *your*, is Kingsolver talking about her own chromosomes or the reader's? Who are *all thin-skinned creatures for all of time*? And a *bottomless thrill* from a *plow*? *Preparedness* for what? The reader continues, seeking answers.

A few sentences later the meaning of *it* becomes clear: knitting. Wait—knitting? Now Kingsolver's description is even more intriguing.

What does a *plow of preparedness* have to do with needlework? Quite a lot, in Kingsolver's view. Picture a pair of knitting needles in action: a small triangle made of thin sticks looping lengths of yarn into neat stitches. A moving shape with a triangular tip, a *point-nosed plow*. Visually, they match.

But Kingsolver has packed more into her description, specifically a blueprint of her essay. Think about the function of a *plow*: to break packed earth into loose clods of soil, pulling lower layers to the surface. That's what Kingsolver's essay does. The phrases "it starts" and "it begins" appear more than a dozen times. Kingsolver's first "start" is the onset of cool weather, when the narrator (presumably Kingsolver herself) sees birds flying south for the winter and plans to "swaddle" her "children in wool." Other "starts" in the essay are "a craving to fill the long evening," a way to endure the boredom of lectures and meetings or to ignore the words that "drub, drub, drub" inside her skull, demanding to be written. Knitting also begins as a distraction from illness, an excuse to get together with friends, an interest in patterns, or an attraction to color and texture. Still more beginnings: raising sheep, shearing them, then spinning and dyeing the yarn. The ultimate "start" of knitting is the earth itself, which "frets and dreams, and knits herself wordless," nourishing sheep on "tart, green blades" of grass as they reproduce, nurture their young, and grow wool.

The *plow* is a focal point of this origin story. For Kingsolver, knitting is the application of human hands to natural material. No megastore craft supplies for her. A *plow* and knitting needles are manmade. The *plow* can't work without nature (the soil), nor can knitters do their work without grass, sheep, and wool. It's a *plow of preparedness*: Nature gives freely, but only those who know how to use its gifts can benefit from them. The products that humans create—knitted garments—signal *preparedness* for winter.

And then there's the yarn, akin to the *two-plied strands of your chromosomes*. Kingsolver sees her DNA (the *two-plied strands*) as *spun by all thin-skinned creatures for all of time*. Once again, the description works on two levels. She's an individual more vulnerable than most to winter, one who watches her children with a "shudder" as they happily eat cold cereal, barefoot, in the first days of autumn. But the fragility of the whole human race is in that phrase, too. We all need protection from the elements; we're all *thin-skinned.* Our *two-plied strands* give us the ability and the need for tool making, creation, and *preparedness.* This is a *bottomless thrill.*

Near the end of her essay, Kingsolver loops back to the description in the featured sentence: "the plied double helices of all creatures that have prepared and justly survived on the firmament of patience and swaddled children." Then comes her last statement, which applies to knitting, the essay, and the description itself: "It's all of a piece. All one thing."

THEME WEAVING

Like Barbara Kingsolver, other authors weave descriptions into their narratives to underscore a theme. In her short story "Mrs. Sen's," Jhumpa Lahiri considers how an immigrant deals with American culture. In this sentence, Lahiri describes the title character's driving:

> Eventually she pressed her foot to the brake pedal, manipulated the automatic gear shift as if it were an enormous, leaky pen, and backed inch by inch out of the parking space.

Mrs. Sen's discomfort behind the wheel mirrors her discomfort in America. She and her husband have moved from their home in Calcutta, India, so he can take a job teaching mathematics at a university on the Atlantic Coast. He's out all day, busy with classes and meetings. She's alone, missing her family and culture. Her clothing and cooking reach toward her home in India, just as her attempts to drive reach toward American life. Neither arrives at its destination. She has no place to go in her best clothes, and she can't find the ingredients she needs in American food markets. Nor can she drive. It's as if her life has been *backed* out of its home *space.*

Mrs. Sen has one companion. She babysits an eleven-year-old boy,

Eliot, every afternoon until his mother returns from work. They're a solitary pair. No other children live nearby, Eliot's mother works fifty miles from home, and his father is "two thousand miles west." Mrs. Sen's adult social life is limited to her husband and the few minutes she spends with Eliot's mother, who wants only to pick up her kid and go.

Mr. Sen and Eliot's mother aren't villains; they're busy. Just as Mrs. Sen tries to manipulate the gear shift, she tries to manipulate them. She pressures her husband to pick up fresh fish from the store, and she prepares elaborate snacks for Eliot's mother each afternoon so the woman can't avoid a short visit. Mr. Sen is not above manipulation either. He takes her and Eliot on an outing, and when she's in a good mood, he tells his wife that she must drive home. She goes a short distance and then pulls over. Her willingness to oblige him has reached its limit: *she pressed her foot to the brake pedal.*

The *pen* in the featured sentence is a writing instrument. But another definition of *pen* is "an enclosure," one that locks Mrs. Sen in and American culture out. For a while, the *pen* is *leaky.* She talks with Eliot and takes trips to the market on a public bus, chatting with the fishmonger. But then she has a minor accident and loses her job minding Eliot. Her isolation deepens.

The confining *pen* image also applies to Eliot and his mother, representatives of disconnected American culture. When Mrs. Sen asks Eliot if he misses his mother, "the thought had never occurred to him." The convivial family gatherings Mrs. Sen describes are far from Eliot's experience. Unlike his mother, who rejects the unfamiliar (she tosses Mrs. Sen's painstakingly prepared food away), Eliot asks questions and pays attention to the answers. He's *backed inch by inch out of* American culture during his time with Mrs. Sen. But he can't get out, really. After the accident he becomes a latchkey kid, home alone. He "said that he was fine" by himself, but the implication is that he's not. Mrs. Sen's judgment of American culture comes, appropriately, while she's attempting to drive: "Everyone, this people, too much in their world."

———

The characters in Joshua Ferris's *Then We Came to the End* are also "too much in their world," and it's not an attractive one. They work in an advertising agency, a soulless set of cubicles and dreary offices, as the economy plummets at the end of the nineties dot-com boom. Ferris uses the pronoun *we* to narrate the story, creating a collective voice that shrinks as employees are laid off. Early in the novel Ferris describes the workforce as

> Goldfish who took a trip every night in a small clear bag of water and then returned in the morning to their bowl.

Ferris's sentence doesn't fit the traditional grammatical definition of completeness. There's a subject, *Goldfish*, and a long description of that subject (*who took a trip . . . then returned in the morning to their bowl*). But *Goldfish* has no matching verb, no action. A standard complete sentence would read:

> Like goldfish, we took a trip every night in a small clear bag of water and then returned in the morning to our bowl.

That version gives the workers (*we*) more agency, making them into people who act. In Ferris's version, they're only described as acting (*took*, *returned*). It's a fine but crucial distinction. Like *goldfish*, the workers can see everything; both the *bag* and the *bowl* are transparent. But also like *goldfish*, they're powerless. They know that they may be laid off, but they can't do anything to help themselves.

Ferris's description (*bag*, *bowl*) emphasizes how *small* the workers' world is. Yet work dominates. A plastic *bag* is a means of transporting fish from the pet store to the home. The *bowl* is where the fish live. In Ferris's sentence, the goldfish *took a trip every night* in the bag. This wording reduces the workers' homes to a temporary stop between workdays. The description also reinforces the concept of confinement. There's not much room in a *bag* or a *bowl*.

One more point: a clichéd sitcom plot involves parents rushing to buy a new goldfish when their child's pet dies. To the parents, the fish are interchangeable. But the child has spent a great deal of time watching "Finny" or "Nemo" swim, and the ruse fails. To the corporate overseers in Ferris's novel, employees are as interchangeable as replacement goldfish. Because Ferris has built individuality into his characters, readers come to know and care about each one. We are, after all, not inside the *bag* and *bowl*.

————

Tim O'Brien calls his short story collection, *The Things They Carried*, fiction. But "Tim O'Brien" is a character in several stories, and other characters share names and fates with soldiers the author served with in Vietnam. In the title story, First Lieutenant Jimmy Cross carries letters from a college girl, Martha:

> In the late afternoon, after a day's march, he would dig his foxhole, wash his hands under a canteen, unwrap the letters, hold them with the tips of his fingers, and spend the last hour of light pretending.

With the tips of his fingers. What care, what fragility, what fear that phrase evokes. Cross knows that Martha writes to him only as a friend, that her sign-off, "Love, Martha . . . did not mean what he sometimes pretended it meant." And *pretending* (a form of storytelling) is the point here, not only for Cross, but for the author as well. According to O'Brien, the truth of war isn't comprehensible through facts alone. To understand it, you need stories. Hence the form of the book, as well as Jimmy Cross's reverence for Martha's letters. They help him create illusions: that she'll return his love someday, that they'll have a future together, and so forth. But illusions shatter easily. When one of his soldiers is killed by a sniper,

Cross blames himself. Had he not been thinking about Martha, he reasons, the soldier would not have been shot. Cross burns the letters, though they remain in his memory.

O'Brien provides no evidence that Cross's vigilance could have saved the man. They're in a war, a particularly dangerous one with no defined battlefields. Yet Cross's belief is understandable. It's natural to pretend that changing one factor (thinking about love) can guarantee safety. Not so, of course. O'Brien's description reflects the fact that such an important illusion requires careful handling, that is, *with the tips of his fingers.*

LOOK SHARP

A really good description catches the reader off-balance a moment before it falls into the "of course!" slot in the brain. Here are a few such descriptions, categorized by purpose.

To illuminate personality
In *The Sisterhood of the Traveling Pants*, Ann Brashares delineates a character who once "trusted what she liked" and then changed:

> Later, if she loved the name Mimi, she would have thought that was a good reason to name her [guinea pig] Frederick.

Adolescent rebellion and confusion have seldom been summed up so neatly.

———

Edith Wharton considers the other end of the life cycle, describing the feelings of an elderly lady in her story "Mrs. Manstey's View." Faced with a construction site that will block her window, Mrs. Manstey thinks:

> She might move, of course; so might she be flayed alive; but she was not likely to survive either operation.

Her reaction may sound extreme, but looking through that window is her only pleasure because her world is so constricted.

————

Anyone who's read Jim Butcher's Dresden novels, or the hardboiled-detective genre they riff on, will recognize this blend of humor and action:

> In some distant corner of my mind, where my common sense apparently had some kind of vacation home, my brain noted with dismay that I had broken into a sprint of my own.

The *sprint* is toward trouble; the novel is *Turn Coat.*

To depict physical traits
P. G. Wodehouse gives this line to Bertie, the hapless employer of the quintessential butler, Jeeves:

> She fitted into my biggest arm-chair as if it had been built round her by someone who knew they were wearing arm-chairs tight about the hips that season.

Bertie's Aunt Dahlia, the *she* in the chair, would not have been pleased with Bertie's description. Fortunately, in a rare moment of discretion, Bertie keeps this thought to himself.

————

So does the narrator of Julia Alvarez's "The Rudy Elmenhurst Story," who thinks of a classmate:

> He grinned, dimples making a parenthesis at the corners of his lips as if the smile were a secret between us.

It's not spoiling the suspense of the story to say that Rudy, the *he* in Alvarez's sentence, is hoping that there will be *a secret between us* and that the secret will involve their bodies.

———

Sound, not sight, is the focus of this description by Bruce Springsteen, referring to a record track that

> . . . had that 747-engine-in-your-living-room rumble, the universe hanging, for one brief moment, in balance as the cosmic chord goes *twang.*

Cosmic chord. A description as inspired as Springsteen's music.

———

Science also gives rise to creative description. Here are two:

> The female giant ichneumon wasp flies, impressively for her near-eight-inch length, with the light buoyancy of cottonwood fluff . . . her thorax is connected to her abdomen by a Victorian-thin waist.
> —Jill Sisson Quinn, "Sign Here If You Exist"

> The slice [of brain tissue] floats in saline solution in a shallow black plastic tray, and at first it looks exactly like a piece of ginger at a good sushi restaurant, one where they don't dye the ginger but leave it pale.
> —Luke Dittrich, "The Brain That Changed Everything"

To recount events
In this sentence from Tayari Jones's *Leaving Atlanta*, parents break the news that they are separating. The older daughter's reaction is not what they hoped for:

He should have said, *Tasha, DeShaun, your mother and I have been playing with matches and your whole life is on fire.*

———

This sentence from Wole Soyinka's *Death and the King's Horseman* refers to a ritual suicide believed to insure safe passage for the king through the afterlife:

Your death will be like the sweet berry a child places under his tongue to sweeten the passage of food.

———

Far less important than the horseman's ordeal is a yacht race, even a premier event like the America's Cup. Ring Lardner covered the 1920 competition:

At high noon the wind was blowing a two-inch gale backwards and neither scow would move, so the starter postponed it till along come a breathe of fresh air, was a ¼ to 2. Then away went the 2 slops like a snail with paralysis.

Lardner was famous for playing with—that is to say, breaking—grammar and spelling rules in order to achieve a distinctive voice. Copy editors infuriated him when they corrected his intentional mistakes, such as changing *slops* to *sloops* and *scow* to a term better suited to an expensive vessel.

———

Another race, this time with horses, via sportswriter Red Smith's interview with a trainer:

He rode that race like he rode this race a hundred years ago and came back to ride this one at eighteen years old.

The *he* is Steve Cauthen, the *race* is of the 1978 Kentucky Derby, in which Cauthen rode the winning horse, Affirmed.

———

Politics isn't ordinarily covered as a boxing match, but Red Smith applied sportswriting conventions to the 1956 Democratic political convention. Whether Averill Harriman or Adlai Stevenson would be the party's presidential candidate was still in doubt when former president Harry Truman stepped up to the podium to support Harriman. Smith describes the moment this way:

This was Harry ("Give 'em hell") Truman, last Democrat to hold the heavyweight title, coming out of retirement now to slug it out with the clever young contender, Ad Stevenson.

Harry Truman may have fought hard, as his nickname implies, but Adlai Stevenson was the winning nominee—and the losing candidate in the general election.

FOR THE WRITER

Some readers see a solid block of description and skip nimbly to the next line of dialogue, avoiding what they think will be a boring paragraph. Show them they're wrong by creating descriptions they'll want to read.

MIX-UPS

Those whose first language isn't English sometimes mix up common expressions. One of my favorites is from a television character who remarks that finding the murder weapon will entail searching for a needle in a needlestack. These mistakes are, at times, more apt than the standard version. After all, finding the right needle in a "needlestack" really would be hard.

Purposely mix up a common descriptive expression. Change one or more words, staying true to the general intent of the original but adding eccentricity. Some possible candidates for renovation:

bent out of shape (annoyed)
under the weather (ill)
on the ball (alert, prepared)
thrown for a loop (shocked)
over the moon (happy)

Bonus: Take the clichéd description to its logical, literal conclusion. What would someone who's *on the ball* look like at work? Squirming to stay balanced on a sponge-rubber sphere? Sitting in an office with a spherical floor, computers and papers sliding toward the wall?

STANDOUTS

Writers such as Tim O'Brien frequently string details together, all giving information. Usually, though, one stands out. In the O'Brien sentence I quote earlier in this chapter, it's *with the tips of his fingers*. In a student essay about grief, it's the fact that the bereaved, cooking pasta, lets her salty *tears drip into the pot*.

Describe a simple action (observed or imagined). Capture a vivid detail that will stand out.

THE OBSERVING EYE

Check the internet or a book for a scientific illustration—a diagram of a physical process or a photo of a plant or animal. With a comparison, describe what you see. An example: A ladybug (ladybird beetle) looks like "a miniature turtle in a couture coat."

SYNESTHESIA

I'd wake and hear the cold splintering, breaking.
—Robert Hayden, "Those Winter Sundays"

Are you reading this during a bitter cold winter? As you wind an extra scarf around your neck, think about *bitter cold*, an expression that draws on taste to describe temperature. It's an example of synesthesia, a neurological phenomenon in which stimulation of one sense also activates another. A small percentage of people are synesthetes. They may see patterns when they hear music, perceive sounds attached to scents, attach colors to numbers, and so forth. But it's likely that everyone has a bit of sensory crossover. Why else would *sharp cheese, sweet sound*, and *salty language*—not to mention *bitter cold*—be so familiar?

Because synesthesia appears often in literature, it's worth considering what the writer—and the reader—gain from this device. I suspect its popularity rests on the fact that writers must use words to convey what is beyond words, nothing less than physical and emotional reality. True, English has a rich vocabulary for what the five senses perceive: *spicy, rancid, loud, green, soft*, and so forth. But those aren't enough. As John Logan wrote in his play *Red*, that color is "rust on the bike on the lawn" and "heartbeart." Red is "a rabbit's nose" and "an albino's eyes." It's "that phone to the Kremlin on the President's desk" and "nick yourself shaving," and many other things as well. By drawing on more than one sense, synesthesia adds nuance and depth, engages the audience more fully, and perhaps reaches a preverbal level of the mind.

Consider Robert Hayden's poem "Those Winter Sundays." The speaker in the featured sentence looks back on his childhood. (I say *his* for convenience and because the poem is frequently viewed as reflecting the hardships of Hayden's childhood. But poets aren't constrained by reality, and the gender of the speaker is never identified.) The father kindles a fire before dawn on "Sundays too" while his family slept. It's no easy task. The father's hands "ached / from labor in the weekday weather." But the speaker doesn't depict a saint. He fears "the chronic angers of that house."

Cold appears three times in this short poem, and each time it's associated with a different sense. First it has a color (blueblack), then a sound (splintering), and last a solid presence that can break and be "driven out." By bringing in several sensory aspects, Hayden takes you into a real moment—a frigid, early morning. Anyone who has experienced winter knows exactly what Hayden means.

The poem does more than describe a time of day or a season, however. It also maps the speaker's changing views of his father. The adult remembers "Speaking indifferently" to his father and says, "No one ever thanked him." The poem ends with a haunting question: "What did I know, what did I know / of love's austere and lonely offices?" *Offices* are "services done for others" or "duties." It's easy to see how Hayden's usage fits the first definition, because the father's actions are done for his family. Perhaps the child would have assigned the second definition, assuming his father lit the fire and polished shoes out of duty. The adult realizes that more than duty is involved and attaches the possessive form *love's* to *offices*. He now sees his father's actions, and by extension his father, as "lonely" and "austere," but loving.

Back to synesthesia: The speaker's childhood relationship with the father was *cold*. The colors Hayden assigns to *cold*—blue and black—are often associated with emotions. Blue is sad: you can have, or sing, the blues. Black is frequently attached to depression. But that *cold* relationship has been *splintering* and *breaking*, if only in the speaker's memory. The father "had driven out" the physical cold, and now the speaker has "driven out" the cold feelings he once had for his father. Subtly employing sight, sound, and touch, Hayden shows a sincere and moving transformation.

MIXING SENSES, POETICALLY

Because they rely on imaginative comparisons, poets are especially likely to turn to synesthetic imagery. Story Musgrave, who is not only a poet but also an astronaut and a trauma surgeon, wrote hundreds of poems while in space. In "Amazonia," he interweaves sight and sound:

> waves of waving purples and yellows, singing chimes upon my
> eyes . . .

―――――――

Back on Earth, Dylan Thomas connects sound, sight, and touch in this line from his poem "Fern Hill":

> The foxes on the hills barked clear and cold.

"Fern Hill" depicts a carefree child joyfully romping through nature, unaware that this period in life is brief. The sound (*barked*) has a visual component (*clear*) and physical sensation (*cold*). Throughout the poem, and especially here, Thomas reminds the reader that childhood ends. Foxes bark when they reach sexual maturity. To the child the sound is *clear*, but the meaning—the end of one stage of life and the beginning of another—isn't. The bark is a *cold* reminder of the relentless progression of time.

―――――――

Edith Sitwell writes these lines in her poem "Aubade":

Each dull blunt wooden stalactite
Of rain creaks, hardened by the light

Every streak of rain is separate and solid, a *dull blunt wooden stalac-tite*, menacing in its fall. But those are physical sensations. With *creaks*, Sitwell crosses into sound, and *light* brings the visual. A well-rounded description of rain, indeed.

———

Robert Frost, in "After Apple Picking," also works with the sense of smell:

Essence of winter sleep is on the night,
The scent of apples: I am drowsing off.

Defining *winter sleep* as the *scent of apples*, the poem presents an exhausted worker whose rest is permeated by the day's task, picking apples.

———

Emily Dickinson wrote of the same season in this poem:

There's a certain Slant of light,
Winter Afternoons –
That oppresses, like the Heft
Of Cathedral Tunes –

Dickinson brings in sight (*Slant of light*), touch (*oppresses*), and sound (*Tunes*).

———

Now to a warmer month:

And the hyacinth purple, and white, and blue,
Which flung from its bells a sweet peal anew
Of music so delicate, soft, and intense,
It was felt like an odour within the sense . . .

These lines from Shelley's "The Sensitive Plant" interlace the colors of the flower with sound (*sweet peal*, *music*), touch (*delicate*, *soft*), and smell (*odour*).

BEYOND POETRY

Synesthesia adds texture to prose, too, in all its forms: novels, stories, plays, and nonfiction. Synesthetic imagery pops up in film and song lyrics, as well as in advertisements. A sampling, some with commentary:

———

Florens, a character in Toni Morrison's novel *A Mercy*, thinks,

Night is thick no stars anyplace but sudden the moon moves.

Florens, an enslaved young woman, has been sent to find a blacksmith who has some knowledge of medicinal herbs. The hope is that he can cure "Mistress" of smallpox. That Florens experiences a time of day as *thick* mirrors the fact that her life is dense, or *thick*, with problems: what will happen to her if Mistress dies, will the blacksmith reciprocate her feelings of attraction to him, and will she even survive the journey? More important to the theme of the novel, Floren's understanding of her past is also *thick* with confusion; she has no one to guide her (*no stars anyplace*). She misinterprets a key childhood moment, when her mother urged her sale to the visiting "Sir," the husband of "Mistress." The reader, but not Florens, discovers the reason in the last paragraph of the novel, a *sudden* shift of illumination.

———

The narrator of Ha Jin's "A Report" is an army officer in China. The entire story is presented as a letter reporting an incident involving paratroopers marching off to war and singing a sad song:

> The words and music, suitable only for lamentation, melted the strength of the soldiers' feet.

The lyrics, the narrator explains, concern a recruit leaving his mother, who is told not to cry. A passerby watching the troops says they resemble "a funeral procession." The officer vows to prohibit anything other than patriotic songs in the future and says the soldiers should have sung about their skills ("Every bullet strikes an enemy dead") and the respect they inspire ("If we have no clothes and food the enemy sends them to us"). Both songs—the one the soldiers sang and the one the official recommends—attest to the power of *words and music*. The sentimental song is a solid object with physical power: It *melted the strength* of the troops. The patriotic song is an obvious lie.

———

A few more examples of synesthesia:

Touch and sound

> They [the words] cut like a dagger.
> —Oscar Wilde, *The Picture of Dorian Gray*

Sight and sound

> Then he crossed his arms over his chest and began to listen to the radiant voices of the slaves. . . .
> —Gabriel García Márquez, *The General in His Labyrinth*

And all the people saw the thunderings...

> —*King James Bible*, Exodus 20:18

The lights grow brighter as the earth lurches away from the sun, and now the orchestra is playing yellow cocktail music....

> —F. Scott Fitzgerald, *The Great Gatsby*

He has occasional flashes of silence, that make his conversation perfectly delightful.

> —Lady Holland, *A Memoir of the Reverend Sydney Smith*

Even the ears must dance.

> —Natalia Makarova (ballerina)

Taste and sight

You've never seen a taste like this.

> —soda advertisement

Taste and sound

Thy voice is wine to me.

> —Oscar Wilde, *Salome*

Like sweet banjo music to your tongue.

> —potato chip advertisement

Music to your mouth.

> —candy advertisement

Smell and sound

I can't hear you over the smell of those fries.
> —*Grey's Anatomy* (television show)

Sight and touch

It is the cold, lifeless hour before the dawn; the night presses solidly down.
—George F. Wear, *Everyman at Dawn* (memoir of World War I)

Oh, land of gold and burning blue,
I'm crying like a child for you!
> —Dorothy Frances McRae, "Homesick"

The sky, a greasy soup-tureen,
Shuts down atop my brow.
> —Rudyard Kipling, "In Partibus"

It [the street] shines in the glare of lamps
Cold, white lamps . . .
> —Amy Lowell, "A London Thoroughfare 2 a.m."

Sense and Ideas

I can't assign one sensory aspect to ideas, because they arise from all senses, and sometimes from no sense at all (pun intended). This statement attaches temperature to a thought:

One cool judgment is worth a thousand hasty counsels.
> —Woodrow Wilson

FOR THE WRITER

If you look through your work, chances are you'll find that synesthesia is already there. Even so, you can hone your skills by practicing synesthetic expression. Take care to avoid clichés such as *tickled pink* for happiness. Here are a few prompts to get you started.

BLUEBERRY

I've chosen a blueberry as a starting point, but feel free to substitute any food item from your cupboard or refrigerator. Warning: This one can be messy.

- Take a blueberry and look at it carefully. List everything you see: color, shape, size, and so forth.
- Now turn your attention to the sense of touch. Run your finger over it. How does it feel? Bumpy, smooth, some of each? What about temperature? Is it cool to the touch? Warm? Room temperature?
- Sniff it. Try listing what you smell, but I should warn you in advance that English has few words for scents. Do try to stretch beyond "the blueberry smells like a blueberry."
- Listen to it. This one is a little ridiculous, but humor me. Shake the berry. Drop it. Drop it on a different surface. Write what you hear.
- Taste it. Yes, you get to eat the exercise. You also get to describe its taste.

Now that you have every possible literal description of a blueberry, look for opportunities to cross senses. Perhaps the blueberry is textured like a love song or has a muted gray tint on its side. Let your imagination roam: the blueberry may smell like the Fourth of July, for example.

CLASSIC, IN A SENSE

Aristotle ranked the senses from least to most important:

LEAST IMPORTANT TOUCH, TASTE, SMELL, SOUND, SIGHT MOST IMPORTANT

In terms of writing, Aristotle may be most accurate at the high end of the scale. It's easy to describe a visual setting and the sounds heard there. On the low end, you may wish to quarrel with Aristotle. Although scent often evokes powerful emotions and memories, it's difficult to describe because English has few "smell" words that don't rely on comparisons. Try to describe the scent of butter, for instance, and you'll see what I mean. Thus few writers bother unless the odor is indicative of the larger meaning, such as rotted food that an impoverished child eats with gusto. Touch and taste tend to be specialized also. In a scene about a dinner date, both serve a purpose, but generally writers can omit these details without losing much.

POEM STRIPPING

Select a poem with synesthetic expressions in it. Robert Hayden's "Those Winter Sundays" is widely available and a wonderful read, but you can easily find other poems for this exercise. Strip the poem of synesthesia. Hayden's *cold* can be "below freezing" but not "blueblack," for instance. Nor can the *cold* be *splintering* or *breaking*. Instead, it's "easing up" or "growing warmer." Read the revised poem. Whether the new version is awful or great, you will have a better grasp of the power and purpose of synesthesia.

FACT AND FICTION

Normally, the distinction between fact and fiction is paramount. For this exercise, however, you can make up details. Find a news story or a paragraph from a textbook that presents a number of factual statements. Underline five or six bits of information and inject some synesthesia. Here's one example:

> ORIGINAL: The penthouse featured a window wall <u>with views of surrounding boroughs</u>.
> REVISION: The penthouse featured a window wall <u>giving a taste of India in Queens County, a hint of Italian delicacies in the Bronx, and a Dodger-era egg-cream soda from Brooklyn</u>.

Now evaluate your revision. Does synesthesia add or subtract from the effect of the paragraph? As important as knowing when to use a literary device is knowing when *not* to use it. In your own work, decide how best to reach your audience.

PART V EXTREMES

MARATHON SENTENCES

But when you have seen vicious mobs lynch your mothers and fathers at will and drown your sisters and brothers at whim; when you have seen hate filled policemen curse, kick, brutalize and even kill your black brothers and sisters with impunity; when you see the vast majority of your twenty million Negro brothers smothering in an air tight cage of poverty in the midst of an affluent society; when you suddenly find your tongue twisted and your speech stammering as you seek to explain to your six-year old daughter why she can't go to the public amusement park that has just been advertised on television, and see tears welling up in her little eyes when she is told that Funtown is closed to colored children, and see the depressing clouds of inferiority begin to form in her little mental sky, and see her begin to distort her little personality by unconsciously developing a bitterness toward white people; when you have to concoct an answer for a five-year old son asking in agonizing pathos: "Daddy, why do white people treat colored people so mean?"; when you take a cross country drive and find it necessary to sleep night after night in the uncomfortable corners of your automobile because no motel will accept you; when you are humiliated day in and day out by nagging signs reading "white" and "colored"; when your first name becomes "nigger," your middle name becomes "boy" (however old you are) and your last name becomes "John," and when your wife and mother are never given the respected title "Mrs."; when you are harried by day and haunted by night by the fact that you are a Negro, living constantly at tip-toe stance, never quite knowing what to expect next, and plagued with inner fears and outer resentments; when you are forever fighting a degenerating sense of "nobodiness"; then you will understand why we find it difficult to wait.
—Martin Luther King Jr., "Letter from a Birmingham Jail"

S tand, in your imagination, at the top of a steep and icy slope. Push off. The feeling that comes next—an intense, unstoppable rush—is what you get the moment you read *But when you have seen.* . . . You can't stop there, or halfway, or anywhere at all in this sentence until you get to the end. That's Martin Luther King's achievement. One of them.

King's marathon sentence is powerful but not unique. Longer-than-usual sentences—not all as lengthy as King's—have a special energy. They give readers no moment to escape from the ideas within. A marathon sentence can be an argument, a journey through a tumultuous event, a train of thought, or a detailed description. It may challenge readers' patience but, if well written, will reward their persistence.

The featured sentence, from "Letter from a Birmingham Jail," is all the more remarkable because when King wrote it he had no notebook, no writing paper, and no typewriter. All he had was a copy of a local periodical that contained "A Call for Unity," a letter from eight white clergymen in Birmingham, Alabama, urging an end to the sit-ins and marches against segregation that were taking place there in April 1963. King and other protestors had been arrested for breaking the law prohibiting these demonstrations. The white clergymen's letter asked protestors to wait and trust that newly elected city officials and the courts would effect change. Writing in the margins of the newspaper, and later on scraps smuggled to him by an African American guard, and finally on a legal pad his lawyer obtained, King composed his answer. The *Letter*, with minor editing changes, appeared in many periodicals and eventually became part of King's 1964 book, *Why We Can't Wait*.

Uniting righteous anger with moral authority and sound logic, King justifies nonviolent civil disobedience as the best way to confront Birmingham's racial injustice. In his letter King notes that Birmingham was "probably the most thoroughly segregated city in the United States" and had "an ugly record of police brutality," and "more unsolved bombings of Negro homes and churches" than any other American city. King addresses several objections from the white clergymen, including, in this sentence, the idea that the demonstrations are "unwise and untimely." They urge a moderate, slower pace of change. It's fitting that this sentence is anything but moderate and slow, because King rejects the clergymen's suggestion. Every African American, writes King, knows that "wait" nearly always means "never."

The letter as a whole draws on theology, philosophy, and history to explain why the protests must continue. In this sentence, though, King speaks from personal experience. He starts the sentence with *but*, a word signaling a change in direction—here, the opposing argument. The clergymen, and by extension anyone supporting their position, have made their case. Now it's King's turn.

Structurally, the sentence is an extended series of *when you* statements, each invoking an unbearable reality: lynching, drowning, curses, kicks, and other offenses. Each lands like a judge's gavel. Readers, like spectators in a courtroom, can't interrupt with counterarguments or justifications. They must let King have his say. More important, they must feel what his words mean.

The pronoun *you* refers to the clergymen King addresses, but it includes King himself, who is processing reality through internal dialogue. He recounts and watches his own memories in passages such as these:

> as you seek to explain to your six-year old daughter why she can't go to the public amusement park

> when you have to concoct an answer for a five-year old son

> uncomfortable corners of your automobile because no motel will accept you

King's *you* encompasses other African Americans, too. He bears witness to their experiences:

> when you have seen vicious mobs lynch your mothers and fathers

when you have seen hate filled policemen curse, kick, brutalize, and even kill

when you see the vast majority of your twenty million Negro brothers smothering in an air tight cage of poverty

He also explains the effects of racist acts, to the clergymen but perhaps also to himself:

unconscious bitterness
harried by day and haunted by night
plagued with inner fears and outer resentments
a degenerating sense of "nobodiness"

All this in one sentence! And within that sentence, significant details that contribute to its power. One example: King refers to *an air tight cage of poverty.* Cages let air flow freely, so this cage is an illusion, more a coffin than a *cage.* The *tip-toe* stance evokes the image of a runner waiting for the starter's pistol or a fighter ready for the first blow. Both are adrenaline-filled moments with uncertain outcomes and therefore serve as a warning: *never quite knowing what to expect next* applies to the victim as well as to the perpetrator.

The sentence also shows King's sadness that he can't fulfill one of the traditional male roles. He can't protect his children (*clouds of inferiority begin to form in her little mental sky*) or tell them the truth (*concoct an answer*). He can't defend the women he loves (*your wife and mother are never given the respected title "Mrs."*). These are heavy burdens.

At the end of the sentence, King changes *when* to *then.* Go through all this, he says, and *then you will understand why we find it difficult to wait.* I doubt the white clergymen, or anyone else counseling patience, can read King's letter without shame. Nor should they.

ON THE MOVE

Marathon sentences are particularly good at relating events that are, or seem, inescapable. In this sentence from *Giants in the Earth*, Ole Edvart Rølvaag takes the reader into a swarm of locusts:

> And now from out the sky gushed down with cruel force a living, pulsating stream, striking the backs of the helpless fold like pebbles thrown by an unseen hand; but that which fell out of the heavens was not pebbles, nor raindrops, nor hail, for then it would have lain inanimate where it fell; this substance had no sooner fallen than it popped up again, crackling, and snapping— rose up and disappeared in the twinkling of an eye; it flared and flittered around them like light gone mad; it chirped and buzzed through the air; it snapped and hopped along the ground; the whole place was a weltering turmoil of raging little demons; if one looked for a moment into the wind, one saw nothing but glittering, lightninglike flashes—flashes that came and went, in the heart of a cloud made up of innumerable dark-brown clicking bodies!

Rølvaag presents an overpowering force of nature in an overpowering sentence. The farmers in this scene can't escape the insect invasion, and neither can readers.

———

Nature seems more benign in this sentence from Helena María Viramontes's story "The Moths." A girl works in her grandmother's garden, punching holes in old cans:

> This completed, my job was to fill them with red clay mud from beneath her rosebushes, packing it softly, then making a perfect hole, four fingers round, to nest a sprouting avocado pit, or the spidery sweet potatoes that Abuelita rooted in mayon-

naise jars with toothpicks and daily water, or prickly chayotes that produced vines that twisted and wound all over her porch pillars, crawling to the roof up and over the roof, and down the other side, making her small brick house look like it was cradled within the vines that grew pear-shaped squashes ready for the pick, ready to be steamed with onions and cheese and butter.

This image of nature overflowing with new life contrasts sharply with the confined, tense atmosphere of the granddaughter's home. The orderly activity and the nurturing (*cradled* emphasizes this point) are exactly what the girl needs. In turn, the granddaughter will fulfill her grandmother's needs.

Here's one from Nora Ephron, who discusses "parenting," a modern invention in which "any time is quality time" if the parent is present:

As a result, you were required to be in attendance at the most mundane activities—to watch, cheerlead, and, if necessary, coach, even if this meant throwing your weekend away by driving three hours and twenty minutes in each direction so that you could sit in a dark, hot locker room next door to a gym where your beloved child was going down to resounding defeat in a chess tournament you were not allowed to observe because your mere presence in the room would put unfair pressure on him or her.

The length of the sentence and its forward momentum suggest an unstoppable force leading to a question parents seldom have time to ask: How did we get here?

Beryl Markham's memoir, *West with the Night*, describes a terrifying night at her horse farm in Africa:

Lion in the paddocks—the bawling of a steer, a cow, a heifer; the rush for hurricane lamps, rifles, the whispering of one man to another; the stillness; the tawny shape, burdened with its kill, flowing through the tall grass; bullets whining away against the wind; the lion leaping, bullock and all, over the cedar fence; the lowered rifles.

The list of actions, each recounted in just a few words, mirrors the lion's speed and the urgency of the human response.

———

Jan Morris, in her travel memoir *Contact*, presents a human invasion in this tale of a restaurant patron:

She screamed, shouted, sang ear-splitting snatches of songs, threw plates about, dropped her hat, made savage faces at the customers, knocked tables over and reduced the whole room to helpless laughter until at last, to crown a splendid entertainment, somebody dialed the wrong number and obtained, instead of the police, the fire brigade whose clanking red engines skidded to a halt outside our windows and whose helmeted officers, trailing axes and hoses, stared in bewilderment through the open doors at the hilarious chaos inside.

In eighty-four words Morris brings the scene to life, capturing the chaos by placing all of those words in a single sentence.

THINK FAST

To represent thoughts, so much faster than the speed of light (let alone the formation of words), many authors turn to a marathon sentence, which zips the reader from one idea to another without pause. This sentence from "Nashville" by Lydia Peele represents a young woman's mind when she drops her phone after a riotous night out:

I turn and squat to get it and my face is inches from a spilled styrofoam container of wings, gnawed-on bones and spattered barbecue sauce like blood, and I think about the dead baby bird and the Tavern Master calling me a monster, and, gosh, maybe I am a monster because I would have left the baby bird there to die, instead of putting it out of its misery, maybe I'm a monster for buying these boots that some kid in China probably died to make, but then all I can think of is *my poor phone my poor phone my poor phone.*

———

Now another young woman, worried that she's not properly dressed, pulled onto the dance floor at a family party. Sandra Cisneros shows the dancer's reaction in *The House on Mango Street*:

And Uncle spins me, and my skinny arms bend the way he taught me, and my mother watches, and my little cousins watch, and the boy who is my cousin by first communion watches, and everyone says, wow, who are those two who dance like in the movies, until I forget that I am wearing only ordinary shoes, brown and white, the kind my mother buys each year for school.

From embarrassment to joy, all in one dance, and all in one jam-packed sentence.

———

What does a young man think about when he test-drives a car he can never hope to afford? Christina Sun, in "I Am Not Jeremy Lin," imagines this:

I was driving smooth along I-205 in the brand new GS F Lexus because I needed a car, not a bike, according to my parents, and Brad's asking me, "Jeremy Lin? Like the basketball player?"

because maybe Brad was wondering if I was the point guard for the Brooklyn Nets, but he didn't want to be racist in case I wasn't, and he was also trying to sell me this car and silent rides weren't good for a sale.

The narrator doesn't buy the car, disappointing the salesman, Brad. The reader, if not Brad, enjoys the ride.

————

Edward O. Wilson describes the process of thinking itself, as practiced by a scientific researcher, explaining first that "Nothing comes harder than original thought":

The rest of the time his [the scientist's] mind hugs the coast of the known, reworking old information, adding lesser data, giving reluctant attention to the ideas of others (what use can I make of them?), warming lazily to the memory of successful experiments, and looking for a problem, always looking for a problem, something that can be accomplished, that will lead somewhere, anywhere.

————

Toni Cade Bambara, in "Sort of a Preface" to her collection of short stories *Gorilla My Love*, allows the reader into the author's mind:

It does no good to write autobiographical fiction cause the minute the book hits the stand here comes your mama screamin how could you and sighin' death where is thy sting and she snatches you up out of your bed to grill you about what was going down back there in Brooklyn when she was working three jobs and trying to improve the quality of your life and come to find on page 42 that you were messin' around with that nasty boy up the block and breaks into sobs and quite naturally your family strolls in all sleepy-eyes to catch the floor show at 5:00 A.M. but as far as your mama is concerned, it is nineteen-forty-and-something and you ain't too grown to have your ass whipped.

Which, Bambara explains, is one reason she writes "straight-up fiction," though she adds, "Mostly I lie a lot anyway."

––––––––

The last example belongs to Shakespeare, who gives this speech to Polonius, a character in *Hamlet*. Polonius can't seem to stop himself as he describes a visiting troupe of actors:

> The best actors in the world, either for tragedy,
> comedy, history, pastoral, pastoral-comical,
> historical-pastoral, tragical-historical, tragical-
> comical-historical-pastoral, scene individable, or
> poem unlimited: Seneca cannot be too heavy, nor
> Plautus too light.

WHEN MORE REALLY IS MORE

Lately there's been much written about simplifying life and decluttering our spaces. Perhaps we need that advice because clutter is all around. And perhaps it's all around because something draws us to excess. Writers pile on descriptive details to satisfy the need for more, more, more.

––––––––

Thomas Pynchon is a good example. Here's just one sentence from a set of three, all marathon length and all describing what's on the desk of Slothrop, the main character in Pynchon's novel *Gravity's Rainbow*:

> Then comes a scatter of paperclips, Zippo [cigarette lighter] flints, rubber bands, staples, cigarette butts and crumpled packs,

stray matches, pins, nubs of pens, stubs of pencils of all colors including the hard-to-get heliotrope and raw umber, wooden coffee spoons, Thayer's Slippery Elm Throat Lozenges sent by Slothrop's mother, Naline, all the way from Massachusetts, bits of tape, string, chalk . . . above that a layer of forgotten memoranda, empty buff ration books, phone numbers, unanswered letters, tattered sheets of carbon paper, the scribbled ukulele chords to a dozen songs including "Johnny Doughboy found a Rose in Ireland" ("He does have some rather snappy arrangements," Tantivy reports, "he's a sort of American George Formby, if you can imagine such a thing," but Bloat's decided he'd rather not), an empty Kreml hair tonic bottle, lost pieces to different jigsaw puzzles showing parts of the amber left eye of a Weimaraner, the green velvet folds of a gown, slate-blue veining in a distant cloud, the orange nimbus of an explosion (perhaps a sunset), rivets in the skin of a Flying Fortress, the pink inner thigh of a pouting pin-up girl . . . a few old Weekly Intelligence Summaries from G-2, a busted corkscrewing ukulele string, boxes of gummed paper stars in many colors, pieces of a flashlight, top to a Nugget shoe polish can in which Slothrop now and then studies his blurry brass reflection, any number of reference books out of the ACHTUNG library back down the hall—a dictionary of technical German, an F.O, *Special Handbook* or a *Town Plan*—and usually, unless it's been pinched or thrown away, a *News of the World* somewhere too—Slothrop's a faithful reader.

Slothrop is an American working with the British military during the London Blitz of World War II. The ellipses appear in the original, hinting that even more is on the desk than appears in this sentence. (Making the point more emphatic are additional descriptions in two other sentences.) Pity poor, neat Tantivy, the officer who shares a cubicle with Slothrop.

———

Evelyn Waugh is only slightly more restrained in this sentence from *Vile Bodies*:

> Masked parties, Savage parties, Victorian parties, Greek parties, Wild West parties, Russian parties, Circus parties, parties where one had to dress as somebody else, almost naked parties in St. John's Wood, parties in flats and studios and houses and ships and hotels and night clubs, in windmills and swimming baths, tea parties at school where one ate muffins and meringues and tinned crab, parties at Oxford where one drank brown sherry and smoked Turkish cigarettes, dull dances in London and comic dances in Scotland and disgusting dances in Paris—all that succession and repetition of massed humanity. . . .

———

All those parties bring food to mind. Here's a description from "Altered Tastes" by Maria Konnikova:

> A plate was silently placed in front of me, or rather, a dark brown platform of what looked at first to be sod (actually a mixture of beetroot and mushroom powder with truffle), adorned with bursts of yellow pollen (a compact butter with truffle, root vegetables, and salt), anchored by a crinkled log (potato-starch paper covered in smoked salt, powdered mushroom, and porcini), punctuated by tiny green leaves (fig leaves), and at the bottom a thin layer of mushrooms (button, anchored by a mushroom stock jelly).

Are you hungry yet?

FOR THE WRITER

Marathon sentences don't have to go on forever (though some seem to!). They do need to pack in a wealth of information and hold the reader's interest. These prompts build your marathon skills.

INDICTMENT

Who or what has enraged you? Don't fight; write. List everything that's gone wrong, every fault, every incident. Now put your grievances in order. Group them into categories. Or, opt for escalation, moving from smaller offenses to larger ones. Then cram every point of your indictment into one sentence. Aim for a slam-dunk ending, rather than simply a slam. If you've built a good case, the reader should feel that your conclusion is inescapable. One word of advice: Don't share your indictment with opponents unless you're prepared to fight for real. And even then,

---

ULTRA-MARATHON

In the sentence world, there's long and then there's *long*. William Faulkner packed 1,288 words into one sentence of *Absalom, Absalom!* That's short compared to the last sentence of James Joyce's novel *Ulysses*, a 3,687-word soliloquy from Molly Bloom. Both pale in comparison to Bohumil Hrabal's *Dancing Lessons for the Advanced in Age*, a novel with just one 160-page sentence (as translated from the original Czech), and Mike McCormack's *Solar Bones*, with its 273-page sentence. Charles Dickens, Marcel Proust, and Virginia Woolf are also reliable ultra-marathoners.

---

stay away from physical expressions of anger, unless you're willing to be indicted yourself.

PLAY-BY-PLAY

I hope you've never experienced a swarm of locusts or a lion attack, but I imagine at one time or another you've been caught up in a fast-paced event. (If not, watch a minute or so of a hockey game and you'll have enough to work with.)

Write everything that happened: what you did, what others on the scene did, what you thought, what you saw or heard or felt . . . in short, all the details you can supply. Arrange them chronologically, from the first moment of the event through to the last. Now fashion a sentence that leads the reader through the event.

THE THINKER

You can be the focus of this exercise, but you can also peer into the mind of a character you've created. Either way, write every thought that pops up in, say, three minutes. Don't worry about punctuation or grammar as you record ideas. Those niceties can come later. Instead, take dictation from your brain. You'll be too slow, of course, to capture everything. Your hands will never be as quick as your mind. Nevertheless, aim for completeness.

Now that you have raw material, apply technique. Select details that reinforce a theme or emotion (regret, amazement, victory, urgency, and so forth). Move the details around and add enough context to help the reader understand what you're trying to express. Refine the wording, and apply grammar and punctuation rules. If your sentence is successful, your reader should have a clear impression of the character's mood or personality.

SIMPLICITY

Aim for grace.

—Ann Beattie, "Learning to Fall"

Writing with simplicity can be a complex process. First, authors must decide what's important. Next, they must ruthlessly omit interesting but extraneous information. Last, they must summon courage, because a whittled-down sentence offers no room to disguise or soften. If authors achieve simplicity, though, the rewards are ample. Simplicity adds depth and contrast. It's a refreshing change for the reader after marathon-length or ornately detailed sentences. And by choosing just the right, simple words, worlds of meaning open up.

Take Ann Beattie's sentence, the last of her story "Learning to Fall." Its three words serve as the capstone to three character arcs: that of the narrator, her friend Ruth, and Ruth's eight-year-old son, Andrew. As the story begins, the narrator picks up Andrew from his home in a suburb of Manhattan for their twice-monthly visit to the city. The narrator likes Andrew, but she admits that the trip is an excuse to see Ray, a man with whom she recently had an affair. Ruth's romantic life is also complicated. Andrew's father left her when she was pregnant and never returned. Ruth's lover visits her while Andrew is out, happy to be alone with her but unwilling to commit himself to a relationship. The boy is also struggling. Injured slightly at birth, Andrew is self-conscious about the paralyzed corner of his mouth and the slow pace of his learning at school.

Andrew and the narrator visit a museum, eat at the boy's favorite restaurant, and pick up some photos for Ruth. They miss their intended train home. Faced with a long wait, the narrator arranges to meet Ray at the station. She says, "I always mean not to call him, but I almost always do." The adults have coffee, Andrew a milkshake. Andrew confides that his mother is "learning to fall" in her dance class. They set out for a walk, and the narrator discourages Ray from holding her hand. Ray drapes an arm around her shoulder, making them "the proper gentleman and the lady out for a stroll." That's when the narrator discovers what "Ruth has known all along: what will happen can't be stopped." Then comes the featured sentence: *Aim for grace.*

The narrator speaks about her day in the present tense, dipping into past tense as she recalls prior events. Present tense suits the narrator's realization that she has little control over the future, or "what will happen." Her marriage may be doomed, and a renewed relationship with Ray may be inevitable. In this sense, the narrator has been "learning to fall" in love. Ruth may also fall someday—literally or figuratively or both. And Andrew will always have a paralyzed mouth and other challenges. The trick, as Ruth has been learning in dance class, is to fall with *grace*.

However, *grace* isn't guaranteed. It's a goal, something they *aim* at and therefore something they may miss. Significantly, the featured sentence is a command. *Aim* even though you don't know "what will happen," Beattie says through her narrator. The simplicity of her sentence strips away illusions and justifications. For dealing with what remains, *aim for grace* is the best option.

REALITY, WANTED OR NOT

A science-fiction writer once defined reality as "that which, when you stop believing in it, doesn't go away." The couple in Ernest Hemingway's story "Hills Like White Elephants" can't ignore reality, but they do their best to sidestep it. Almost every sentence in the story is a terse statement or question. Implied is that the woman is on her way to have an abortion. The man continually tries to reassure her that "it's simple." She asks him over and over if "it will be nice again" afterwards. She tells him:

I don't care about me.

The candor of her comment shakes him. He counters with "I care about you." She acknowledges his love, repeats her earlier statement, and tells him that she'll "do it and then everything will be fine."

What's apparent from their conversation is that she truly doesn't care about herself. Rather, she cares about the relationship, the one she had with him before becoming pregnant and the one she wishes she could have with him and their child. At one point she gestures to the land around the station: "And we could have all this . . . we can have everything." The reader knows that she's not talking about the view. The man seems to agree, but he's talking about a life unencumbered by a child. She says that "once they take it away, you never get it back."

What they both really want is *to want* the same thing, but that's impossible. He tells her several times, "I don't want you to do anything that you don't want to do." Yet when she says, "We could get along," implying that family life is manageable, he answers, "I don't want anybody but you." There's no way out of this dilemma for them, but he continues to look for one. The story and the quarrel have no resolution, just the stark honesty of *I don't care about me* and the equally stark dishonesty of her last words in the story: "I feel fine."

———

Dissonance is also a factor in *Eliot: A Soldier's Fugue*, a play by Quiara Alegría Hudes about a military family. The grandfather (Grandpop) served in the Korean War, the father (Pop) in Vietnam, and the son (Eliot) in Iraq. The mother, too, is a veteran. She was a nurse in Vietnam, where she met Pop.

As the play begins, Eliot is home on leave with a severe but healing leg wound. Civilians praise him as a hero, a label Eliot rejects. The family has never discussed their military service, but after serving in Iraq,

Eliot pressures Pop for information. Eliot is desperate to contextualize his experience there, but Pop is still unwilling to speak.

The story floats around in time, with characters frequently narrating the stage directions that govern their own actions. At one point, Grandpop says:

A boy enters.

and then comes on stage in full combat gear. The line hits hard. The audience sees a soldier, ready to kill and to die for his country. But he's a *boy*. As an old man looking back at himself, Grandpop acknowledges his immaturity. His grandson is barely eighteen when he leaves for Iraq, but his stage direction, which he reads out loud, is "a man enters." The audience hears that line but sees a kid posing in front of a mirror, playfully pretending to trash-talk rivals. This is before Eliot's service begins, when he idealizes war as glorious and manly. Pop is somewhere in the middle. His stage direction is "a young man enters."

Regardless of the terms the characters use, the audience witnesses the toll war takes on soldiers. Whether it happens to *a boy* or to someone who thinks of himself as "a man" or "a young man," the pain is the same. The simplicity of Hudes's line gives the audience no escape from this truth.

OPENING DOORS

Though simplicity sounds like the ultimate form of direct expression, a sentence with this trait can carry many levels of meaning. In a restaurant review, for instance, Ligaya Mishan begins:

A momo is a dumpling, and yet.

And yet? That's a door to more information, which the article goes on to provide, including the form, taste, history, and cultural significance of momos. *And yet* encompasses an Indian politician who burned momos in effigy because the popular dumplings were a "threat to national identity," YouTube videos with recipes for new momo flavors, and much more. The critic's opening sentence draws readers in and makes them (or me, at least) yearn to try *a dumpling*, preferably one with *and yet*.

————

A simple question can also evoke a sweeping judgment. In her story "Fredo Avila," Gina Apostol recounts the title character's dream to be a contestant on *The Price Is Right*. Fredo and his neighbors idealize Beverly Hills, where the show is taped, as the opposite of the rural Filipino town they live in. Fredo actually gets on the show, winning a "high-tech, 4-speed, mirrored bubblegum machine" and a few other small prizes. When he returns, he asks the narrator one question:

Danny, did you know there is dust in America?

Dust: not the hallmark of luxury or perfection. With that question, Fredo's disillusionment becomes evident. Soon after, he dies. Another character, Eusebia, remarks tersely that "dreams are wounds."

————

In the face of an overwhelming event, simplicity makes a strong statement. *New York Times* reporter A. M. Rosenthal knew this when he visited the concentration camp at Auschwitz fourteen years after the end of World War II. It was, Rosenthal said, "a place of unutterable terror." He was struck by the incongruity of what he saw at the gates: a sunny day, green grass, and children playing. The title of Rosenthal's article sums up his reaction:

There is no news from Auschwitz.

An apt title, for really, what could adequately memorialize the suffering and death that the Nazis perpetrated at Auschwitz? Rosenthal noted that not to write "would somehow be a most grievous act of discourtesy" to the millions who died there. And so he wrote. The simplicity of Rosenthal's sentence isn't an evasion; it's an evocation of unspeakable evil.

CHARACTER DEVELOPMENT

People are seldom simple, but the sentences that best illuminate their characters—and in some cases the communities they belong to—often are. Such is the case with Thomas Cromwell, the protagonist of Hilary Mantel's historical novel *Wolf Hall*. In one scene Cromwell recalls his boyhood visits to the house of Cardinal Morton, where his uncle is a cook. Young Cromwell spends a lot of time in the kitchen, hoping to secure leftover food, and frequently runs errands for the staff. One day he brings "a wheaten loaf" to Thomas More, who is a page in Morton's household, a position awarded to the teenage sons of upper-class families. Cromwell lingers until More makes it clear that he is unwelcome. Mantel writes:

But he did not throw anything at him.

The *he* in this sentence is More, the *him* Cromwell. (The story is told from Cromwell's point of view.) In that short sentence, the effects of Cromwell's upbringing as the child of an abusive, alcoholic father are apparent. Cromwell lingers in More's chamber because he covets the status More has by birth. Even though Cromwell eventually rises to the highest levels of the English court, he never leaves his violent past behind, and for many years his tendency to anticipate threats serves him well.

———

Margaret Schlegel, a character in E. M. Forster's *Howards End*, is anything but violent. Her line, indeed her philosophy of life, is simplicity itself:

Only connect.

These days, *only connect* is the preferred bromide offered to the socially isolated, but the sentence has a more specific meaning in Forster's novel. Margaret represents England's cultural elite. Her fiancé, Henry Wilcox, is a pragmatic materialist. If they can *only connect*, Forster implies, the nation will be stronger. But Margaret's sentence also says much about her character as an individual. With *only connect*, she's giving herself a command. She knows that Henry has never resolved the tension between his body's desires and his spiritual views. She must *only connect* the two in him, she believes, and then he will no longer be "a little ashamed of loving a wife." Margaret's crusade is simple and, she thinks, "need not take the form of a good 'talking.'" Rather, she plans to lead by "quiet indications," building a bridge to "span their lives with beauty." Margaret's plan arises from naive idealism. *Only connect* is much more difficult than she realizes.

––––––

No one would call Sam Spade idealistic. He's the protagonist of Dashiell Hammett's *The Maltese Falcon*, a hard-boiled detective who has seen everything. When he discovers that his lover has killed his partner, he talks with her in a "soft, gentle" voice:

If they hang you, I'll always remember you.

She, not surprisingly, has hoped that he'll ignore her crime because he loves her. She's not comforted by his opinion that she'll serve only twenty years. Spade's line perfectly reflects his cynicism, which comes from hoping for the best but expecting the worst of human nature.

––––––

Faye Travers is cynical, too, at the beginning of Louise Erdrich's novel *The Painted Drum*, constructed from three interwoven story lines. Faye's sister died when the siblings were little, and Faye has tried to shield herself from further pain by keeping others at bay. Faye notes that her house in New England can be reached by

No true path.

Faye's sentence has no verb, because she's allowed herself no *true* movement in her life. She's stuck until she steals the "painted drum" of the title and travels to the Ojibwe reservation, where the drum was made, to return it. There Faye learns more about the drum's history. Eventually she confronts her restricted life and realizes that "you have to love" and "you are here [on earth] to risk your heart." Erdrich's choice of *path* emphasizes that understanding oneself and forming relationships is not a single event, but a journey.

FOR THE WRITER

No writer turns to simplicity in every sentence, except perhaps in parody. But well-placed simplicity accomplishes what no other sort of writing can. My advice: dare to be simple, sometimes, no matter how hard it is.

SCREENWRITER

Television's most famous feminist of the 1970s, Maude (from the show of the same name), summed up her goals in one sentence: "I want it all." The plotlines of the series cast doubt on the feasibility of that goal, but her statement captured the character. So did Dirty Harry's "Go ahead, make my day." Played by Clint Eastwood, the line epitomized the character's toughness and willingness to shoot the bad guys of *Sudden Impact*.

Your goal is to formulate a sentence that reveals character. Your line can be for a film, show, or story written by someone else, or it can be the basis for a character you create.

REALITY, SIMPLIFIED

Search your memory or check the news. Focus on an important event—or one that's important to no one but you. Of the many things you can say about the event, select one key fact. Now write a sentence to express the fact. Keep it simple. Here's an example:

SITUATION: The Cathedral of Notre Dame is on fire. Millions around the world watch firefighters battle the blaze. The roof with its wooden supports is engulfed by flames, and the spire topples.
SENTENCE: History is burning.

Later, if you wish, you can write a full narrative to expand on the idea of your initial sentence.

SIGNIFICANT DETAIL

Think of your writing as a camera lens. For some shots, you want a wide angle; for others, a tight focus. For this exercise, select a significant detail. Express it in a no-frills sentence. For example, suppose you're writing about a birthday party for a ten-year-old. There are five guests, all the same age. Then

Sheila inhaled two slices of pizza.

The next event, as I witnessed it, wasn't a trip to the emergency room. It was a rush to party games.

RADICAL HONESTY

Imagine a conversation between two people you know. (Insert yourself as one of them, if you wish.) Strip away all qualifiers, all evasions. Write a line of dialogue that states the truth baldly. An example:

THE CONTEXT: Bill wants to know why Henry didn't tell him about his new job.
HENRY'S LINE: I didn't want to deal with your jealousy.

Ouch! But refreshing, too. Warning: You may want to password protect this exercise if it reflects a real relationship. Simplicity has its downside.

CONTRADICTION

It's heavy, this lightness.

—Margaret Atwood, "Orphan Stories"

"A foolish consistency is the hobgoblin of little minds," wrote Ralph Waldo Emerson in his essay "Self-Reliance." A fair number of writers and artists seem to have beaten that hobgoblin (a folklore creature often seen as wicked) and opted for contradiction. And why not? To consider another point of view, to acknowledge complexity, and to take into account emotion as well as logic—all of these are good ideas, most of the time. Not always. Expecting that would be foolish consistency indeed.

Consider the contradiction in Margaret Atwood's four-word sentence, which appears in one section of "Orphan Stories," a meditation on the appeal of (do I need to say it?) orphan stories. In a series of quick takes, Atwood examines the role of orphans in fiction: They're dangerous outsiders or hapless victims, objects of charity that gratify the giver or blank slates on which to project fears and desires. In one section of "Orphan Stories," Atwood compares orphans to snails, who carry nothing with them but their homes, empty shells. They travel light, but as Atwood notes, *It's heavy, this lightness.*

By definition, *lightness* can't be *heavy*. Neither can emptiness. But who hasn't experienced or witnessed the *heavy* feeling of disconnection, of solitude, of rootlessness? In a figurative sense, *lightness* can very well be *heavy*. That's, of course, the sense of *lightness* Atwood employs. But to make her point, she had other choices at her disposal:

It's hard to be alone.

To have nothing to call your own is a burden.

Without connections and possessions, a house is not a home.

All of these statements work, but none contradict themselves. So what does Atwood gain from that option? A nod to that favorite English-teacher topic, appearance versus reality, for one. In the midst of clutter, bareness appeals. A net of family and friends can feel confining and the open road inviting. But snip the threads of the net and you register, immediately or eventually, the lack. The net may weigh you down, but it also anchors you.

Atwood's contradictory sentence also calls the concept of *lightness* into question. Remember, Atwood is talking about orphans. But every orphan has a past, even if it is unknown. Atwood writes that the snail's home, its shell, is filled with "nothing but yourself." No one's "self" grows in a vacuum. The people an orphan encounters and everything an orphan experiences leave a residue; *lightness* is an illusion or, at most, a temporary state.

Heavy can also be defined as "striking with force or violence," as in a *heavy* blow. Atwood hints at this meaning, too. After the featured sentence are these words: "it's crushing, that emptiness." A snail shell feels like protection, but it's brittle. Inside is the vulnerable creature, the self. With "nothing but yourself," what can really protect you? Not a shell. Only a net.

It's hard to read this passage from "Orphan Stories" without thinking of Atwood, the writer. To sit inside a shell in *lightness* with "nothing but yourself" sounds like the default state of poets and fiction writers, who spin ideas out of nothing but their own minds. Consider, then, how *heavy* it feels for writers to be without ideas. Every writer has blanked at least once, and it's a *heavy* feeling.

One more point: Atwood rejects the more conventional sentence *this lightness is heavy*. She begins with a vague pronoun-verb contraction (*it's*, short for *it is*). When you read *it's heavy*, you naturally expect *it* to stand in for something like lead, bricks, sorrow, duty . . . something immediately recognizable as *heavy*. Instead, you run into a contradiction. The word order keeps the reader—and the hobgoblin of consistency—off-balance.

LOVE AND CONTRADICTION

Is there anything more contradictory than love? Lovers reach the heights of joy and the depths of despair, sometimes simultaneously. Consider two of the world's most famous teenagers, Romeo and Juliet, who exhibit every stereotype associated with their age group. In the Shakespearean play named after them, they rebel against their families, jump to conclusions, and act without thinking. In the first scene, before he's even met Juliet, Romeo examines the spot where a fight has just occurred. He notes that the brawl has "much to do with hate but more with love," establishing a link between the two extreme feelings that fuel the action of the play. He continues:

> Feather of lead, bright smoke, cold fire, sick health,
> Still-waking sleep, that is not what it is.

Romeo is speaking of his unrequited love for Rosaline, a young woman who has pledged chastity. His words exhibit a trait often celebrated in the sonnets of the Elizabethan era (and earlier): intense passion directed to an idealized, unattainable person. Romeo's contradictory statements suggest that he isn't thinking clearly. And he's not. Within a day, his intense "love" for Rosaline is over because he's found a new one—Juliet. "Sweet sorrow" ensues. Romeo is, as Juliet puts it, "My only love sprung from my only hate!" Their families are sworn enemies.

Shakespeare's images—*feather of lead, bright smoke, cold fire, sick health, still-waking sleep*—are at war with reality because the lovers are. One glance, one evening, a speedy marriage, and a quick death—does that add up to love? Perhaps. The beauty of Shakespeare's poetry easily carries his audience into Romeo and Juliet's belief in their love, which may be Shakespeare's belief also. It's worth noting, though, that Romeo and Juliet die before daily life has a chance to step in. Would their infatuation, if that's what it is, have matured into true love? Shakespeare doesn't have to supply an answer.

Feather and *lead* are on opposite ends of the weight scale, just as *cold* and *fire* are on a thermometer. These contradictory phrases express a truth about the lovers: they're willing to go to extremes. *Bright* implies clarity, and *smoke* the opposite. Both Romeo and Juliet believe that they understand what's happening, but they don't. Juliet thinks that she can solve all her problems by feigning death; she can't. Romeo kills himself because he believes that Juliet is dead; she's not. The last two contradictory pairs, *sick* and *health* and *waking* and *sleep*, can't coexist. Neither can Romeo and Juliet exist as a couple. Their families won't allow the match, nor will society condone it. Shakespeare's language fits the theme of *Romeo and Juliet* and ensures that these lovers, who never lived, live on.

———

So, too, do Arthurian legends endure. "Lancelot and Elaine" is one section of *Idylls of the King*, a reimagining of Arthurian legends by Alfred Lord Tennyson. He sets up an impossible situation in "Lancelot and Elaine"—more a love rectangle than a triangle. Elaine is in love with Lancelot and nurses him back to health even though she knows he's in love with Guinevere, the wife of King Arthur. Lancelot feels a great deal of affection for Elaine and says that "had he seen her first," they might have made a good match. But

The shackles of an old love straitened him,
His honour rooted in dishonour stood,
And faith unfaithful kept him falsely true.

The *old love* is Guinevere, and he must be true to her because his *honour* is at stake. Because she's married, that *honour* is *rooted in dishonour.* He must be faithful to her, but the adulterous nature of their relationship makes his *faith unfaithful.* Still, he keeps his promise to Guinevere and stays *falsely true* to her. Contradictions abound in these phrases, as they do in the situation.

CONTRADICTORY EVENTS

Charles Dickens's famous sentence about the French Revolutionary period is a master (some would say monster) example of contradiction:

> It was the best of times, it was the worst of times, it was the age of wisdom, it was the age of foolishness, it was the epoch of belief, it was the epoch of incredulity, it was the season of Light, it was the season of Darkness, it was the spring of hope, it was the winter of despair, we had everything before us, we had nothing before us, we were all going direct to Heaven, we were all going direct the other way—in short, the period was so far like the present period, that some of its noisiest authorities insisted on its being received, for good or for evil, in the superlative degree of comparison only.

A Tale of Two Cities highlights duality in its title and elaborates on that theme with paired places (London and Paris) and paired characters. Sydney Carton and Charles Darnay bear a strong physical resemblance. Carton is a drunken wastrel, but he redeems himself by smuggling Darnay out of France and submitting to the guillotine in Darnay's place. Darnay, a member of an aristocratic family, renounces them and makes his life in England. Darnay's uncle exemplifies the arrogance of the French nobility, displaying no guilt when his carriage kills a poor child. His cruelty matches that of the revolutionary Madame Defarge, who will be satisfied only when all aristocrats have been executed.

The novel's duality fits well with the contradictory pairs Dickens chose: *best* and *worst, wisdom* and *foolishness, belief* and *incredulity, Light* and *Darkness, hope* and *despair*, and so forth. Dickens doesn't write "good" and "bad." He needs *best* and *worst* (the superlative degree of comparison) to fit the intensity of the French Revolution.

Dickens employs independent clauses (statements that can stand alone as complete sentences) to make his point forcefully: *It was the best of times, it was the worst of times* is more emphatic than "It was the best and worst of times." The sentence's length also adds force. The reader expects a break, but the sentence won't allow a pause, just as a revolution affords no chance to rest.

After ten *it* statements, Dickens abruptly switches the pronoun to *we*. The reader's inside the moment, attempting to evaluate what's happening (*we had everything . . . other way*). Dickens includes himself in that pronoun. The extreme injustice that gave rise to the French Revolution captured his sympathy, but the violence of the rebels disturbed him. He was caught in the middle of contradictory emotions, which his contradictory statements reflect but don't resolve. Instead, the massive sentence ends with a comparison to *the present period. A Tale of Two Cities* was published in 1859, many years after the French Revolution had succeeded and then failed. Today's readers may see the turbulence of our times, *the present period*, in Dickens's sentence as well.

———

Sportswriter Mike Royko, less wordy than Dickens, also notes contradictory feelings. Royko attended a baseball game when he was fifteen, during Jackie Robinson's first season in the major leagues. Robinson, an African American, had broken the barrier of segregation. As Robinson comes on the field, Royko observes:

A tall, middle-aged black man stood next to me, a smile of almost painful joy on his face, beating his palms together so hard they must have hurt.

To see a barrier fall brings *joy*, a noun, which is more important than its modifier, *painful*. Royko's description shows that the positive emotion dominates, but it's marred by the suffering that segregation has inflicted on the *middle-aged black man* and on Robinson himself.

————

A few more contradictory responses to events:

> If I could drop dead right now, I'd be the happiest man alive.
>   —Samuel Goldwyn (film producer)

> It's a step forward although there was no progress.
>   —Hosni Mubarek (president of Egypt, 1981–2011)

> I didn't do it, nobody saw me do it, there's no way you can prove anything.
>   —Bart Simpson, *The Simpsons*

YES! NO! BOTH!

Reality seems so simple, to a computer. A zero or a one, a yes or a no. But reality to a human being (and increasingly to advanced computers) is more complicated. Take this statement from Isaac Bashevis Singer:

> We must believe in free will—we have no other choice.

Though he contradicts himself, Singer's comment makes sense. If everything in life is predetermined, then everyone is a robot, moving on a path laid down by fate. But no one who claims to hold that belief can live accordingly. Free will may be an illusion, but it's one we can't live without. The most significant word in Singer's sentence is *other*. It's a nod to the array of possibilities we so often have in front of us: chocolate or vanilla, paper or plastic, stability or change, and so on. Extract *other* from the sentence, and you're left with compulsion. The overall meaning is the same, but the *other*-less sentence lands more robotically than Singer's version.

———

So, too, does artist Andy Warhol make sense of a contradiction:

I am a deeply superficial person.

Warhol insisted that anyone who wanted to know him should "look at the surface of my paintings and films and me, and there I am." But there's more to Warhol's "surface" than is immediately apparent. Consider his many images of cultural icons, such as Campbell's soup cans and celebrity portraits (Mao, Che Guevara, Elizabeth Taylor, and Jacqueline Kennedy, to name a few). The subjects are immediately recognizable (that's the *superficial* part) and thus represent the society they arise from (there's the *deeply*). Both *deeply* and *superficial* are descriptions, *deeply* an adverb and *superficial* an adjective. As parts of speech, adjectives and adverbs are usually equal in importance. In a sentence like "I skillfully drew a blue pig," the adverb *skillfully* and the adjective *blue* give information of similar importance. In Warhol's sentence, though, *deeply* modifies *superficial*, making *superficial* the key concept. This ranking bolsters Warhol's emphasis on "the surface"; however, *deeply* also changes the meaning of *superficial*. The contradiction makes sense because, as one art historian put it, Warhol "elevated the common to the unique."

———

Poet Edna St. Vincent Millay writes:

I like humanity, but I loathe persons.

Don't bother pointing out that *persons* are part of *humanity*. Instead, focus on how easy it is to care about groups large enough to become abstractions while treating one's neighbors and colleagues with indifference or disgust. Millay is not alone in her attitude, I suspect.

———

George Hegel's statement also rings true:

We learn from history that we do not learn from history.

How many wars could have been avoided, unwise laws rejected, or economic downturns prevented if Hegel were wrong! But history shows that too often he's right. "This time it will be different" is far too common an assumption.

———

A few more contradictions, some serious and some not:

No one goes there anymore, it's too crowded.
—Yogi Berra (baseball player)

A joke is an extremely serious issue.
—Winston Churchill

He could smell them and he could feel their eyes seeing him and not seeing him.
—Andre Dubus III, *Townies*

It usually takes me more than three weeks to prepare a good impromptu speech.
—Mark Twain

It [the wind on the Great Plains] is at once the most violent and placid motion in the universe.
—N. Scott Momaday, *The Names*

The best cure for insomnia is to get a lot of sleep.
—W. C. Fields

FOR THE WRITER

Check the day's news and most likely you'll find a contradiction . . . or a thousand contradictions. To develop your own contradictory powers, focus on words, not on situations.

DECISION TIME

Life poses many questions, and most of us spend quite a bit of time coming up with answers. But if you pose the same question to several people, you may end up with some contradictory answers. In fact, a contradiction may appear in a single answer. So—fashion some questions that invite contradictory answers. Then answer them. For example:

> QUESTION: Do you have trouble making up your mind?
> ANSWER: Well, yes and no.

If you wish, expand your answers into a monologue justifying each part of the contradiction, as you see here:

> I make a snap decision when I open my closet, because it's not worth my time to fret about the blue or the red shirt. Who cares? But ask me which movie I want to see, and I am paralyzed. There are so many out there I haven't seen, and I have limited time. What am I missing? FOMO, I guess.

FOMO, in case you don't text-abbreviate, means "fear of missing out."

ANTONYMS

Select some antonyms: *love* and *hate*, *asset* and *liability*, *generosity* and *selfishness*, *interest* and *boredom*, and so forth. How do they combine in the same person or situation? Write a sentence or two showing the contradiction. You don't have to use the words you chose, as long as the reader perceives the qualities they represent. Here's one to start you off:

Sydney was my best friend and would do anything for herself.

ALL-IN-ONE

Can you create a single word out of contradictory terms? Some already exist: *frenemy* (both a friend and an enemy) and *dramedy* (a show or story with elements of comedy and drama). Find some antonyms. (Your word-processing program might help here, or any dictionary.) Now blend the words together. Write a definition for the contradictory term.

DOUBLE TALK

In *1984*, George Orwell's imagined world, the government issues statements such as "War is Peace" and "Freedom is Slavery." Look for current events that have propaganda or political spin attached to them. Now write some double-talk of your own. It may help to imagine that you're writing in the voice of someone with an opposing view.

TIME

When she was small, her granny owned the house she will remember best.

— Karen Salyer McElmurray, "Consider the Houses"

You can name it and number its parts, but you can see nothing of it except its effects. You can attempt to disregard it, in life as well as in writing, but you'll never be free of it. Time doesn't work that way.

Writers deal with time, well, all the time. They may follow time on an arrow path forward or loop it around until it resembles yarn a cat tangled with. Some speak of time directly; others show its passage on the body, in a place, or through a sequence of actions.

Karen Salyer McElmurray, in "Consider the Houses," spirals time into a set of remembered dwellings. She takes the reader on a dreamlike tour of them, including the one that *her granny owned*, which *she will remember best*. The essay gives few clues to tether events to a specific time period. The first paragraph, for example, has no verbs, and therefore no verb tenses. Because tense is a grammatical way to indicate time, a verbless paragraph floats free from clock and calendar.

Which is not to say that time and verb tense don't appear in the essay. The featured sentence contains three verbs: *was, owned*, and *will remember*. The first two are in the past tense, the third in future tense. There is one anchor point, *small*, but it's vague. A baby and a toddler and a preteen child are all *small*. Context would help, but McElmurray withholds information. The reader knows only that the *small* narrator (McElmurray) has a *granny*, not how old each was. From that hazy starting point, the third verb (*will remember*) projects into the future. McElmurray seems to be there already, explaining what happened after she was no longer *small*. She now knows which house she *will remember best*, though McElmurray doesn't explain when "now" is.

McElmurray selects verb tenses and time clues carefully, intentionally muddling the time line to reflect how memory works. In this story, the progression of time is the creation of memories. McElmurray flashes light for just a moment on physical objects or events in the houses she asks the reader to *consider*. After allowing a glimpse, she moves on. The house *her granny owned*, for instance, has a hidden stash of letters, deeds, and "one X-ray of a hand," all bringing the more distant past into a *small* girl's memory of that place.

Matching form with theme, McElmurray surfs waves of time, moving backward and forward freely as she recounts dreams, which are themselves remembered bits of thought. She cites a house with a collection of antique shoes that she visits "much later on." How much later? McElmurray doesn't explain. At "another time" there's a house in "a college town" where her father calls her to remind her to "give some time" to Jesus. What other time? How much time? Again, no answers appear. Her concern isn't the houses but rather her experiences of them, which become memories as they occur.

The essay ends with the statement that "her house will have sunlight and love and the reach of hands across the clean, clear glass of windowpanes." Is she in the past, projecting what awaits her? Or is she in the present, expressing a hope that in the future she will attain her ideal house? The reader can't be sure, and that's exactly the effect McElmurray wants. She writes that we "are never real historians, but always near-poets." Poetry relies on figurative language to express reality, just as the images of houses in this essay capture time. Even seen through "clean, clear glass," her memories won't achieve clarity. Memories never do.

TRACKING TIME

Marking time by its effects, Rumer Godden begins her novel *Take Three Tenses* with an "inventory" of a house belonging to a family that can trace its roots far earlier than the construction of their home:

> "We existed before you, you see," the family might have said to the house; and the house, in its tickings, its rustlings, its creakings as its beams grow hot, grow cold—as the ashes fall in its grates, as its doorbells ring, as the trains in passing underneath it vibrate in its walls, as footsteps run up and down the stairs—as dusters are shaken, carpets beaten, beds turned down and dishes washed—as windows are opened or shut, blinds drawn up, pulled down—as the tap runs and is silent, as the lavatory is flushed—as the piano is played and books are taken down from the shelf, and brushes picked up and laid down again on the dressing-table, and flowers are arranged in a vase—as the medicine bottle is shaken; as, with, infinite delicate care, the spillikins are lifted in the children's game—as the mice run under the wainscot—the house might steadfastly reply, "I know! I know. All the same, in me you exist."

This marathon sentence contains the whole of daily life, as experienced by the house. Any one action moves time forward (*blinds drawn up, pulled down*, for example), but nothing changes. Everyday life, in this passage, is a succession of repetitive activities.

———

E. L. Doctorow, in his short story "All the Time in the World," records time through construction:

> After a flag tops things off as if they were all sailing somewhere, they load in the elevator, do the wiring, the plumbing, they tack

on the granite facing and set in the windows through which you see they've walled in the apartments, and before you know it there's a canopy to the curb, a doorman, and upstairs just across the street from my window, a fully furnished bedroom and a naked girl dancing.

The flag Doctorow refers to is the one traditionally hoisted when construction workers frame the top floor of a building. The building is complete when residents begin their lives in it, like the *naked girl dancing*. Here's one more from the same Doctorow story:

It dawns on me metaphorically that I have never appreciated the bus stop for the ancient invention it is.

A place to load and unload sledges, hand-carts, chariots . . . Doctorow draws a straight line from them to modern public transport.

———

Don DeLillo records the passing of time with water from a kitchen faucet in his novella *The Body Artist*:

It [the water] ran silvery and clear and then in seconds turned opaque and how curious it seemed that in all these months and all these times in which she'd run water from the kitchen tap she'd never noticed how the water ran clear at first and then went not murky but opaque, or maybe it hadn't happened before, or she'd noticed and forgotten.

This single moment expands into months, as the title character questions the accuracy of her observation and DeLillo muses on the nature of time, which another character calls "the force that tells you who you are."

———

Nora Ephron, in "My Cookbook Crushes," describes the passage of time in a comical way:

> This [her marriage] was right around the time arugula was dis-
> covered, which was followed by endive, which was followed by
> radicchio, which was followed by frisée, which was followed by
> the three M's—mesclun, mache, and microgreens—and that, in
> a nutshell, is the history of the past forty years from the point of
> view of lettuce.

———

Alice Walker's story "Advancing Luna—and Ida B. Wells" situates a point in time in the most somber way possible:

> John Kennedy and Malcolm X had already been assassinated,
> but King had not been and Bobby Kennedy had not been.

———

And then there's the timekeeping of adultery. A character in Lillian Hellman's play *Watch on the Rhine* remarks:

> Fashions in sin change.

The character who says this is perplexed that someone has chosen a French lover. "In my day it was Englishmen," she explains.

———

Jorge Luis Borges, in "The Threatened," charts time through a relationship:

To be with you and not to be with you is my measure of time.

––––––––

and Cormac McCarthy, in *All the Pretty Horses*, through the body:

Scars have the strange power to remind us that our past is real.

––––––––

In *On Photography*, Susan Sontag describes how a camera captures time:

Precisely by slicing out this moment and freezing it, all photographs testify to time's relentless melt.

––––––––

Donald Hall in *Life Work* traces time's passage through his ancestor's business:

From hired hand he became middleman, founding the Hall Dairy—that would grow, expand, combine with Charlie Brock's to become Brock-Hall Dairy, wax over southern Connecticut, acquire moribund family dairies, metamorphose stables of workhorses into fleets of delivery trucks . . . and finally fail, *fail*, as supermarkets with loss-leader half-gallon milk cartons knocked out home delivery in the 1950s and 1960s.

––––––––

Arata Isozaki muses on time as expressed in his profession:

Like the universe, architecture comes out of nothing, becomes something and eventually becomes nothing again.

TIME ZONES

As in the featured sentence, authors often write in two or more time periods simultaneously, recollecting the past or pondering the future, both from the present. In this sentence from Charles Dickens's *Great Expectations*, the narrator considers how a seemingly small event can have long-lasting repercussions. Speaking directly to the reader, he says:

> Pause you who read this, and think for a moment of the long chain of iron or gold, of thorns or flowers, what would never have bound you, but for the formation of the first link on one memorable day.

———

In her novel *Leaving Atlanta*, Tayari Jones looks at the transition from childhood to puberty:

> But that was before last summer's rains changed the girls.

Changed how? All the girls started the new school year wearing new "pink training bras."

———

A few more time-slips:

> I wondered whether our marrying should really be this notch in the belt of time.
>
> —Lorrie Moore, "One Hot Summer,
> or a Brief History of Time"

He already had the music at the ends of the sentences which he hadn't yet begun.

—Théophile Gautier (poet), describing Flaubert (novelist)

The future came and went, in the mildly discouraging way that futures do.

—Neil Gaiman and Terry Pratchett,
*Good Omens: The Nice and Accurate
Prophecies of Agnes Nutter, Witch*

But it was like I aimed my fork at the fish but kept accidentally skewering something else—my future reminiscence of it.

—Charles Comey, "Against Honeymoons"

Andy Kaplan is going to turn out the sort of spatial brilliant that can rotate irregular objects in his head, but for now he's just a pale sprout of a guy with spittle on his braces.

—Gish Jen, *Mona in the Promised Land*

———

Many authors tackle the impossible: understanding the unremembered past or the unforeseeable future. Here's another character from Tayari Jones's *Leaving Atlanta*:

With closed eyes you try to trace memory to its origin, to the instant you were born.

———

and one from Edith Wharton's short story "A Cup of Cold Water":

It was certainly curious to reflect, as he leaned against the door-way of Mrs. Gildermere's ball-room, enveloped in the warm

WHAT TIME IS

Not content with telling time through stories and characterization, some authors can't resist making philosophical statements about time itself:

All we have to decide is what to do with the time that is given us.
—J. R. R. Tolkien, *The Fellowship of the Ring*

It is the time you have wasted for your rose that makes your rose so important.
—Antoine de Saint-Exupéry, *The Little Prince*

The past is never dead. It's not even past.
—William Faulkner, *Requiem for a Nun*

Time is an illusion.
—Albert Einstein

People assume that time is a strict progression of cause to effect, but *actually* from a non-linear, non-subjective viewpoint—it's more like a big ball of wibbly wobbly . . . time-y wime-y . . . stuff.
—Steven Moffat, *Doctor Who*

Time folds you in its arms and gives you one last kiss, and then it flattens you out and folds you up and tucks you away until it's time for you to become someone else's past time, and then time folds again.
—Margaret Atwood, "Heritage House"

Time takes it all, whether you want it to or not.
—Stephen King, *The Green Mile*

atmosphere of the accustomed, that twenty-four hours later the people brushing by him with looks of friendly recognition would start at the thought of having seen him and slur over the recollection of having taken his hand!

Wharton's narrator thinks he understands what will happen in the next *twenty-four hours*, but he doesn't.

––––––––

This unrealistic fantasy is from the narrator of Margaret Atwood's "Life Stories," who has "discovered the virtues of scissors" that snip away eras of her existence:

> Adolescence can be discarded too, with its salty tanned skin, its fecklessness and bad romance and leakages of seasonal blood.

All that remains, when Atwood's narrator finishes cutting, is *I*, the essential self.

––––––––

To sum up, a philosophical stance from the Doors, from their song "Roadhouse Blues":

> The future is uncertain and the end is always near.

FOR THE WRITER

You're dealing with time in your writing (not to mention time *for* your writing) whenever you have an idea to express. The trick is to do so in an artful way, selecting verb tense or descriptions that reveal more than what's on the clock. I must note, as someone who cares about proper grammar, that only when you know the standard meanings of each tense can you bend or break the rules to achieve the effect you intended.

TIME WITHOUT A CLOCK

Practice telling time without a clock by placing cultural references into your sentences instead of dates. For example:

> I met Alex just as Mamie Eisenhower bangs gave way to the Jacqueline Kennedy bouffant.

This sentence situates your reader around 1959–60. The danger of this technique is that it may work perfectly with some readers and not with others. My example is incomprehensible to people who never saw photos of these first ladies. Similarly, references to Bruno Mars and Beyoncé may befuddle those who don't listen to current music. But it's fun to experiment. In addition to hairstyles and musicians, try these time markers: fads, the hot toy for a holiday gift, the most popular tech gadget, films or television shows, dance crazes, or clothing styles. Write sentences that span a few time periods identified by cultural allusions.

SWEET SPOT

The "sweet spot" is what I call the period of time between two undesirable alternatives. For instance, between pimples and age spots or between begging for a later bedtime and desperately trying to carve out a few more hours of sleep from the workweek.

Look for your own "sweet spots" and attach them to characters who are in, just past, or still looking forward to them. If you're ambitious, write their stories.

ONE FOR THE AGES

Try your hand at communicating the age of a character without resorting to numbers. Gish Jen, for example, sums up the awkwardness of preadolescence as "chin-to-chest disease." A former student referred to old age as the time when "everyone's glasses get bigger" (presumably to accommodate progressive lenses). The Sphinx's riddle refers to four legs in the morning (babyhood, when the child crawls), two legs in the afternoon (adulthood, walking upright), and three legs in the evening (old age, with a cane).

SPLITS

Stories that weave two time periods together in alternating bands are popular, and not just in print. Films and television shows also play with time. Create a sentence or two that might appear in a plot from one or more of these patterns:

- Flashback (interrupt an event with a scene from an earlier point in the character's life)
- Flash-forward (insert a teaser about the future)
- Paired characters living in different eras (two children with the same home, one in 1860 and one in 1960, for example)
- Time travel (not just for science fiction!)

Eager for more? Turn your plotline into a fully developed story.

IMPOSSIBILITY

Who would have thought that a little old baby could harbor so
much rage?

—Toni Morrison, *Beloved*

What is it about the impossible—science fiction, magical realism, fantasy, legend, myth—that's irresistible? Is it the reach beyond one's grasp? The idea that another universe exists—somewhere that's anywhere but here? Perhaps it's that individual words or short phrases expressing the impossible sometimes say more about reality than facts do.

The featured sentence comes from Toni Morrison's novel *Beloved*, a work that nods to magical realism, a genre presenting the impossible in minute, seemingly realistic detail. In *Beloved*, the ghost of a murdered baby haunts her family and eventually takes on the physical body of a young woman. *Beloved* isn't an ordinary paranormal tale, however. It's a study of the effects of trauma, specifically the trauma of slavery. In that light, the novel isn't magical realism, but rather psychological realism.

A *baby* can be *little*, but not *old*. True, *little old* can be a single description, one of mock humility ("little old me") or endearment ("my little old house"). In the featured sentence, the second usage makes some sense. The sentence comes from the thoughts of Sethe, who escaped from a plantation called "Sweet Home" that was anything but sweet or a home. Enslaved since birth, Sethe has just twenty-eight days of freedom before the plantation overseer finds her. As he approaches, Sethe hustles her four children into a shed. Rather than see them subjected to the horrors she experienced, Sethe attempts to slit her children's throats. She succeeds in killing one. That child is known only by the word Sethe orders carved on her tombstone, *Beloved.* The word reflects Sethe's motive: she killed because she loved.

But *little old baby* means much more than endearment. The *baby*, filled with *so much rage*, stays in Sethe's house. There she wreaks havoc on Sethe and her remaining family. The community shuns them because of Sethe's crime. Twenty years later, Paul D., who was enslaved on the same plantation as Sethe, arrives. That's when Beloved takes physical form.

Beloved, the *old baby*, is the personification of Sethe's trauma—the degradation of rape, the pain of whipping, the guilt of infanticide. The *old baby* also embodies Beloved's trauma—her violent murder and the loss of a free life with a loving mother. The *old baby* is the trauma of Paul D. and Sethe's remaining daughter, too, and by extension, of the community they live in. A key word in the sentence is *harbor*, a verb that may mean "shelter" or "protect." Although Sethe's act begins as an attempt to protect her daughter, her home shelters *rage.* Isolation and unspoken horrors nurture the *rage*, as do repressed emotions. And like a baby, the *rage* grows. They must all confront what happened, on the plantation and afterward, before they can expel the *rage* of the *old baby* and begin to heal.

It's significant that the featured sentence is a question, not a statement. *Who would have thought?* applies to the consequences of the murder, of being enslaved, of severing the bonds of community, and more. Nor are these consequences solely in the past. Morrison implies that our national trauma of slavery remains. In an introduction to the novel she writes that *Beloved* is an invitation to readers and to herself to enter "the repellant landscape" that is "hidden, but not completely; deliberately buried, but not forgotten": an *old baby* whose needs must be tended.

ESSENTIAL TRUTHS

In her poem entitled "Poetry," Marianne Moore begins by saying, "I, too, dislike it" before making the case that poetry offers something essential. She asserts that poetry presents "an imaginary garden with real toads in it." Through the unreal (the *imaginary garden*), truth (*real toads*) emerges.

———

Ken Kesey probably never met Marianne Moore, but he would have agreed with her on this point. His novel *One Flew Over the Cuckoo's Nest* is narrated by Chief Bromden, who acknowledges that readers may not believe him because he was a patient in a mental hospital, the setting for the story he is about to tell. He adds:

But this is true, even if it didn't happen.

Bromden tells the story of Randle McMurphy, who conned his way into the hospital in order to avoid jail time. McMurphy foments rebellion against Nurse Ratched, the manipulative, sadistic ward overseer. When he realizes that he can't be released from the hospital without her approval and that she can subject him to dangerous treatment, McMurphy complies with her orders for a brief period. However, the other patients need his support to resist her power. McMurphy resumes his defiance, sacrificing himself to save them; Nurse Ratched has him lobotomized (a surgery that, in the novel, robs patients of free will).

What is *true, even if it didn't happen* in the world Kesey created? That power, wielded cruelly, must be opposed. That rebels who defy authority for the sake of justice are heroes for doing so. That one inspirational figure can make a difference. And that Chief Bromden isn't mentally ill at all. His delusion is that the "Combine" (a mega-corporation) controls everything. At the end of the novel, Bromden escapes the mental hospital, which Kesey depicts as an institution whose goal is to control everything in the patients' lives.

————

John Lennon and Paul McCartney's song "I Am the Walrus" also makes a philosophical statement:

I am he as you are he as you are me and we are all together . . .

Lennon repeatedly claimed that the song was nonsense, the product of drugged dreams and an attempt to thwart those who searched for deep meaning in the Beatles's songs. Yet so much of what the Beatles wrote calls for people to give up self-imposed restrictions and "come together"—the title of another of their songs. Instead of a divisive "us versus them" mentality, this sentence argues that *we are all together* in this life. All those pronouns (*I, you, me, he, we*) give a universal quality to this statement. It's not just some individuals who are connected; it's everyone.

SETTING BOUNDARIES AND BREAKING THEM

Impossible situations are often used to define a boundary, one that appears unbreakable. W. H. Auden, in his poem "As I Walked Out One Evening," characterizes the limit of love this way:

I'll love you till the ocean
Is folded and hung up to dry . . .

————

And Robert Burns thus:

And I will luve thee still, my dear,
Till a' the seas gang dry.

Climate change notwithstanding, *the ocean* isn't going to hang anywhere to dry. Nor will *the seas*. Thus the time limit of love is forever.

The title character of Henrik Ibsen's play *Brand* is bound by his sense of right and wrong. His mother resorts to the impossible to express her feelings. Here are her words, as translated by C. H. Herford:

Bid fire be sever'd from its heat,
Snow from its cold, wave from its wet!

The mother wants her son, a minister, to absolve her of her sins so that she can go to heaven when she dies. The son says he will do as she wishes if she will give up all her worldly possessions and "naked to the grave descend." She can't accept that condition and orders him, "Ask less!" It's significant that the name of the son, *Brand*, comes from the word for "fire." Brand can't be separated from what he believes is morally right, even later in the play when his mother begs him to come to her death-bed. She offers half her wealth, then more. But nothing less than all of it is acceptable to Brand, and he refuses to go. It's his nature to be uncompromising, just as it's in the nature of *fire* to have *heat*, *snow* to be *cold*, and a *wave* to be *wet*.

Power, though, sometimes makes the impossible possible. In Lewis Carroll's *Through the Looking-Glass*, Alice tells the Red Queen that "one can't believe impossible things." The Red Queen is undaunted, remarking that Alice hasn't "had much practice." The Queen, on the other hand, practiced believing the impossible "for half-an-hour a day" when she was young. She continues:

Why, sometimes I've believed as many as six impossible things before breakfast.

The cold logic—and absolute power—of the Red Queen go a long way toward making her assertion believable.

————

A similar situation occurs in *Animal Farm*, George Orwell's satire of the Russian Revolution. The animals have overthrown the human farmer who mistreated them, writing seven principles of "Animalism," the most important of which is "all animals are equal." After a number of conflicts, Napoleon the pig emerges as the supreme leader and the seven principles are reduced to one:

> All animals are equal, but some animals are more equal than others.

————

But even power has limits. After the title character kills the king, Macbeth looks at his blood-stained hands. Shaken, he asks:

> Will all great Neptune's ocean wash this blood
> Clean from my hand?
> No, this my hand will rather
> The multitudinous seas incarnadine,
> Making the green one red.

Macbeth, figuratively, never again has clean hands. The whole kingdom suffers under his rule. In a sense, he does make the *seas incarnadine* because in slaying the rightful king, Macbeth has subverted nature. Only when the king's murder is avenged and power is restored to a legitimate heir is the "blood" staining Scotland washed away.

————

On a more personal level, many of us can relate to the impossible situations these two writers describe:

"Well, I can't relax when I'm anxious about relaxing," I would (accurately) reflect. . . .

> —Charles Comey, "Against Honeymoons"

. . . so I was trying not to think about the fact that I was eating, which is a form of thinking about it.

> —John Green, *Turtles All the Way Down*

Has anyone heard "Don't panic!" without panicking? I doubt it.

IMPOSSIBLY VIVID

In addition to many other reasons for making impossible statements, writers know that this device attracts attention. A few examples:

Trying to define yourself is like trying to bite your own teeth.

> —Alan Watts, *Life*

It rained all night the day I left,
The weather it was dry,
The sun so hot, I froze to death . . .

> —Stephen Foster, "Oh! Susanna"

I close my eyes so I can see
I burn a fire to stay cool.

> —Fugazi, "Shut the Door"

Late at night, it got so frigid that all spoken words froze solid afore they could be heard.

> —"Babe and the Blue Ox" (folktale as retold by S. E. Schlosser)

All right, everyone, line up alphabetically according to your height.

> —Casey Stengel (baseball manager)

There was no hurry, for there was nowhere to go, nothing to buy and no money to buy it with, nothing to see outside the boundaries of Maycomb County.

—Harper Lee, *To Kill a Mockingbird*

I was quaking from head to foot, and could have hung my hat on my eyes, they stuck out so far.

—Mark Twain, *Old Times on the Mississippi*

And again I say unto you, It is easier for a camel to go through the eye of a needle, than for a rich man to enter into the kingdom of God.

—*King James Bible*, Matthew 19:24

It's finished. I have only ten more pages to write.

—Théophile Gautier, reporting a comment from Flaubert

FOR THE WRITER

In 2008, scientists on the television show *Mythbusters* built a lead balloon that could fly. If they can achieve what appears impossible, so can you. Try these prompts to access your impossible powers of writing.

FEBRUARY 30TH, PART 1

As anyone with a calendar knows, February 30th doesn't exist. What else is impossible? Think personally: an amiable conversation with Aunt Mildred, completing a school or work assignment before deadline, finally decluttering the basement . . . whatever. Also think globally: flattening the Alps, redistricting Congress without argument, crossing the Sahara on a bicycle, and so forth. Look at your list to see if anything there might develop into a longer piece of writing.

FEBRUARY 30TH, PART 2

What would you do on February 30th, if a science-fiction gap in the space-time continuum opened around you? Make a list. Some activities may reflect real goals you never have time to achieve, such as reading the 184 back issues of your favorite magazine you've been saving. Others may be impossible but desirable, such as brokering peace between always-at-odds political parties. Again, use the list as a source for your writing.

SURREALISM

Take a long look at a surrealist painting, such as René Magritte's portrait of a man facing a mirror and seeing his own back. Other good Magritte prompts: his shrouded lovers and suited businessmen falling through a city sky. Write a story based on the painting. Other artists to consider: Salvador Dalí, Frieda Kahlo, Giorgio de Chirico, and Leonora Carrington. Instead of writing a story, you might try distilling the impossibility expressed in the artwork into a descriptive phrase or sentence. Magritte's businessmen, for example, might be "accountants slicing the clouds into ledger columns."

THE SKY IS NOT THE LIMIT

Despite what the cliché says, the sky is no longer the limit in this era of space travel. But what is the limit? Make two columns, one for the boundary you want to define, and one for the impossible definition. Let W. H. Auden and Robert Burns inspire you, but don't feel obliged to focus on love. Instead, go for hate, fame, fortune, friendship . . . and everything else. For example, here's one on fame: "He was instantly recognized on every planet in the Milky Way galaxy, and on some major planets in other galaxies, too."

VISUAL PRESENTATION

> *What* on earth have you done?
> What *on* earth have you done?
> What on *earth* have you done?
> What on earth *have* you done?
> What on earth have *you* done?
> What on earth have you *done*?

—Nicky Enright, *What on Earth (have you done)?*

You know how to read and write English: top to bottom, left to right, on straight lines (or straight-ish, in handwriting). Space between words, pause at a comma, stop at a period. Lift at the end for a question, clap of thunder for an exclamation point. Brief rest at a semicolon. Those are the rules, right? Right. Except for artists.

When I say artists, I refer to more than painters, sculptors, or photographers. Writers who consciously create with words are artists, too, whether or not they concern themselves with visual presentation. Those who do—and who break the rules—produce spectacular effects: Roy Lichtenstein's cartoon-bubbled images. Tauba Auerbach's nonlinear, punctuation-free sentences. Jenny Holzer's text-projections. John Hollander's word-picture of a swan and its shadow. Jeff Kinney's playful fonts and layout in *The Diary of a Wimpy Kid*. And many more rule-breaking art creators.

Such as Nicky Enright, author and artist of the featured sentence, which is actually a panel of six sentences, identical in words and punctuation but not in italicization or meaning. Enright describes *What on Earth?* as an exploration of "the subtle yet intense relationships between visual text, aural sound, and literal meaning." Motivated by the environmental crisis, he asks the same question six times. By italicizing a different word in each sentence, Enright adjusts the meaning.

All the iterations of Enright's question are open to more than one interpretation. I recommend that you read them aloud and decide for yourself how they differ before you read my analysis.

Ready? Here's what I hear in the first: a parent's voice (Mother Earth?) discovering a mess a child has made. So, dismay. Or, inquiry: *What* have you done to clean up that mess? You're on the spot either way, chastised or prodded to act.

Now the second, with an italicized *on*: this iteration challenges intellectuals and the spiritually inclined. It's fine to nurture the life of the mind and the soul, but practicality has value, too. The answer to this question should be a list of actions: trees planted, trash recycled, pollutants cleansed.

Moving on to number three, in which *earth* is the focus: I hear outrage, the sort of scream that a doomsday scenario inspires. Alternative: it's a call to focus attention on our home planet. Trips to Mars and habitats in space are great ideas, potentially permitting a few people to evade disaster. But you are here, now, on Earth. How much attention have you paid to this planet?

The fourth, with *have* in italics, is skeptical. Oh, you say that you're an environmentalist? That's nice. What *have* you done to earn that label? Another point: the verb *have done* is in present-perfect, a tense with ties to the past and the present. This version evaluates your past actions but also offers hope. The present is now; you still have time to act.

You, number five, makes the reader squirm. *You* are in the spotlight, not others. Relentless in its focus, this sentence calls *you* to account. *You* must report your deeds, and *you* will be judged for them.

Now to *done*: Disbelief enters the picture, with a dose of despair. The damage is *done*. It can't be un*done*.

Enright's visual presentation creates a seventh sentence. Read diagonally, the italicized words convey intense urgency. It's also worth noting that while Enright conceived of this piece as an environmental statement (and indeed it is), other meanings are possible. *What on earth* is a common phrase, one expressing surprise or shock. Taken this way, Enright's sentences may apply to other situations that, like our planet-in-trouble, require action and accountability.

STARRING PETER

Anyone who reads Beatrix Potter's *The Tale of Peter Rabbit* without knowing the title nevertheless understands immediately that Peter is the star. The first sentence gives Peter that distinction with its layout:

> Once upon a time there were
>   four little Rabbits, and their
> names were —
>   Flopsy,
>   Mopsy,
>   Cotton-tail,
>   and Peter.

First, *Peter* is last. Potter's gentle curve of names—which mimics Peter's tail when her illustrations show his profile—guides the reader's eyes through the *four little Rabbits*, each meriting a separate line. Peter's line is the tip of the tail. With that position, plus the extra length of *and*, the eye lingers on *Peter* longer than on the other bunnies. Peter certainly needs that extra attention because, in this tale, he's always getting into trouble. The other *Rabbits* obey their mother's orders to play elsewhere and to avoid "Mr. McGregor's garden," where their father "had an accident" and consequently was "put in a pie by Mrs. McGregor." Peter, unconcerned about this awful fate and "very naughty," of course heads straight for the forbidden. A series of narrow escapes ensues, with Peter eventually arriving home, minus his jacket and shoes, feeling "not very well." His mother isn't surprised (he's lost his clothes before) and calmly puts him to bed with a spoonful of medicinal tea. The good little bunnies get berries and milk for supper.

Like many children's classics, Potter's story is anything but tame. Death is real (the father-filled pie). Bystanders are no help: an old mouse shakes her head when asked where the gate is because she's carrying food in her mouth and can't speak. Peter's mother is kind, but busy. She's at the store the morning of Peter's adventure and has three other offspring to feed that evening. Peter, shivering and scared, is on his own— in the story as well as in the first sentence.

SPRINGING IT

Edward Eslin Cummings (E. E. Cummings) enjoyed flouting the rules of grammar, capitalization, poetry, and pretty much everything else. His poems are aural experiences, to be sure, but often they're visual objects as well. "in Just-"—the first line of the poem that also serves as its title— dances down the page like the characters in it. It's difficult to say where one sentence begins and another ends in this poem, as hyphens and apostrophes are the only punctuation marks, and neither separates one thought from another. In fact, it's possible to read the entire poem as a single sentence. It may also comprise two. Relying on content, here's the first:

in Just-
spring   when the world is mud-
luscious the little
lame balloonman

whistles   far   and wee

and eddieandbill come
running from marbles and
piracies and it's
spring

when the world is puddle-wonderful

Off-balance, are you? That's the point, or part of it anyway. The second half of the poem is also one long sentence. (Again, I'm judging by content, though *when the world is puddle-wonderful* may attach to either half.) The subsequent lines also totter and sprawl down the page, with "bettyandisbel" and "the goat-footed balloonMan" analogous to *eddie-andbill* and *the little / lame balloonman*. Spring is a season of possibility, of new life, and therefore of change—not to mention sex—all factors that disrupt, just as the poem's form disrupts a standard line reading.

Cummings places his characters in childhood: *eddieandbill* could be any two boys who play *marbles and / piracies* and find the world *puddle-wonderful*. Some readers leave it at that, picturing a happy playground scene with a friendly balloon vendor. However, Cummings layers more into the poem, hinting that change is on the way. The boys are running to *the little / lame balloonman*, who's "goat-footed" later in the poem. The *balloonman* is an allusion to Pan, the Greek god associated with spring, music, the wild, and sex. Like Cummings's sentence, there's not much balance in Pan, whose name gave rise to the word *panic*.

The process of growing up is also uneven: regressions, leaps forward, and wrong turns abound. Hence the odd spacing and line breaks. The first line, *in Just-*, cuts *Just-* from *spring*. Elsewhere in the poem hyphens create compound words (*mud- / luscious* and *puddle-wonderful*). Likewise, *Just-spring* may be a single term, broken off at the end of the line like *mud- / luscious*. So it's *Just-spring* that the boys—and in the second half of the poem, the girls—are experiencing. And that's enough to change them.

What about those *whistles   far   and wee*? They're spaced out, again a nod to the uneven pace of change but also to the summons to maturity. Of course, *eddieandbill* heed the call. They can't do otherwise while they're *in Just-spring*.

SUMMER

John Allman's poem "Biology" ends in August, but its spiral structure exists in every season and in every organism, including us. In a later poem, "Syntax," Allman writes, "Nothing steps out of nature." In "Biology," he elucidates and illustrates this point with words, margins, and line breaks. "Biology" doesn't follow standard capitalization and punctuation rules. Instead, sentences begin when the speaker turns to a new thought. Here's the end of the poem:

my instinct travels

to attract

your

touch

where you tie up

wandering

morning-

glory's

mauve trumpets

The layout spirals like DNA, the basis for all life and a pattern consistent throughout the poem. With this presentation, Allman's thesis sits in plain sight: all living beings share DNA and the instinctive drive to survive and procreate. The poem moves easily back and forth between humans and nature, with exquisitely detailed descriptions of sea cucumbers, pelicans, horseshoe crabs, algae, and many other animals.

The speaker in "Biology" makes frequent references to a spouse. The two unite "dirt from Irish fields" and "the fields of Krk" (an island on the Croatian coast). As the poem progresses, the couple travels: to Charleston, to an island, to Dogwood Lane, to home. Interwoven with observations of wildlife are equally sharp depictions of the couple's experiences together: how a thunderstorm served "to move us closer / to each other" or when they sang their "road / songs" and "spilled the last coffee / from a broken thermos."

The featured sentence follows two stanzas about bees communicating, with a "waggle dance," where food may be found. The bees' actions are hardwired, their communication visual. They parallel the speaker's *instinct* that *travels / to attract / your / touch* as the spouse, connected to nature, works in a garden. In *morning- / glory's / mauve trumpets*, both humans and bees find beauty, attraction, and growth. This sentence, like the poem as a whole, reflects Allman's stated belief that science makes the world "comprehensible" while beauty makes it "desirable." He sees commonality between human and animal natures, which he expresses visually in the spiral DNA of the poem's lines.

IN THE MIDDLE

Marsha Pomerantz's poem "The *Illustrated* Middle" is exactly that: lines laid out with a split in the center, resembling the human thorax. Each sentence is read from left to right in the traditional way, crossing over the gap. In that empty space much meaning resides, whether the speaker is talking about a stroke, a bookmark, internal struggles, or opposable thumbs.

That mean streak in stroke	where the live side
meets dead flesh	at the sternum.
Line of	last resort for
waves breaking each other	between two breakwaters.
Where Mommy's half met Daddy's	half of me.
Where my hair	must opt to drop
over one ear	or the other.
Where the bookmark	holds the abandoned
res,	in case.
Where I was monkey	and things flew over
my head into	the hands of others.
Defiant finger with	two on either side,
one op	posable.
Where you can't	decide which way to
dash to	dodge a car.
Where doubts	redouble and
redoubts	resound.
Internal	edge,
cae	sura,
un	centered.
This post-*ovum*	pre-*corpus*
state,	stanza.
This still thorax	with voluble wings.
This	.

Within the poem is this sentence about a childhood game:

Where I was monkey   and things flew over

my head into   the hands of others.

"Monkey in the Middle" (also known as "Keep Away") is simple. Two or more kids toss a ball to each other, while one, the "monkey," stands in the middle and tries to intercept. It's not easy being the monkey. If the throw-catch pair can achieve a high arc, only an athletic leap and grab can thwart them.

Look closely at Pomerantz's "middle." *When I was monkey* refers to childhood, and to a specific frustration of that age. *Things* do fly over a child's *head*, a ball in this sentence but much more than that: adults' discussions and decisions, for example. A child's endless questions—why? how? when? what if?—arise from this gap, and many remain unanswered for what, to a child, seems like forever. The middle is also a powerless spot, with *the hands of others* controlling everything. How much anger sits in that blank space, the "illustrated middle"!

In other lines, Pomerantz moves beyond childhood to feelings present during every stage of life, relating them to art:

This post-*ovum*   pre-*corpus*

state,   stanza.

She expresses universal bewilderment through a specific instance:

Where you can't   decide which way to

dash to   dodge a car.

Her final line, with the single word "This" on one side and a period on the other, pushes the reader to think about the middle, which, while empty, is where we spend much of our time.

WEDGED

Each stanza of Sharon Kunde's poem "Prodigal" is a wedge, the long first line forming a right angle at the top, gradually tapering to a short, two- or three-word line. The first stanza describes the arrival of a slate slab, which the speaker's father prepares for its function as the undersurface of a pool table. In the second stanza, the speaker, in a "room upstairs," listens to the father and other "prairie men" playing billiards. The final stanza describes the father, shrunken with age, watching television with the speaker, who is now the same size. This sentence appears in the first stanza, mid-wedge:

> I stopped
> my play and floated over, eyes high
> as the bright table, enchanted:
> I had never seen you touch
> a thing you loved.

The form of Kunde's poem echoes its meaning. The father "bent to the table like an avid lover" as he spread wax over "every divot." When the table's in use, billiards players hunch over the edge. In both images, the reader sees wide upper torsos supported by solid but thinner legs, akin to a wedge shape. There's a wedge between the father and his offspring, too. The speaker *had never seen* his love expressed and wonders "What / taught you to check / this kind of care, / to stow it away, / not squander it." While the grown men play, the young speaker hears the father's "tough lullaby." Later in life, when the speaker is an adult and the father has been diminished by age, they're together physically but not emotionally. The television has a "glassy surface"; it, and their relationship, look smooth, but that's the surface—the appearance and not the reality. Like the pool table, their bond is "shrouded" and etched with "number-less / fine cracks," though they present "brave / stony faces." The table and the shape of the poem mirror the relationship.

FOR THE WRITER

Tinkering with the visual presentation of a sentence is a little like throwing paint around until you like what you see. Have at it!

STRAIGHT = BORING

Take a sentence, capitalize every letter, strip it of punctuation, and whip it around the paper. See what happens. For example:

ORIGINAL: This is reality.

CAPITALIZED AND STRIPPED: THIS IS REALITY

WHIPPED-1: Place the words in a triangle, with each word forming a side.

WHIPPED-2: Draw the words off-line without creating a discernable geometric shape.

WHAT HAPPENS: The reader can't determine where the sentence begins. It might be "IS THIS REALITY" (a question without the question mark) or "REALITY THIS IS" (a Yoda-esque reversed-order statement).

Magnetic poetry sets are good for this exercise, but pencil and paper suffice. The computer may be a bit tougher unless you're good with word-art functions.

TOGETHER AND APART

Like E. E. Cummings, you too can squash words together and spread them apart. You can also stretch out sound with hyphens. For example:

Ernie swallowed, picked up his notes, and said, "Iwouldbeagoodpresidentpleasevoteforme."

He waited as the seconds ticked by, m-o-r-e and m-o-r-e and then *m-o-r-e* seconds.

The squashed words show Ernie's desire to finish as fast as possible; the stretched words and italics reveal his anxious wait for the audience's reaction.

PICTURE PERFECT

Choose a picture, take a photo, or create an image yourself. Insert a sentence, word by word, into the visual element. Slant the words, pop up a letter or two in the middle if appropriate (aLPs), or go vertical, as in this arrangement superimposed on a suburban lawn:

```
        O   T   C
    M   V   I   U
G   O   E   M   T
R   W   R   E
A   I   D       I
S   N   U   T   T
S   G   E   O   !
```

CREDITS

ONOMATOPOEIA

Excerpts from *The Little Engine That Could: The Complete, Original Edition* by Watty Paper, copyright © 1976, 1961, 1954, 1945, 1930 by Platt & Munk, Publishers, a Grosset & Dunlap imprint of Penguin Young Readers Group. *The Little Engine That Could*, engine design, and "I THINK I CAN" are trademarks of Penguin Putnam, Inc. Used by permission of Grosset & Dunlap, an imprint of Penguin Publishing Group, a division of Penguin Random House LLC. All rights reserved.

"In the Marvelous Dimension," © Kate Daniels.

MATCHING SOUNDS

"Alabanza: In Praise of Local 100." Copyright © 2003 by Martín Espada, from *Alabanza: New and Selected Poems 1982–2002* by Martín Espada. Used by permission of W. W. Norton & Company, Inc.

REPETITION

"I Shall Be Released," written by Bob Dylan. Copyright © 1967, 1970 by Dwarf Music; renewed 1995 by Dwarf Music. All rights reserved. International copyright secured. Reprinted by permission.

"Do Not Go Gentle into That Good Night" © Dylan Thomas Trust.

"Do Not Go Gentle into That Good Night" by Dylan Thomas, from *The Poems of Dylan Thomas*, copyright © 1952 by Dylan Thomas. Reprinted by permission of New Directions Publishing Corp.

"Back Back Back," written by Ani DiFranco, © 1999 by Righteous Babe Music (BMI). Used with permission.

NEGATIVITY

"The Rising" by Bruce Springsteen. Copyright © 2002 by Bruce Springsteen (Global Music Rights). Reprinted by permission. International copyright secured. All rights reserved.

INDEX OF AUTHORS AND
SENTENCE SOURCES

ABOUT THE AUTHOR

Asked to describe herself in "100 words or less," Geraldine Woods is more likely to wonder why people tend to say "less" instead of "fewer," which some grammarians insist is the correct word, leading her to question why anyone worries about "less" and "fewer" when no one even considers saying "100 words or much." Which is all you need to know about her, except for the fact that she's taught every level of English from grade 5 through Advanced Placement, most recently at the Horace Mann School, and written more than fifty books. She posts wry commentary on language at grammarianinthecity.com and lives in New York City. This is her first book for W. W. Norton.